The Edinburgh Goldsmiths I:
Training, Marks, Output and Demographics

Also by Rodney and Janice Dietert

Compendium of Scottish Silver vols 1 & 2

The Edinburgh Goldsmiths I: Training, Marks, Output and Demographics

Present and former officers of the Incorporation of Goldsmiths of the City of Edinburgh. From left to right: Henry Steuart Fothringham O.B.E., Historian; Henry Roy Tatton, freeman, master and former deacon; Mary Michel, secretary; Michael Laing O.B.E., present deacon.

Photograph by Janice M Dietert

Rodney R Dietert, Ph.D.
Janice M Dietert

www.lulu.com

Cover Art by: David Kessler
http://www.flickr.com/welcome/3273751/517342/

The Edinburgh Goldsmiths I: Training, Marks, Output and Demographics/

ISBN 978-0-6151-4456-6

Acknowledgements

Note that any errors present in this book are solely the responsibility of the authors and should in no way reflect on those who have graciously helped with this endeavor.

We want to thank Incorporation officers, Mary Michel, Deacon Michael Laing O.B.E, D. L. and former deacon, Henry Tatton, for their assistance. The help of George Dalgleish, Curator of History of the National Museums of Scotland, as well as Irene Mackay in the museum's silver department and Helen Osmani in the picture library is also gratefully acknowledged. We most gratefully thank Robert B. Barker and Wynyard Wilkenson for their suggestions, and Mrs. F. Hooper of the George Watson's College and Mr. Fraser Simm of the George Heriot's School for their timely assistance. We also thank John Davis, curator, and John Hyman, associate curator, of Colonial Williamsburg for their timely assistance.

The cover-art work produced by David Kessler and the text help provided by Adriana Rovers were invaluable to the book's preparation.

It is with much gratitude that we acknowledge the following individuals, firms and institutions who generously allowed us the use of maker's mark images:

Alastair Dickenson Ltd.,
anotherdirtydancer (EBAY seller)
Argentum – The Leopard's Head, San Francisco at http://www.argentum-theleopard.com
B. Silverman, London at http://www.silverman-london.com
Beth Leintz
Bryan Douglas Antique Silver at http://www.bryandouglas.co.uk
Chuck Cordero
Colin Fraser
Daniel Bexfield Antiques at http://www.bexfield.co.uk and The Silver Spoon Club of Great Britain
David Bevan, Lord of the Manor of Dycheforde
Derek Douglas Esquire
EBAY sellers who donated marks but wish to remain anonymous
FitzSimon Antiques at http://www.rubylane.com/shops/fitzsimonantique
Gavin Mullen at Charente Antiques at: http://stores.ebay.com/CHARENTE-ANTIQUES
George Dalgleish, curator, National Museums of Scotland
George R. Schrager and Schredds Antiques of Portobello at http://www.schredds.com
Giovanni Ciceri of Argenti Inglesi at http://www.argentinglesi.com
Global Collectables at http://stores.ebay.co.uk/Global-Collectables
Goodwin's Antiques, Ltd. of Edinburgh at http://www.goodwinsantiques.com
H.R. Mendes Da-Costa
Hayward and Stott Antiques at http://www.scottishsilver.com
Henry Steuart Fothringham
I. Franks Antiques, London at http://www.ifranks.com
John Davis, curator, and John Hyman, associate curator, Colonial Williamsburg

Acknowledgements (cont.)

leeofbarna (EBAY seller)
Merced Antiques Mall
Mick Guy, Mixed-Lot EBAY store http://www.ebay.co.uk/Mixed-Lot
Michael Lee
Nicholas Shaw Antiques at http://www.nicholas-shaw.com
One of a Kind Antiques at http://www.oneofakindantiques.com
porringer9 (EBAY seller)
Ray Fuller at http://stores.ebay.com/Antique-Silver
S. J. Phillips, Ltd., London at http://www.sjphillips.com
Stephanie Bates of the Forrest of Dean in Gloucestershire
The Bedford Gallery
The National Museums of Scotland
Tim Zekki

Dedication

To Henry Steuart Fothringham

This project could not have been accomplished except for the meticulous transcriptions and generous sharing of records by Henry Steuart Fothringham, O.B.E. and Historian of The Incorporation of Goldsmiths of the City of Edinburgh. We are forever grateful to him.

Contents

Brief Guide to the Goldsmiths: The Apprentices and Freemen of Edinburgh

A complete transcription of the early Incorporation practices regarding apprentices and freemen can be found in Fothringham, HS, *Edinburgh Goldsmiths' Minutes 1525-1700*, Scottish Record Society New Series v29, 2006. Additionally, further details of the rules surrounding the booking of apprentices and the granting of freedom will accompany the biographies in volume II of the present work.

Apprentices of The Incorporation of Goldsmiths of the City of Edinburgh were boys most commonly between the ages of 13 and 16, although occasionally younger or older apprentices were taken. The boys were bound by indentures to the freemen, Edinburgh goldsmiths who were Incorporation members. Indentures were two sets of contract papers. Detailed demographics of the apprentices and freemen masters are shown later in the volume. Guides of conduct for the apprentices were also part of the contract. The duration of the indentures was typically for seven years. The freeman had to make certain payments at the time the indentures were presented to the Incorporation members. Following the successful discharge of the indentures and a period as a journeyman goldsmith, the former apprentice could request an essay (crafting of silver and/or gold pieces and an oral examination). If he passed this, obtained a burgess ticket and found a financial guarantor of his work (termed a cautioner), he could be admitted as a freeman of The Incorporation of Goldsmiths of the City of Edinburgh.

Freemen could book an apprentice every three years and this general pattern can be seen in the training diagrams of some freemen with long careers. But exceptions to the three-year rule were made for booking scholars of George Heriot's Hospital and George Watson's Hospital, both schools in Edinburgh, as well as for the booking of freemen's sons. Additionally, the rule was not uniformly enforced over the centuries. When apprentices died or left the indentures before their expiration, new apprentices could be booked to take their place.

This volume of the two-volume work provides a comprehensive look at over four centuries of Edinburgh's goldsmiths by tracking instruction in the art and craft of goldsmithing across 15 generations of training. This tradition of master-apprentice instruction in Edinburgh impacted not only the crafting of gold and silver in that city, but also throughout the British Isles, the British Empire and her trading partners.

Introduction to the Training Diagrams: Pedigrees of Edinburgh's Apprentices and Freemen

Organization: Similarity to Family Trees

The training histories of Edinburgh apprentices are depicted in the same way one might diagram a family tree or pedigree across four centuries. In this case the master-apprentice relationship in the diagrams becomes equivalent to that of a parent and child in a family tree. Lines and directional arrows show the training relationship from the master to the apprentice. When a master booked several apprentices, these are organized chronologically under the master and displayed similarly as one would the birth order of children. As the training progresses chronologically involving more apprentices becoming masters themselves and training future generations, the entries flow onto additional branches. However, the generation numbers continue in sequence. Therefore the generations originating with a single early master can be tracked vertically in exactly the same way as in a family tree. Instead of moving from an individual to child, to grandchild, to great grandchild, etc. one moves from a master to apprentice, to "grand" apprentice, to "great grand" apprentice in each succeeding generation. There are up to 15 sequential generations tracked in this manner (e.g. the Daniel Crawford tree and branches). More than 1200 apprentices plus additional early and late freemen whose training is uncertain are organized among these diagrams.

Trees vs. Branches

The diagrams are named either trees or branches. Trees begin with a master whose own training was not specified in the available records. While most trees start in the 16th or 17th centuries, a few begin in the 19th century because the history of the particular master is not known. Branches flow directly from trees and are usually given the name of a prominent apprentice who himself became an important master. For example, Edward Cleghorne (1) appears on the Crawford Tree in the third generation. But as a master Cleghorne trained so many important apprentices that it was necessary to place his training records onto a separate page into a branch of the Crawford Tree that was named Cleghorne-Yorstoun. A separate branch also linked to the Crawford Tree is named Crawford-Reid. It follows the master-apprentice bookings of Daniel Crawford's apprentice, Alexander Reid (1). In this way, trees may divide into several branches as apprentice "children" become masters and have their own "children".

Indexes of the Apprentices, Masters and Freemen in this Book

The earliest entries in the diagrams begin in the early 1500s and the training sequence progresses to the present. Names, dates, and diagram positions of 1200-plus apprentices and freemen are provided in a list. The index is organized alphabetically by name of the apprentice and/or freeman. Note that approximately 30 early Edinburgh goldsmiths are not included among the indexes or diagrams. Because no information connecting them to other apprentices or goldsmiths was found, their inclusion would not offer additional insights. However, a list including these goldsmiths can be found in the Nominal Roll of the Incorporation [*Fothringham, Edinburgh Goldsmiths' Minutes*].

Diagram Abbreviations

For convenience, diagrams are designated with a two-letter abbreviation. A directory of these abbreviations also follows this introduction. For example the abbreviation used for James

Penman's branch is "PE" and that for James Ker's branch is "KE". The Daniel Crawford Tree is termed "CF" and the Foulis-Kirkwood Tree is indicated as "FK". Among the diagrams there are 88 trees and branches.

Dividing Diagrams into Sections For Presentation

One further subdivision was needed to permit the training data to be displayed. Many trees and branches were simply too large to show on one page. To overcome this, it was necessary to divide the tree or branch chronologically. In most cases this was done by using left and right halves. For example, the Cleghorne-Yorstoun Branch is displayed on two pages since it was divided into left and right halves. In one case, that for the Penman Branch, three chronological sections were needed: left, center and right. Finally for the Mosman Tree the halves were divided as early and late generations rather than left and right halves. With these extra subdivisions, the 87 trees and branches form 110 pages of diagrams. When tree and branch division was necessary, the halves are shown on succeeding pages in the book.

Navigating Between Trees and Branches and Using the Global Maps

Note that moving among branches is not difficult. Each tree or branch has prompts and headings at the top and bottom of the diagrams directing the reader to the other connected diagrams. The training line and generation numbers continue through those other diagrams. Overall maps illustrating how the trees and branches are connected are shown on two pages essentially as global maps. These precede the alphabetical presentation of the trees and branches. One global map illustrates the Daniel Crawford tree and associated branches. The second displays the remaining trees and branches such as those involving the Heriots and Dennistouns.

How to Find an Apprentice

Apprentices and freemen have been given one or more personal identification (PIN) numbers indicating their precise location in one or more diagrams. These PIN numbers are systematic and are composed of 4-7 characters/spaces. They always begin with the two-letter tree/branch abbreviation followed by a dash. Then the generation number follows and is a number between 0-15. This apprentice will be found within that generation of the particular diagram. Finally, if the branch has been subdivided onto more than one page, one or two letters will follow the generation number. They indicate the diagram half or section and are abbreviated as follows:

L = Left
C = Center (Only used for the Penman Branch)
R = Right
L&R = Left and Right (only used for a master starting both halves of the tree or branch).
EA = Early (only used for the Mosman Tree)
LT = Late (only used for Mosman Tree)

Want to find James Ker, his father and his son?

James Ker was a second-generation trainee of James Penman and was apprenticed to his father, Thomas Ker, in 1709. James Ker's apprentice-related PIN number is PE-6L. That means that as an apprentice, Ker is located in the Penman Branch diagram at generation number 6. In this case the "L" that follows the generation number means that one should refer to the left section page of the Penman diagrams to find him. Not surprisingly, James Ker's father, Thomas Ker, appears in generation 5 of the Penman diagram with a PIN number of PE-5L. James Penman himself is in generation 4. On this diagram showing James Ker, the arrow from James Ker's listing says "To Ker Branch, KE". This indicates that James Ker has his own branch containing his trainees and a second PIN number reflecting his location in that branch. It is

KE-6L&R. This indicates that Ker's branch is divided into left and right halves. He is shown as the starting master in both halves still at generation number 6. James Ker booked one of his sons, William, as an apprentice in 1731. William Ker has the PIN number of KE-7L. Therefore he is located under James Ker in generation #7 on the left half diagram of the Ker Branch.

Getting the Most From Each Apprentice Entry (Including Abbreviations)

The following extract shows part of the Penman Branch left section illustrating James Penman, Thomas Ker and James Ker. Each apprentice and freeman entry has information on the year of the apprentice booking. This is indicated as "P" followed by the year. If the apprentice became a freeman, his name appears in capitol letters. Also the freedom year is indicated as "F" followed by the year. A "*c*." before the year indicates it is an approximation and the precise date was not specified, and "bef" is used as an abbreviation for before. If an apprentice died during the indentures or was transferred to a new master, this is indicated. Death is abbreviated as "d." followed by the year. The testament is abbreviated as "Test." "NR" stands for the Nominal Roll of Freemen and the NR # provides some indication of chronology for the early members of the Incorporation of Goldsmiths. Years indicated as 1662/64 reflect either confusion over the booking entry in the Incorporation minutes or in most cases, the transfer of the apprentice among masters. Transfer itself is abbreviated in the diagrams as "Tr." It should be noted that a second volume of this series is planned, which will contain biographies of the apprentices and freemen included in volume one. Those entries will provide additional details concerning transfers, etc.

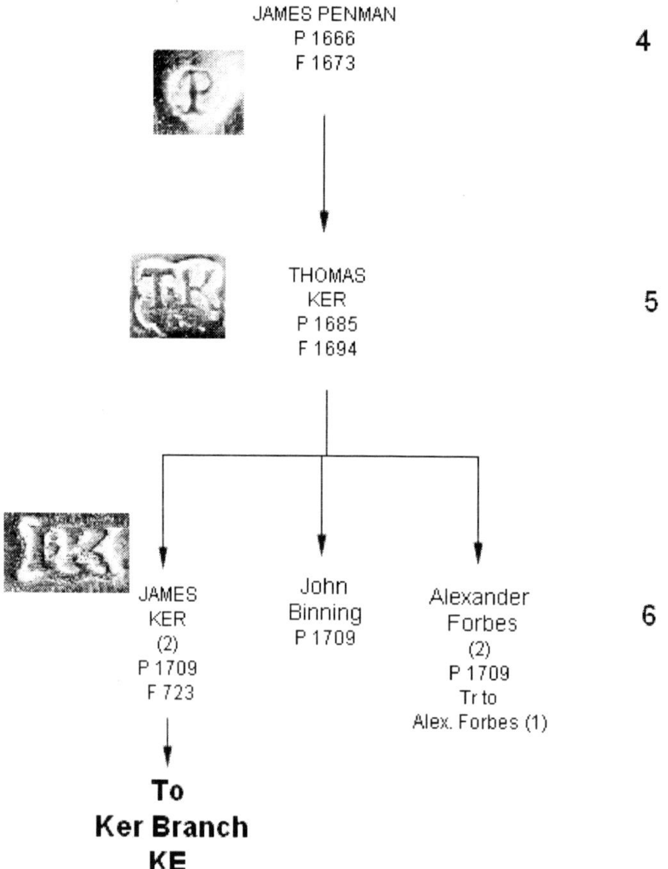

To Pedigree the Apprentices

Using the guidelines, pedigrees of the masters and apprentices can be tracked by each generation by using the prompts in each branch and progressing via the originating tree and its branches. For example, Henry Roy Tatton, the last of the masters, appears in both the Crichton Branch and in his own branch at generation 14. His pedigree can be tracked back to the 1500s and Daniel Crawford. This continuous line runs from the Crawford Tree and progresses through the Crawford-Reid, Seaton, Mungo Yorstoun, McKenzie, Nasmyth and Crichton Branches. Similar pedigree mapping can be done for any apprentice.

Cautionary Note for Early Freemen and Their Apprentices

A number of very early freemen have been included in various early trees (e.g. Allane, Stalker, Rynd) in either the 0 or 1st generations. They are also included in the volume II biographies and are presented here since some evidence suggests they worked as goldsmiths. They also have the same surname as several freemen who follow in these trees. It is likely they were related to subsequent generations of goldsmiths of the same name. In some instances, we do have evidence of a relationship but may not know if the earliest freemen booked any relatives as apprentices. If alive at the time, it is probable they trained sons or nephews as apprentices. However, only those master-apprentice relationships connected by solid lines are supported by information in the available records. Those early freemen and apprentices connected with dashed lines are speculative and are presented here only as suggestions or possibilities. Therefore those potential relationships should be viewed only in that context.

Additionally another early tree, the Mosman Tree, has entries in the minutes where some family member names appear to have been confused by the recorder. This has resulted in some uncertainty in assigning precisely which James or John Mosman was the master for a given apprentice.

Inclusion of Maker's Marks

When available, maker's marks of Edinburgh-trained apprentices and freemen have been included in the training diagrams. Many individuals, firms and organizations generously provided images of marks for this purpose and they are listed in the acknowledgements section at the beginning of this book.

The mark shown is not necessarily the only one associated with that maker. In fact, several goldsmiths had more than one mark during the course of their careers. An example would be James Ker's mark as a freeman, which chronologically overlapped with the mark used by the partnership of James Ker and his son-in-law, William Dempster (Ker & Dempster). In all cases, we have shown only one mark next to the maker's name in the diagrams. It should not be assumed that this was the only mark used by the individual and not even the most commonly seen mark for this maker.

In some cases, particularly during the 19th century, marks are found for Edinburgh apprentices who apprenticed to freemen, made and marked silver in Edinburgh, but never themselves became freemen. A handful of these are included as well and can be identified as a group by the font of the maker's name (not in ALL CAPS as was used to indicate freemen in the diagrams). Additionally, several marks are shown for former Edinburgh apprentices who made silver after migrating to other Scottish towns and/or to other countries. For these individuals, the name of the town or location is indicated below the mark depicted. All other marks without such designation are from Edinburgh. Note that for Charles Dickson (1), his Edinburgh mark is not certain at present. Therefore, the mark illustrated is one he used when working at his second location in Dundee.

By viewing the marks in the context of the training diagrams, it becomes apparent that several apprentices employed a mark stylistically modeled after that of their master. An example of this can be seen in the case of marks from James Mitchell and his apprentice, James Welsh. The marks of Thomas Ker and his son/apprentice, James Ker, also show striking similarities.

Propagation of the Craft

The diagrams enable the Edinburgh freemen to be viewed not only as craftsmen but also as premier teachers of their craft. It should also permit novel style development to be tracked among the specific training lines. The diagrams suggest that several masters were pivotal trainers of future generations of Edinburgh freemen (e.g. James Penman, Edward Cleghorne (1), Thomas Cleghorne (1), Thomas Yorstoun, Alexander Reid (2), James Tait). Still others trained few Edinburgh freemen but educated a surprising number of craftsmen who became goldsmiths elsewhere (e.g. Colin Campbell, Charles Duncan). Finally, many of the masters were exceptional goldsmiths considering their output [see *Compendium of Scottish Silver*]. However, for some reason they trained few freemen or emigrated craftsmen (e.g. Robert Bruce, Robert Gordon).

It is hoped that the training data will prove useful in examining the evolution of the Edinburgh-associated goldsmith craft across the centuries.

Directory of the Trees and Branches

Tree/Branch	Code	Tree/Branch	Code
Aitchison Branch	AI	Davie Branch Left Right	DA
Allane Tree	AL	Dempster Branch	DE
Annand Branch	AN		
Aytoun Branch Left Right	AY	Dennistoun-Lamb Tree Left Right	DL
Bartane Tree	BA	Dickson Branch Left Right	DI
Bethune Branch	BE	Douglas Branch	DO
Blair Branch	BL	Early Fragments	EF
Borthwick Branch	BO	Edmonstoun Branch	ED
Bruce Branch	BR	Fairbairn-Cockburn Branch	FC
Campbell Branch	CA	Fenwick Tree	FE
Cleghorne-Scott Branch	CS	Forbes Tree	FO
Cleghorne-Yorstoun Branch Left Right	CY	Foulis-Kirkwood Tree	FK
Cokkie Tree	CO	Gairdner Branch Left Right	GA
Colin McKenzie Branch	CM	Ged Branch	GE
Craig Tree	CG	George Crawford Branch Left Right	GC
Crawford Tree	CF	George Heriot (3) Branch	GH
Crawford-Reid Branch Left Right	CR	Gilbert Tree	GI
Crichton Branch	CT	Gilchrist Branch	GL
Cunningham Branch Left Right	CU	Gilmore Branch	GM

Directory of the Trees and Branches (cont.)

Tree/Branch	Code	Tree/Branch	Code
Gordon Branch	GO	Mitchell Branch	MI
Grierson Branch	GR	Mitchelson Branch Left Right	MT
Henry Tatton Branch	TT	Mosman Tree Early Late	MO
Heriot Tree Left Right	HT	Muir Branch Left Right	MU
Hewitt Branch Left Right	HE	Mungo Yorstoun Branch	MY
Inglis Branch	IN	Nasmyth Branch Left Right	NA
James Inglis Branch	JI	Oliphant Branch	OL
James McKenzie (2) Branch Left Right	JM	Penman Branch Left Center Right	PE
Jamieson-H. Penman Branch	JP	Rae Branch	RA
John Law Branch	JL	Robb Branch	RB
Ker Branch Left Right	KE	Robert Dennistoun Branch	RD
Lerro Branch	LE	Robertson Branch Left Right	RO
Lindsay Branch	LD	Rynd Tree	RY
Lothian Branch	LO	Scott Branch	SC
Main Branch	MA	Seaton Branch Left Right	SE
Marshall Branch	MS	Sheldon Tree	SH
McAulay-Law Tree	ML	Stalker Tree	ST
McHattie Tree	MH	Syme Tree	SY
McKay Branch Left Right	MK	Symontoun Branch	SM
McKenzie Branch	MZ	Tait Branch	TA
Mellinus Tree	ME	Thomas Mitchell Branch	TM

Directory of the Trees and Branches (cont.)

Tree/Branch	Code	Tree/Branch	Code
Threipland-Reid Branch	TR		
Ure Branch	UR		
Walker Crichton Branch	WC		
Welsh Branch	WE		
William Law (2) Branch	WL		
William Taylor Branch	WT		
Yorstoun (George) Branch	YO		
Ziegler Branch Left Right	ZI		

Alphabetical Index of Apprentices and Freemen in the Maps

Apprentice/Freeman	Map Position(s)	Apprentice Year	Freedom Year
Abercromby, Robert	MY-8	1717	
Adams, Andrew	ZI-10R	1811	
Adie, John	DA-9L	1770	
Aikenhead, George	AI-9	1781	
Aikenhead, Thomas	WL-6	1709	
Aikman, John	SM-6	1671	*c.* 1681
Aikman, Thomas (1)	WL-6	1699	
Aikman, Thomas (2)	SE-6L	1701	
Aikman, William	SH-2	1819	
Aitchison (Achesoune), John	CF-3	1644	
Aitchison, Alexander (1)	SE-7R; AI-7	1733	1746
Aitchison, Alexander (2)	AI-8	*c.* 1763	1770
Aitken, Alexander	OL-9	1767	
Aitken, John	KE-9L	1763	
Alexander, Robert	RO-9R	1768	
Alison, David	RA-8	1742	
Alison, James	ZI-11R	1816	
Allan, Charles	CA-7	*c.* 1724	
Allane, Adam (1)	AL-2		*c.* 1540
Allane, Adam (2)	AL-3		*c.* 1560
Allane, George	AL-1		*c.* 1520
Allane, Robert	AL-1		*c.* 1520
Allen, James	JM-10R	1806	
Alves, James	SE-6R	1717/18	
Anderson, James	BL-7	1720/21	1729
Anderson, John (1)	EF		*c.* 1501
Anderson, John (2)	CR-5	1684	
Anderson, John (3)	LO-8	1753	1763
Anderson, John (4)	JM-10R	1818	
Anderson, Robert (1)	DO-12	1817	
Anderson, Robert (2)	MU-11L	1819	
Anderson, Thomas	DE-4	1753	1764
Anderson, William	AI-9	1778	
Annand, James	HT-3R	1591	
Annand, Michael	GH-4	1595	
Annand, Thomas	GI-2; AN-2	*c.* 1564	1576
Arnot (Arrot), David	KE-7R	1758	
Arnot, James (1)	SY-3	1589	

Apprentice/Freeman	Map Position(s)	Apprentice Year	Freedom Year
Arnot, William	GH-4	1589	
Auchinleck, William	PE-5L	1675	
Auld, George (1)	TM-7	1740	1754
Auld, George (2)	TM-8	1778	
Auld, James	TM-8	1792	
Auld, John	SM-6	1666/68	
Auld, William	TM-8	1782	1788
Aytoun, Andrew	TA-7	1708	
Aytoun, James	RD-4	1626	1636
Aytoun, William	GE-7; AY-7L&R	1706	1718
Bailey, Richard	SC-5	1661	
Bairdner, Archibald	TM-7	1761	
Balfour, David	AY-8-L	1721	
Bannerman, John	AY-9R	1763	
Bartane, James	BA-2	1603	
Bartane, John (1)	BA-1	*c.* 1561	1573
Bartane, John (2)	GH-5	1605	
Baxter, William	MK-11L	1826	
Bayne, George	DE-4	1780	
Beattie, William	MK-10R	1815	1840
Beech, George	DA-8R	1759	1770
Beech, Lindsay	DA-9R	*c.* 1786	
Beech, Patrick	WE-9	1762	
Bell, Robert	RA-7	1704	
Bell, William	RO-11L	1816	
Bell, William Stephen	ZI-10R	1818	
Bennet, James	MT-7R	1739	
Bennet, William	KE-8L	1747	
Bethune, Henry	PE-5R; BE-5	1694	1704
Binning, John	PE-6L	1709	
Blackadder, Adam	DE-4	1763	
Blacklaw, James	RO-9L	1752	
Blair, Charles	YO-6; BL-6	1697	1707
Blair, Joseph	ZI-10L	1808	
Blair, William	CF-4	1653	
Blaw, James or Archibald	HT-3R	1599	
Blyth, William	UR-6	1784	
Bogie, William	RA-9	1751	
Boige, Charles	SC-5	1654	
Boige, David	FC-4	1642	1653

Apprentice/Freeman	Map Position(s)	Apprentice Year	Freedom Year
Bone (Bain), John	ZI-11R	1817	*c.* 1825
Bonthron, Alexander	DA-9L	*c.* 1763-75	
Borthwick, John	BO-6	1662	1675
Borthwick, Patrick	GC-5L; BO-5	1625	1642
Borthwick, Thomas	WT-10	1766	
Boston, John	JM-10R	1808	
Boston, William	MZ-11	1809	
Bowie, Charles	WE-9	1766	
Bowman, James	MZ-9	1768	
Bowman, Robert	UR-5	1767	1780
Boyes, Andrew	CF-2	1593	1610
Braidwood, James	FO-3	1753	
Brock, Thomas	SM-5	1663	
Brodie, Alexander	GA-9R	1802	1814
Brodie (Broddie), John	FK-2	1635	
Brown, Alexander (1)	CF-3	1630	
Brown, Alexander (2)	MT-7R	1745	
Brown, Charles (1)	OL-9	1760	
Brown, Charles (2)	CU-11L	1803	
Brown, David	GR-11	1810	
Brown, Gavin	KE-7R	1743	
Brown, George (1)	WL-6	1701	
Brown, George (2)	SE-7R	1737	
Brown, George (3)	ZI-10R	1812	
Brown, Hugh	TA-8	1741	
Brown, James	BR-7	1702	
Brown, John	GH-4	1590	1602/03
Brown, Robert (1)	WT-9	1767	
Brown, Robert (2)	MU-11L	1816	
Brown, Robert (3)	NA-12R	1857	
Brown, Thomas (1)	CF-3	1630	
Brown, Thomas (2)	YO-7	1701	
Brown, Thomas (3)	AI-10	1786	
Brown, William	CU-11R	1816	
Bruce, Abraham	BA-2	1590	
Bruce, Alexander	LO-8	1747	
Bruce, David	BR-7	1705	
Bruce, Patrick	RY-3	1552	
Bruce, Primrose	SH-2	1819	
Bruce, Robert (1)	FC-6; BR-6	1673	1688
Bruce, Robert (2)	BR-7	1715	

Apprentice/Freeman	Map Position(s)	Apprentice Year	Freedom Year
Bruce, William (2)	RO-9L	1759	
Brydie, Mungo	EF	*c.* 1549	1561
Brysone, Richard	PE-5L	1678	
Buchanan, Andrew	TR-7	1708	
Buchanan, Benjamin (1)	CA-9	1767	1802
Buchanan, Benjamin (2)	MS-10	*c.* 1807	
Buchanan, Robert	MZ-10	1802	
Buchanan, Walter	DA-8L	1742	
Burden, Archibald	SE-6L	1694	
Burnet, William	CY-4L	1653	
Burns, John	NA-11R	1825	
Burrell, Andrew (1)	CS-4	1632	1642
Burrell, Andrew (2)	CR-5L	1670	
Burrell, John (2)	BA-3	1608	
Burrell, John (3)	CS-5	1657	
Burton, William	JL-5	1688	1700
Caithness, James	CR-4L	1636	
Calder, Hugh	HE-6R	1802	
Calder, William	RA-9	1769	
Callander, Edward	AY-8R	1734	
Callender, Davidson	MU-11R	1822	
Cameron, John	IN-6	1701	
Cameron, Kenneth	ZI-10L	1808	
Campbell, Alexander	JI-7	1722	1738
Campbell, Archibald	CA-7	1734	
Campbell, Colin (1)	CM-6; CA-6	1702	1712
Campbell, Colin (2)	CA-7	1734	
Campbell, Colin (3)	JI-8	1740	
Campbell, Colin (4)	KE-8L	1742	
Campbell, David	MT-8L	1744	
Campbell, James (1)	CA-7	*c.* 1727	1734
Campbell, James (2)	FE-2	1818	
Campbell, John (1)	TR-6	1679	
Campbell, John (2)	JI-8	1740	
Campbell, John (3)	KE-7R	1753	
Campbell, Robert	MA-6	1699	
Campbell, William	FC-6	1670	
Carnegie, Robert (1)	DI-4L	1748	
Carnegie, Robert (2)	MH-2	1818	
Carruthers, Andrew	IN-6	1706	

Apprentice/Freeman	Map Position(s)	Apprentice Year	Freedom Year
Carruthers, John	GA-10R	1814	
Carson, John	ZI-11L	1815	
Carstairs, George	NA-11L	1814	1845
Carstairs, William Cooper	NA-12L	1844/46	1865
Caw, David	RO-10R	1805	
Caw, John Blackwood	CU-11L	1805	1815
Chaip, Andrew	DL-3R	1600	
Chaipe (Cheape), Robert	BE-6	1713	
Chalmers, John	UR-5	1765	
Chisholm, Alexander Anslie	GR-11	1813	
Chisholm, Colin	CM-6	1720	
Christie, George	HE-5R	1782	1791
Clark, Alexander	WL-6	1690	
Clark, Andrew (1)	PE-6R	1719	
Clark, Andrew (3)	DO-11	1804	
Clark, Francis	UR-5	1783	
Clark, John (1)	RA-8	1734	1751
Clark, John (2)	MK-10L	1811	
Clark, Robert	WT-9	1754	1763
Clark, William	GA-9R	1797	1805
Cleghorne, Edward (1)	CF-3; CY-3L&R	1637	1649
Cleghorne, Edward (2)	PE-5L	1687/88	1694
Cleghorne, George	CF-3	1630	1641
Cleghorne, Samuel	CF-3	1634	
Cleghorne, Thomas (1)	CF-2	1691	1606
Cleghorne, Thomas (2)	BO-6	1659	1665
Cleghorne, Thomas (3)	CY-4R	1679	1689
Clephan, Thomas	AY-9L	1743	
Cochran, David Wood	NA-12R	1860	1888
Cochran, John (1)	MO-5LT	1601	
Cochran, John (2)	AI-8	1751	
Cockburn, George	RO-10L	*c.* 1800	
Cockburn, James (1)	FC-5	1661	1669
Cockburn, James (2)	BR-7	1702	
Cockburn, John (1)	GC-7L	1646	1666
Cockburn, John (2)	FC-6	1693	

Apprentice/Freeman	Map Position(s)	Apprentice Year	Freedom Year
Cockburn, John (3)	UR-5	1748	
Cokkie (Cok), James (1)	CO-1		*c.* 1520
Cokkie, Archibald	CO-3	1590	1605
Cokkie, James (2)	CO-2	*c.* 1545	1557
Cokkie, James (3)	CO-3	*c.* 1561	1574
Cokkie, James (4)	EF	1577	
Cokkie, Robert	CO-3	1577	1594
Cokkie, William (1)	CO-2	*c.* 1550	1561
Cokkie, William (2)	CO-3	*c.* 1562	*c.* 1586
Colquhoun, John (3)	SH-2	1816	
Colveill, William	ML-2	1577	
Comb, Caleb Hogan	AI-10	*c.* 1815	
Cooper, Alexander Palmer	JM-10R	*c.* 1806	1818
Cooper, Patrick	MO-4LT	1595	
Coutts, Benjamin	FO-3	1727	1754
Coutts, David	CA-8	1739	
Cowie, William	HT-4L	1594	
Craig, Adam	CG-2	*c.* 1550	*c.* 1562
Craig, David	GA-9R	1784	
Craig, James (1)	MY-8	1738	1754
Craig, James (2)	CU-11L	1807	1817
Craig, John (1)	CG-1		*c.* 1550
Craig, John (2)	CG-3	1588/89	
Craig, John (3)	SE-6R	1711	
Craig, Robert (1)	CG-1	*c.* 1514	1526
Craig, Robert (2)	CG-3	1577	
Craig, Robert (3)	JP-7	1729	1746
Cranstoun, Jonaphas	HT-3L	1577	
Craw, William	AI-8	1753	
Crawford, Abraham	CF-2	1614	
Crawford, Alexander	AN-4	1612	
Crawford, Daniel	CF-1	*c.* 1577	1589
Crawford, George (1)	AN-4; GC-4	1591	1606
Crawford, George (2)	GC-6R	1643	
Crawford, James (1)	AN-3	1582	1591
Crawford, James (2)	GC-5R	1635	
Crawford, James (3)	ZI-10L	1810	
Crawford, Thomas	CF-2	1607	1616
Crawford, William (1)	GC-5R	1614	1627
Crawford, William (2)	ZI-10R	1810	
Crichton, Alexander	WC-12	1854	1876

Apprentice/Freeman	Map Position(s)	Apprentice Year	Freedom Year
Crichton, George (1)	MS--10	1825	1845
Crichton, George (2) yngr.	NA-12; CT-12	1862	1876
Crichton, George Duncan	CT-13	1893	1904
Crichton, George Ian Elkron	TT-15	1961	1971
Crichton, George Wilfred Menzies	CT-14	1930	1941
Crichton, John (1)	LE-10	1814	1829
Crichton, John (2)	WC-12	1854	1882
Crichton, John (3)	CT-13	1875/79	1885
Crichton, Michael	MS-11	1868	1882
Crichton, Michael Hewin (1)	NA-11R	1830	1845
Crichton, Michael Hewin (2)	WC-13	1898	1911
Crichton, Walker	MK-11L; WC-11	1826	1853
Crichton, William (1)	RD-3	1606	1619
Crichton, William (2)	AY-9L	1750	
Crichton, William Miller	MS-11	1862	1874
Crookbone, John	GO-8	1748	
Crooks, William	OL-9	1765/68	
Cross, James	GA-11R	1841	1865
Cross, William	GA-10R	1814	1839
Cumming, Alexander	ED-10	1772	
Cumming, James	UR-5	1752	
Cumming, John	SE-6L	1708	1720
Cumming, Thomas (1)	TR-6	1678	
Cumming, Thomas (2)	HE-5L	1761	
Cumming, William	TM-8	1766	
Cunningham, James	GC-6L	1624	1635
Cunningham, John (1)	SY-2	*c.* 1575	1588
Cunningham, John (2)	RO-10R	1792	1798
Cunningham, John (3)	RO-10L	1804	
Cunningham, John Sinclaire	CU-11R	1833	
Cunningham, Murdoch	RO-10L	*c.* 1796	
Cunningham, Patrick (1)	RO-9R	1766	1775

Apprentice/Freeman	Map Position(s)	Apprentice Year	Freedom Year
Cunningham, Patrick (2)	RO-10R	1792	*c.* 1808
Cunningham, Robert	GO-8	1752	
Cunningham, ?	GO-8		
Cunningham, Simon	RO-10L	1792	*c.* 1800
Cunningham, Simpson Andrew	MZ-9	1764	
Cunningham, William (1)	RO-9L	1757	1776
Cunningham, William (2)	RO-10R; CU-10L&R	1792	1802
Dalgarno, John	CY-4R	1675	
Dalgleish, Charles	ZI-10R	1806	1814
Davidson, David	AI-11	1824	
Davidson, John	FK-3	1614	
Davidson, William (1)	BL-7	1733	1749
Davidson, William (2)	HE-6R	1806	
Davie, Adam	DA-8L	1750	1760
Davie, William	TA-7; DA-7L&R	1724	1740
Deas, Joseph	MT-7R	1755	
Dempster, James	DE-4	1756	1775
Dempster, William	DI-3L; DE-3	1732	1742
Denham, William	MZ-9	1755	
Dennistoun, Andrew	DL-3R	*c.* 1624	1636
Dennistoun, David (1)	DL-1L&R	*c.* 1549	1561
Dennistoun, David (2)	CS-4	1626	
Dennistoun, David (3)	FC-4	1654	
Dennistoun, James (1)	DL-2R	*c.* 1587	1598
Dennistoun, James (2)	DL-3R	1610	
Dennistoun, James (3)	DL-3R	1637	
Dennistoun, John	RD-3	1620	
Dennistoun, Robert	DL-2L; RD-2	*c.* 1585	1597
Dewar, Alexander	MU-11R	1820	
Dewar, Henry	BE-6	1717	
Dick, Alexander	JM-10R	1814	
Dick, Charles	DI-4L	1750	
Dick, George	WE-9	1744	
Dick, William	RO-10L	*c.* 1801	*c.* 1807
Dickeson, Andrew	DL-4R	1647	
Dickson, Alexander	CY-6R	1754	
Dickson, Charles (1)	FO-2; DI-2L&R	1702	1719
Dickson, Charles (2)	DI-3L	1730	1738
Dickson, James	GA-9L	1755	

Apprentice/Freeman	Map Position(s)	Apprentice Year	Freedom Year
Dickson, John (1)	SM-5	1646	
Dickson, John (2)	DI-3L	1730	
Dickson, Robert (1)	DI-3L	1720	
Dickson, Robert (2)	DI-4L	1740	
Dickson, Robert (3)	WT-10	1763	
Dickson, William	DI-3R	1733	
Dingwell, John	KE-7R	1738	
Donaldson, James	RO-11L	1804	
Doughty, Benjamin	SH-2	1819	
Douglas, Alexander	EF	1554	
Douglas, Archibald	DO-11	1800	1806
Douglas, James (1)	GL-8	1748	
Douglas, James (2)	WT-10; DO-10	*c.* 1778	1785
Douglas, William (1)	CR-5L	1674	
Douglas, William (2)	OL-9	1748	
Dowie, William Brown	NA-13L	1866	1889
Downie, Charles Stewart	GL-9	1788	
Downie, David	GL-8	1753	1770
Downie, James	DA-9R	1792	
Downie, Robert	JL-5	1679	
Drummond, Alexander	WL-7	1721	
Drummond, Andrew	CM-6	1704	1754
Drummond, William	AY-9R	1752	1760
Drysdale, David	MH-2	1824	
Drysdale, Thomas	MY-8	1731	
Duff, John	CS-5	1642	
Duffus, John	DA-9R	1793	
Duffus, Thomas	DE-4	1767	1780
Dugeal, William	WL-6	1703	
Dunbar, Benjamin	MS-10	1806	
Duncan, Alexander	PE-6R	1734	
Duncan, Charles	PE-5R	1691	1706
Duncan, John (1)	AN-3	*c.* 1578	1592
Duncan, John (2)	ME-4	1725	
Duncan, William (1)	CO-3	1573	1580
Duncan, William (2)	PE-6R	1724	
Durhame, Hercules	MY-7	1711	
Edmond, Alexander	RO-11L	1805	
Edmond, David	AY-9R	1755	
Edmond, John	AY-9R	1746	
Edmonstoun, Alexander (1)	RA-7; ED-7	1712	1721
Edmonstoun, Alexander (2)	GL-9	1759	1779

Apprentice/Freeman	Map Position(s)	Apprentice Year	Freedom Year
Edmonstoun, Alexander (3)	GL-10	*c.* 1800	1807
Edmonstoun, Balfour	MZ-10	1800	1808
Edmonstoun, Hugh	ED-8	1741	
Edmonstoun, John	ED-8	1736	1753
Edmonstoun, William	GL-10	*c.* 1810	1817
Edward, Henry	LO-9	1766	
Edward, James	ZI-11R	1817	
Edward, Thomas	GL-9	1776	
Eiking, Thomas	CS-5	1643	
Elder, Adam	MK-10L	1804	1823
Elder, John	MZ-11	1809	
Elliot, James	LD-4	1618	
Elliot, John	SE-6R	1721	
Elliot, William	MI-8	1712	
Ellis, Samuel	GH-5	1618	
English, John	WE-9	1747	
Ewing, Thomas	EF		*c.* 1545
Fairbairn, James	DL-3; CR-3R; FC-3	1630/32	1641
Fairly, Robert	HT-3R	1586	1597
Falconer, David	KE-7R	1731/35	
Farquharson, Alexander	AY-8L	1725	1734
Farquharson, Charles Henry	MH-2	1825	
Farquharson, James Russell	JM-10L	1804	
Farquharson, Lewis	WE-9	1761	
Feddes, John	MI-8	1761	
Fender, David	RD-3	1599	
Fender, Edward	RD-3	1600	
Fenwick, George (1)	FE-1	*c.* 1788-95	1810
Fenwick, George (2)	FE-2	1812	1820
Fergusson, Henry	RA-7	1709	
Fergusson, James	TM-7	1717	
Finlay, Robert	KE-9L	1759	
Finlayson, Henry (1)	CF-3	1621	
Finlayson, Henry (2)	DA-9L	1760	
Finlayson, John	CR-3L	1622	
Fisher, John	DO-11	*c.* 1805	
Foot/Fytt, David	AY-9R	1738	
Foot/Fytt, John	IN-7	1739	
Foote, James	MZ-11	*c.* 1809	
Forbes, Alexander (1)	FO-1	*c.* 1680	1692
Forbes, Alexander (2)	PE-6L	1709	
Forbes, Alexander (3)	AI-8	1765	

Apprentice/Freeman	Map Position(s)	Apprentice Year	Freedom Year
Forbes, George	FO-2	1718	1731
Forbes, William	FO-2	1705	
Forman, Thomas	FC-4	1649	
Forrest, William	DA-8L	1746	
Forsyth, Samuel	DO-11	1792	
Fortune, John	CU-11R	1813	
Foulaire, Robert	EF	*c.* 1501	
Foulis, David	HT-4R	1609	
Foulis, George (1)	FK-1	*c.* 1582	1594
Foulis, George (2)	FK-2	1623/25	
Foulis, Henry	FK-0		*c.* 1550
Foulis, Robert	CF-2; CR-2	1617	
Foulis, Thomas	GI-2	*c.* 1569	1581
Fouller, James	DI-4R	1749	
France, James	CU-12L	1820	
Frances, Matthew	EF	1573	
Fraser, John (1)	FK-3	1611	1624
Fraser, John (2)	MH-2	1817	
Fraser, John (3)	MK-10R	1818	
Fraser, William	FK-4	1642	
Frethman, Gavin	EF	*c.* 1549	1561
Frier, James	ZI-11L	1825	
Frogg, John	ME-3	1693	
Gairden or Garden, Robert	CY-4L	1657	
Galbraith, John	GI-3	1587	1601
Gardner, Alexander	AY-8R; GA-8L&R	1744	1754
Gardner, John (1)	MA-6	1691	
Gardner, John (2)	GA-6	1773	
Ged, Dougal	AY-8L	1718	1734
Ged, Thomas	LO-8	1736	
Ged, William	IN-6; GE-6	1696	1706
Gibb, John	NA-12R	1869	
Gibson, James	NA-11R	1834	
Gibson, Robert (1)	ML-3	1610	1628
Gibson, Robert (2)	ML-4	1655	
Giddes, Charles	LO-8	1739	
Gilbert, Alexander	GI-0		*c.* 1530
Gilbert, David	GI-2; ML-1	1577	1590
Gilbert, John (1)	GI-1	*c.* 1536	*c.* 1550
Gilbert, John (2)	ZI-11R	1819	
Gilbert, Michael (1)	GI-0		*c.* 1530
Gilbert, Michael (2)	GI-1	*c.* 1537	*c.* 1550
Gilchrist, Archibald	MI-7	1716	
Gilchrist, George	GL-8	1749	
Gilchrist, William (1)	TA-7;GL-7	1718	1736

Apprentice/Freeman	Map Position(s)	Apprentice Year	Freedom Year
Gilchrist (or Guthrie), William (2)	DI-3L	1720	
Gillespie, James	IN-6	1686	
Gillies, Hugh	CU-12L	1826	
Gilliland, James	UR-4	1736	1748
Gilmore (Gilmour), Andrew	FC-6; GM-6	1677	1686
Gilmour (Gilmore), Thomas Jr.	JM-10L	1805	
Gladstaines, Adam	SY-3	1592	
Glass, Thomas	MU-11R	1822	
Glen, James	MT-8L	1737	
Goodsman, John	RO-9R	1767	
Gordon, Adam	ME-2	*c.* 1688	1696
Gordon, Alexander (2)	IN-8	1758	
Gordon, Alexander (3)	AI-10	1797	
Gordon, George	ED-8	1727	
Gordon, Hugh	SE-6R	1717	1727
Gordon, Peter	TA-7	1727	
Gordon, Robert	TA-7; GO-7	1731	1741
Graham (Graeme), John (1)	FO-2	1705	
Graham (Graeme), Patrick	GE-7	1714	1725
Graham, Alexander	WL-6	1695	
Graham, Alexander Aitken	MK-11L	1824	
Graham, John (2)	RO-9R	*c.* 1790/91	
Graham, John (4)	CU-11R	1813	
Graham, Robert	FC-7	1714	
Graham, Symon	CO-3	1589/90	
Grant, Alexander	UR-5	1786	
Grant, George (1)	WL-6	1714	
Grant, George (2)	SH-2	1818	
Grant, Thomas	GL-9	1760	
Grant, William	AY-9R	1758	
Gray, David	DO-11	1792	
Gray, James	GR-11	1820	
Gray, John	MZ-10	1792	
Gray, Robert	CY-4R	1679	
Gray, William (1)	MO-5LT	1652	
Gray, William (2)	TR-6	1675	
Greig, David	KE-8L	1747	
Greig, James Gibson	AI-10	1811	1852

Apprentice/Freeman	Map Position(s)	Apprentice Year	Freedom Year
Grier, James	CY-5R	1702/03	
Grierson, Robert (1)	JM-10L; GR-10	*c.* 1798	1805
Grierson, Robert (2)	GR-11	1807	
Grierson, Robert (3)	GR-11	1813	
Grieson, Robert (4) Jr.	GR-11	1819	
Guthrie, Robert	BL-7	1742	
Guthrie, William	DI-3	1720	
Guthry, James	PE-6L	1700	
Hairt, Edward	CO-3; ML-1	*c.* 1563	1575
Haldane, David	HT-4L	1607	1624
Haliburton, James	GO-8	1753	
Haliday, John	CU-11R	1816	
Halkerston, Robert	MT-7R	1742	
Hall, Robert and/or John	RO-9R	1772	
Hally, James (1)	KE-7L	1723	1738
Hally, James (2)	KE-8L	1749	
Hamilton, Alexander	GC-7R	1649	
Hamilton, Arthur	MI-7	1709	
Hamilton, George	GI-3	1590	
Hamilton, Hugh	CA-7	1712	
Hamilton, John	DA-8R	1762	
Hamilton, Robert	RO-10L	1787	1798/99
Hamilton, Thomas	CR-5	1686	
Hamilton, William	GA-9L	1765	
Hardisty, George	MU-11L	1814	
Harlaw, James	AN-4	1623	
Hartholm, David	KE-7R	1735	
Hathorn, Henry	MI-7	1731	
Haxton, James	NA-12L	1825	
Hay, Andrew	MY-8	1719	
Hay, Michael	ED-8	1733	
Hay, Robert	JL-6	1689	
Hay, Thomas	GM-8	1701	1719
Hector, John	GA-9L	1768	
Henderson, Alexander	HE-5R	*c.* 1785	1792
Henderson, George	EF	*c.* 1563	1575
Henderson, James	CA-8	1743	
Henderson, John	GO-8	1745	
Henderson, Michael	LO-8	1759	
Henderson, Robert	LO-8	1733	
Henderson, William	MZ-11	1809	
Henrie, Robert	LD-4	1589	

Apprentice/Freeman	Map Position(s)	Apprentice Year	Freedom Year
Hepburn, George	ME-2	1679	
Heriot, Alexander	HT-4L	1611	1642
Heriot, David	HT-3L	1573	1592/93
Heriot, George (1)	HT-1L&R		*c.* 1540
Heriot, George (2)	HT-2L&R		*c.* 1562
Heriot, George (3)	HT-3L; GH-3	*c.* 1576	1588
Heriot, George (4)	CY-4L	1657	
Heriot, James (1)	HT-3L	1563	
Heriot, James (2)	HT-3R	1581	1594
Heriot, Joseph	TA-7	1739	
Heriot, Patrick	HT-3R	1586	
Hewitt, James	DE-4; HE-4L&R	1746	1760
Hewitt, William	HE-5L	1770	1778
Hill, George	HT-4L	1601	
Hill, James	DI-3R	1736	1746
Hill, William	CA-9	1770	
Hog, Charles (1)	PE-6L	1700	
Hog, Charles (2)	OL-9	1761	
Home, Andrew	FO-2	1697	
Home, James	AL-4	1596	
Home, John	FO-2	1694	
Home, Patrick	HT-3R	1604	
Hope (Hoip), David	CO-4	1595	1609
Hope, Alexander	DI-4R	1755	
Hope, John	GE-8	1733	
Hope, Robert	BE-6	1729	1743
Horn, ? (illegible)	GE-7	1755	
Houston, Alexander	CU-11L	1807	
Howden, Francis	AI-9	*c.* 1773	1781
Howden, John	AI-10	1814	*c.* 1822
Howden, William	RO-11L	1801	1816
Howieson, Alexander	FC-6	1687	
Howieson, Richard	PE-6L	1694	
Humphrey, James	JP-7	1741	
Hunter, James	YO-6	1685	
Hunter, John	MU-11R	1823	
Hunter, John Adam	GA-9L	1770	
Hunter, Matthew	DL-3L	1596	
Hunter, William	AY-9R	1742	
Hutchison, James (or Thomas)	ZI-11L	1832	
Hutchison, John	LE-10	1811	
Hutchison, Thomas	TR-6	1676	1687
Hutton, John Archibald	RB-13	1885	1903

Apprentice/Freeman	Map Position(s)	Apprentice Year	Freedom Year
Hutton, John Pears	RB-12	1856	1870
Hutton, Robert	HE-7R	1855	
Inglis, Alexander	IN-6	1724	
Inglis, James (1)	PE-6C; JI-6	1710	1720
Inglis, James (2)	IN-6	1712	
Inglis, Robert (1)	CY-5L; IN-5	1677	1686
Inglis, Robert (2)	PE-6L	1703	
Inglis, Robert (3)	IN-6	1712	
Innes, Robert	GE-8	1725	
Irving, Emelius	BE-7	1731	
Irving, John (1)	PE-6C	1702	
Irving, John (2)	DI-4R	1753	1768
Irving, Robert	FO-4	1755	
Ivir, David	AI-8	1755	
Jackson, Alexander (1)	GC-6L	1630	
Jackson, Alexander (2)	RA-8	1750	
Jackson, Orlando	WE-9	1750	
Jamieson, Henry	MK-10R	1830	
Jamieson, James	IN-8	1747	
Jamieson, William	PE-6R; JP-6	1718	1729
Jeffrey, William	AY-8R	1751	
Jervey, Thomas	ED-9	1765	
Johnston, Andrew	JL-5	1692	
Johnston, Archibald	CF-4	1656	
Johnston, John (1)	RO-9L	1756	
Johnston, John (2)	ZI-11L	1824	
Johnston, Patrick	DE-4	1760	
Johnston, Robert	MH-2	1814	
Justice, John	ML-4	1647	
Kay (Key), Thomas	BL-7	1729	1742
Keir, Alexander	RB-13	1868	1885
Keir, Charles Edward Fraser	WC-13	1904	
Keir, George Handysid	MK-10L	1810	
Keir, Thomas	CS-5	1653	
Kennedy, Archibald	KE-7R	1740	
Kennedy, William	PE-6L	1698	
Ker, ? (indistinct)	KE-7R	1750	
Ker, Alexander	BR-8	1708	
Ker, Daniel	CA-8	*c.* 1736	1764
Ker, James (1)	JL-6	1694	
Ker, James (2)	PE-6L; KE-6L&R	1709	1723
Ker, Robert	CY-5R	1694	1705

Apprentice/Freeman	Map Position(s)	Apprentice Year	Freedom Year
Ker, Samuel Archibald	HE-5R	*c.* 1782	1789
Ker, Thomas	PE-5L	1685	1694
Ker, William (1)	KE-7L	1731	
Ker, William (2)	OL-8	1750	1760
Kettle, David	ED-9	1762	
Kilpatrick (Kirkpatrick), Thomas	CR-5L	1675	
Kincaid, Alexander	ME-2	1683	1692
Kincaid, Archibald	ME-3	1699	
Kincaid, John (1)	ME-3	1709	1726
Kincaid, John (2)	ME-3	1728	
Kirkwood, David Wilson	TT-15	1960	
Kirkwood, Gilbert	FK-2	1596	1609
Kirkwood, Henry Bruce	NA-12R	1863	1879
Kirkwood, James (1)	NA-11R	1815	1852
Kirkwood, James (2)	NA-12R	1855	
Kirkwood, Lawrence	FK-4	1637	
Kirkwood, Thomas	FK-3	1620	1632
Kyle, James	EF		*c.* 1520
Kyle, John	EF		*c.* 1550
Kyle, Robert	FC-6	1689	
Kyle, Walter	EF	1554	
Laing, George (1)	JI-8	1744	
Laing, George (2)	SH-2	1819	
Laing, Thomas	MH-2	1817	
Lamb, Adam	RD-3	1609	1619
Lamb, John	GI-3	1591	1597
Lauder, David	CY-6R	1707	
Lauder (or Cawder), Gilbert	DL-3L	1590	
Lauder, William	BL-7	1726	
Laurie, George	CU-12L	1821	
Laurie, John	HE-6R	1810	1821
Lauson, Andrew	HT-4R	1611	
Law, Alexander	ZI-10L	1807	
Law, Andrew	JL-5	1683	1694
Law, Hugh	JL-6	1694	1703
Law, John (1)	ML-4; JL-4	1649	1662
Law, John (2)	SM-6	1679	
Law, Robert (1)	CS-5	1646	1658
Law, Robert (2)	JL-6	1694	
Law, William (1)	CS-5; SM-5	1650/54	1662
Law, William (2)	JL-5; WL-5	1672	1686

Apprentice/Freeman	Map Position(s)	Apprentice Year	Freedom Year
Law, William (3)	BR-7	1694	1703
Leishman, John	CS-5	1633	1662
Leisk, Alexander	ST-2	1601	
Leitch, Charles	CM-6	1708	
Lennox, David	DE-4	1742	
Lerro, George	GA-9R; LE-9	1797	1810
Lerro, William	MZ-11	*c.* 1813	1820
Leslie, Thomas	CY-5R	1703	1712
Letham, George	ZI-11R	1817	
Lindsay, Gavin	LD-4	1626	
Lindsay, George (1)	LD-4	1595	
Lindsay, George (2)	ED-9	1754	
Lindsay, Henry	GH-5	1609	
Lindsay, Hugh	CO-3; LD-3	1577	1587
Lindsay, John (1)	GH-4	1592	1600
Lindsay, John (2)	GH-5	1631	
Lindsay, Patrick	GE-7	1718	
Lintoun, William	CY-4R	1675	
Lithgow, Gilbert	MY-7	1719	
Little, Robert	RA-9	1763/65	
Livingston, Henry	FO-3	1757	
Livingston, James	LD-4	1599	
Livingston, John	LD-4	1605	
Livingston, William (1)	SC-5	1663	
Livingston, William (2)	TA-7	1714	
Logan, Robert	GE-8	1729	
Lothian, Edward	MI-7; LO-7	1720	1731
Lothian, George	LO-8	1750	
Low, Francis	NA-13L	1871	
Low, John	KE-8L	1742	
Low, Robert	KE-7R	1732	1742
Lowie, John	PE-6C	1701	
Lumsden, James (1)	GI-2	*c.* 1573	1577
Lumsden, James (2)	CA-9	1791	
Lyall, George	FE-2	1823	
Lyon, Thomas	MU-11R	1825	
Lyon, William	GH-5	1613	
Madder, William	CA-7	1714	
Main, George (1)	CY-5L; MA-5	1676	1688
Main, George (2)	MA-6	1714	
Main, James	MA-6	1701	
Main, John	MA-6	1714	1729
Main, Robert	MA-6	1705	
Malcolm, Robert	CA-9	1760	

Apprentice/Freeman	Map Position(s)	Apprentice Year	Freedom Year
Manuel, Thomas	RO-9R	1765	
Marshall, David	CA-8	1757	1782
Marshall, John	CU-11R	1817	
Marshall, John Nicholson	NA-12R	1866	
Marshall, Robert Paton	CU-11R	1817	1857
Marshall, Thomas	PE-5R	1701	
Marshall, William (1)	UR-4	1718	1734
Marshall, William (2)	GL-9; MS-9	*c.* 1791	1802
Marshall, William Calder	MS-10	1828	
Martin, Robert	GA-9L	1757	
Martine, George	AI-8	1762	
Mason, (Maisone), Alexander (1)	EF		*c.* 1530
Mason, Alexander (2)	DI-4R	1763	
Mastertoun, Alexander	CR-5L	1678	
Mathie, James	HE-6R	1814	
Mathie, Peter	DA-8R	1759	1774
Mathie, Thomas	DA-9L	1761	
Maxwell, Robert	NA-11R	1817	
McAulay, James (1)	ML-2	*c.* 1586	1598
McAulay, James (2)	ML-4	1630	1644
McBayne, Thomas	NA-11R	1823	
McConchie, Bethram? (illegible)	MK-10R	1814	
McCulloch, Andrew	CF-4	1652	
McDonald, Alexander (1)	RO-10R	1811	
McDonald, Alexander (2)	WC-12	1836	
McDonald, Donald	CM-6	1717	
McDonald, James (1)	RO-10R	1805/08	1815
McDonald, James (2)	WC-12	1835	
McDonald, John	CM-6	1712	
McDonald, Ronald	ED-9	1757	1768
McDougal, George	MT-7R	1733/36	
McDowell, William	NA-11R	1823	
McDuff, John	RA-9	1767	
McEwan, Andrew	UR-5	1762	
McEwan, Daniel	WL-7	1715	
McFarland, James	TM-9	1817	
McFarland, John	ML-3	1605	

Apprentice/Freeman	Map Position(s)	Apprentice Year	Freedom Year
McFarlane, Thomas	MI-7	1708	
McGill, David	GC-5R	1616	
McGowen, George	RO-10R	1807	
McGregor, Colin	AI-10	1803	
McGregor, Robert Anderson	AI-11	1824	
McGrew, John	MK-10R	1816	
McHardie, Charles	DA-8R	1768	
McHattie, George	MH-1	*c.* 1786	1811
McIlriach, James	SH-2	1819	
McIntosch, Alexander	BR-8	1703	
McIntyre, Hugh	JM-10L	1799	
McKay, Alexander	MK-10R	1828	
McKay, Donald	TM-9	1805	
McKay, James (1)	GA-9R; MK-9L&R	1783	1793
McKay, James (2)	MK-10R	1812	
McKay, William	MK-11L	1824	
McKell, John	JM-10R	1805/08	
McKenzie, Charles (1)	MT-7L	1717	1726
McKenzie, Charles (2)	MY-8	1733	
McKenzie, Colin (1)	PE-5L; CM-5	1686/88	1695
McKenzie, Colin (2)	CM-6	1708	
McKenzie, George	JM-10R	1817	
McKenzie, James (1)	MY-8; MZ-8	1731	1747
McKenzie, James (2)	MZ-9; JM-9L&R	1759	1775
McKenzie, James (3)	MZ-10	1790	
McKenzie, John	CM-6	1699	
McKenzie, John (2)	CM-6	1730	
McKenzie, John (3)	MU-11L	1814	
McKenzie, John Donaldson	SH-2	1817	
McKenzie, Kenneth	MY-7	1706	1714
McKenzie, Norman	RA-9	1759	
McKenzie, Roderick	CM-6	1712	
McKenzie, William (1)	MZ-9	1773	1783
McKenzie, William (2)	MZ-10	1801	1807
McKenzie, William (3)	JM-10L	1805	
McKerter, James	KE-9L	1755	
McKinnon, Martin	IN-8	1764	
McLaughlain, James	CA-7	1746	
McLaymond, James	GA-9L	1762	
McLean, Charles James	NA-12R	*c.* 1885	1913
McLean, Daniel	ZI-10L	1804	

Apprentice/Freeman	Map Position(s)	Apprentice Year	Freedom Year
McLean, George (1)	CU-11R	1816	1849
McLean, George (2)	CT-14	1923	1933
McLean, Ian Hargreaves	CT-14	1923	1938
McLean, John Craig	NA-11R	1849	1876
McLean, John Montgomery	CT-13	1880	1893
McLean, Laughlan	MZ-9	1752	
McLean, Robert	AI-10	1804	
McLean, William	MI-7	1703	
McLeod, Angus	ZI-11L	1825	
McLeod, Duncan	LO-8	1759	
McNaughton, John	HE-7R	1815	
McPhail, Archibald	BL-8	1749	
Meane, John	JL-5	1674	
Meickle, Samuel	DL-4R	1653	1663
Mein, David	AY-9L	1735	
Meldrum, John	KE-7R	1747	
Meldrum, Peter	RB-13	1863	
Mellinus, Zaccharias	ME-1		1672
Melvill, William	SE-6L	1694	
Menzies, John	WL-7	1718	
Mercer, John	ST-1	1577	
Merstoun, Andrew	SC-5	1649	1668
Metcalf, Matthew	UR-6	1780	
Metcalf, Solomon	RO-10R	1801	
Middleton, Alexander	BR-7	1698	
Middleton, Charles	CM-6	1694/95	
Miller, John	AY-8R	1732	
Milligan, John	MK-10L	1803	
Milne, David	MO-3LT	*c.* 1561	1573
Milne, John	MO-4LT	*c.* 1632	1644
Milne, Robert	MO-4LT	1600	
Mitchell, David	IN-6; MI-6	1690	1700
Mitchell, Henry James	FE-2	1820	
Mitchell, James (1)	IN-6	1725	1736
Mitchell, James (2)	WE-9	*c.* 1760	
Mitchell, John Lawrence	SH-2	1819	
Mitchell, Thomas	PE-6L; TM-6	1696	1709
Mitchell, William Cunningham	ZI-11L	1818	
Mitchelson, James (1)	MA-6; MT-6L&R	1696	1706
Mitchelson, James (2)	MT-7R	1736	
Mitchelson, John (1)	BR-7	1697	
Mitchelson, John (2)	MT-7R	1736	

Apprentice/Freeman	Map Position(s)	Apprentice Year	Freedom Year
Mitchelson, Walter	WL-7	1750	
Mochie, John	GR-11	1819	
Moore, Archibald	MY-7	1715	
Moore, Robert	CA-8	1744	
Morgan, Peter	MH-2	1821	
Morrison, Charles	DI-4R	1760	
Morrison, David	BE-6	1726	
Mortimer, Patrick	CR-5	1680	
Mosman, Alan	MO-0EA		*c.* 1505
Mosman, Alexander	MO-0EA		*c.* 1530
Mosman, Hugh	MO-2EA		*c.* 1560
Mosman, James (1)	MO-0EA		*c.* 1525
Mosman, James (2)	MO-2EA<	*c.* 1542	*c.* 1554
Mosman, James (3)	MO-3LT	*c.* 1575	*c.* 1585
Mosman, James (4)	MO-4LT	1586	
Mosman, John (1)	MO-1EA		*c.* 1540
Mosman, John (2) elder	MO-2EA	*c.* 1552	1564
Mosman, John (3) younger	MO-3LT	1564	1575/76
Mosman, Thomas (1)	MO-1EA		*c.* 1554
Mosman, Thomas (2)	MO-2EA		*c.* 1578
Muir, Andrew	TA-7	1705	
Muir, George	ME-2	1672	
Muir, James	JM-10L; MU-10L&R	1799	*c.* 1810-13
Muir, John	GA-9L	1760	
Muir, Thomas	BO-6	1649	
Munro, James	HE-6R	1794	1806
Murdoch, William	IN-7	1748	
Murray, Alexander	RO-10L	1796	
Murray, Andrew	FK-4	1632	
Murray, Anthony	AY-9L	1738	
Murray, George	DI-4R	1746	
Murray, James (1)	MY-7	1702	
Murray, James (2)	DE-4	1754	
Murray, Lewis	NA-11R	1830	
Murray, Mungo	CM-6	1720	
Murray, Patrick (1)	FC-6	1692	1701
Murray, Patrick (2)	FC-7	1718	1728
Murray, Patrick (3)	RA-7	1718	1732
Murray, Richard	CU-11R	1822	
Murray, Robert (1)	ST-0		*c.* 1554
Murray, Robert (2)	AY-9L	1735	
Murray, William	RA-8	1738	
Nairn, Robert	AY-9L	1735	
Napier, James	ME-3	1720	

Apprentice/Freeman	Map Position(s)	Apprentice Year	Freedom Year
Nasmyth, Charles James	NA-11R	1840	
Nasmyth, James	MZ-10; NA-10L&R	1803	1813
Neilson, Alexander	ME-3	1698	
Neilson, Peter	RD-4	1635	1647
Neilson, Robert	DI-4R	1765	
Nicholson, John	DE-5	1766	
Nicholson, William	HT-4R	1599	
Nicoll, John	ML-4	1652	
Nisbit, Lewis (Luis)	ME-2	1675	
Nisbit, Patrick	MY-7	1710	
Ochiltree, Archibald	ED-9	1760	1772
Ochiltree, Charles	GO-8	1756	
Ogill, Archibald	DL-4R	1642	
Ogilvee, James (1)	DL-3L	1596	
Ogilvee, James (2)	MI-8	1761	
Oliphant, Ebenezer	MT-7L	1727	1737
Oliphant, James	KE-8L	1751	1760
Oliphant, Lawrence	GE-7; OL-7	1710	1737
Ord, Robert	HT-4L	1605	
Orrock, William	PE-6C	1703	
Oswald, David	IN-6	1692	
Palmer, David (1)	HT-3L	1564	1578
Palmer, David (2)	GC-5R	1621	
Palsen, Patrick	FO-3	1740	
Park, James Snodgrass	NA-12R	1852	1903
Park, John	BR-7	*c.* 1688-94	
Parlen, Watson	NA-12L	1825	
Paterson, Alexander	FO-3	1740	
Paterson, George	MA-6	1693	
Paterson, Robert	ST-2	1588	
Paton, Alexander	ED-8	1751	
Paton, George	MH-2	1817	
Paton, Neil	UR-5	1757	1783
Pearson, David	ZI-11L	1817	
Peat, William Scott	DO-11	1802	1813
Penman, Edward	PE-5C	1692	1700
Penman, Hugh	PE-6C; JP-6	1720	1734
Penman, James	CY-4L; PE-4L,C&R	1666	1673
Penman, John (elder)	CY-5R	1690	1702
Penman, John (younger)	PE-5C	1689/90	1703
Phillip, John	ME-3	1703	
Pine, Thomas	ED-10	1777	
Pirie, Thomas	CF-4	1647	

Apprentice/Freeman	Map Position(s)	Apprentice Year	Freedom Year
Pollock, Archibald (1)	RB-12	1849	1860
Pollock, Archibald (2)	CT-13	1883	
Pollock, David (1)	ST-3	1620	
Pollock, David (2)	DO-12	1815	1847
Pollock, John	MI-8	1719	
Pollock, Thomas Valentine	RB-13	1893	1919
Porter, Thomas	RA-9	1762	
Preston, Edward Hall	MU-11R	1827	
Preston, George	CY-5L	1674	
Preston, Richard	JL-6	1695	
Pringle, Andrew	MT-7L	1707	
Pringle, John	CA-8	*c.* 1755	
Pringle, William	YO-6	1691	
Provand, James	BA-2	1586	
Rae, Richard	PE-6L; RA-6	1691/94	1703
Rae, William	CR-5L	1665	1673
Raeburn, Henry	UR-5	1771	
Rait, Robert	MU-11L	1818	
Rait, William Skirvin	MK-11L	1826	
Ramage, Alexander	TM-9	1805	1821
Ramage, John	DA-9R	1805	
Ramsey, George	HT-3R	1592	
Ramsey, James	BL-7	1714	
Rankin, Gabriel	SE-6L	1698	
Reid, Alexander (1)	CF-2; CR-2L&R	1604	1618
Reid, Alexander (2)	CR-4L&R	1644	1660
Reid, Alexander (3)	CR-5L; TR-6	1668	1677
Reid, Alexander (4)	CR-5; IN-6	1692/1699	
Reid, Alexander (6)	LO-8	1750	1760
Reid, Christian	DA-8R	1769	
Reid, James	DA-8L	1747	1760
Reid, John	MT-8R	1760	
Reid, Thomas	PE-6L	1703	
Renton, Robert	ME-3	1696	
Rhind, William	CA-9	1769	
Richardson, James	MY-8	1752	
Richardson, John (1)	MK-10L	1811	
Richardson, John (2)	NA-11R	1819	
Rigg, Alexander	BR-7	1689	
Ritchie, Joseph	RO-9L	1761	
Ritchie, Nicoll	AI-10	1799	
Robb, Charles	CU-11L; RB-11	1815	1844
Robb, Thomas	RB-12	1844	1857
Robertson, Alexander	WT-10	1763	

Apprentice/Freeman	Map Position(s)	Apprentice Year	Freedom Year
Robertson, Alexander	WT-10	1763	
Robertson, Andrew	HT-3R	1607	
Robertson, George (1)	GC-5L	1607	1616
Robertson, George (2)	GC-6L	1634	1643
Robertson, George (3)	GC-7L	1663	
Robertson, George (5)	MT-8L	1740	
Robertson, James (1)	GC-6L	1617	
Robertson, James (2)	UR-6	1793	
Robertson, John (1)	CY-5L	1682	
Robertson, John (2)	MA-6	1688	
Robertson, John (3)	MT-7R	1747/49	1758
Robertson, Marcus	SC-6	1681	
Robertson, Patrick	LO-8; RO-8L&R	1743	1751
Robertson, Robert	FC-6	1694/95	1706
Robertson, Thomas (1)	BO-6	1647	
Robertson, William (1)	CR-5L	1662	
Robertson, William (2)	RO-9R	1783	1789
Rodger, Alexander	DA-9R	*c.* 1796	
Rolland, George	BO-6	1660	1675
Rollo, John	BE-6	1723	1731
Rollo, Robert	LO-8	1742	
Rose, Arthur	RA-8	1759	
Ross, Adam	MS-10	1805	
Ross, George	ME-3	1717	
Ross, William	FO-3	1731	
Row, John	TR-6	1684	
Roxburgh, John	GO-8	1751	
Rudaiman, John	ED-9	1766	
Russell (or Burrel), Alan	GA-9L	1775	
Rutherford, James	OL-8	1737	1748
Rutherford, John Crichton	CU-12L	1825	
Rynd, Edward	RY-3	1563	
Rynd, George	RY-1		*c.* 1530
Rynd, Michael (1)	RY-2	c1533	1545
Rynd, Robert	RY-1		*c.* 1530
Rynd, Thomas (1)	RY-0		*c.* 1520
Rynd, Thomas (2)	RY-2	1544	
Rynd, William	RY-0		*c.* 1520
Sandeland, Charles	BE-6	1710	
Sanders, Archibald	DE-4	1751	
Sands, James	UR-5	1756	
Saunders, George	WE-9	1760	
Saxon, Joseph	MT-8R	1760	
Scott, Alexander (1)	CS-4; SC-4	1637	1649

Apprentice/Freeman	Map Position(s)	Apprentice Year	Freedom Year
Scott, Alexander (2)	SC-5	1662	
Scott, Andrew	PE-6R	1709	
Scott, Donald	MU-11R	1824	
Scott, George (1)	SC-5	1668	1680
Scott, George (2)	GM-7	1687	1697
Scott, James (1)	PE-6L	1694	
Scott, James (2)	MT-7L	1709	1722
Scott, John (1)	CF-3; CS-3	1611	1621
Scott, John (2)	SC-5	1677	
Scott, Robert	ME-2	*c.* 1689	1697
Scott, Thomas	CS-4	1641	1649
Scott, Walter (1)	JL-5	1677	1686
Scott, Walter (2)	BR-7	1690	1701
Scott, Walter (3)	MI-7	1720	
Scott, William (1)	SC-5	1677	
Scott, William (2)	FC-6	1684	
Seaton, Andrew	BE-6	1706	
Seaton, Christopher	SE-6R	1715	
Seaton, George	AN-4	1592	
Seaton, John	CR-5R; SE-5L&R	1677	1688
Sempil, Thomas	WE-9	1769	1791
Seymour, George	MT-7L	1712	
Shand, James	SE-6L	1704	
Shanks, Martin	NA-11L	1814	
Sharp, Patrick	CO-4	1603	
Sheills, Gavin	KE-7L	1727	
Sheldon, Richard	SH-1		*c.* 1816
Short, John Campbell	NA-12L	1862	
Simpson (Sympsone), James (1)	CY-4R	1677	1687
Simpson, Alexander	MI-7	1700	1710
Simpson, James (2)	FK-3	1636	
Simpson, John Swinton	RO-10L	*c.* 1781	1786
Simpson, William	PE-6R	1713	
Sinclair, John	RB-13	1867	1900
Sinclair, William (2)	SE-7R	1740	
Skeen, Edward	FC-7	1710	
Sligh, James	MK-10L	1805	
Small, Peter	FE-3	1816	
Smith, Alexander	TM-8	1761	
Smith, John Lyon	AI-10	1810	
Smith, Thomas	SH-2	1816	
Smiton, Alexander	KE-8L	1754	
Smiton, James	BE-6	1720	

Apprentice/Freeman	Map Position(s)	Apprentice Year	Freedom Year
Smyt, John	SC-5	1665	
Sommervail, Francis	DA-9L	1760	
Sommervail, James (1)	BL-7	1708	
Sommervail, James (2)	KE-8L	1739	1754
Sorreck, Henry Strabach	FE-2	1812	1818
Sorreck, Simon Joseph	NA-11L	1814	
Spaulding, Alexander	LO-8	1759	
Spaulding, Peter	MI-7	1737	1753
Spence, Alexander	DA-8R	1767	1783
Spence, James (2)	HE-5R	1792	
Spence, John	DA-9R	1804	
Spence, Robert	DA-9R	1800	
Stalker, Andrew	ST-2	*c.* 1585	1597
Stalker, Henry	ST-0	*c.* 1551	1563
Stalker, James (1)	ST-0		*c.* 1557
Stalker, James (2)	ST-2	1595	1618
Stalker, John	ST-1	1554	
Stalker, William (1)	ST-1	*c.* 1564-74	1586
Stalker, William (2)	ST-2	1590	1600
Steel, Alexander	CU-11R	1813	
Steel, James	ZI-11L	1814	
Steel, Thomas	SM-6	1680	
Steven, George	TM-9	1791	1817
Steven, John	AY-8R	1737	
Stevenson, Alexander	SM-6	1674	
Stevenson, James (1)	FK-4	1637	
Stevenson, James (2)	TR-7	1704	
Stevenson, John (1)	JL-5	1669	
Stevenson, John (2)	TR-7	1704	
Stevenson, William	FE-2	1812	
Stewart, Alexander	CA-8	1761	
Stewart, Fraser	MK-10R	1821	
Stewart, Gilbert	GL-8	1749	
Stewart, James	JI-9	*c.* 1799	
Stewart, John	GL-10	1809	
Stewart, Robert (1)	UR-5	1778	
Stewart, Robert (2)	RO-10R	1806	
Stewart, William (1)	AY-9L	1735	
Stewart, William (2)	GL-8	1772	
Stirling, Archibald	GI-3	1595	
Stirling, John	MZ-9	1749	
Storie, John	HE-6R	1796	
Strachan, Alexander	SC-5	1675	
Straitoun, Robert	AN-4	1597/98	
Straitoun, William	CO-4	1594	1609

Apprentice/Freeman	Map Position(s)	Apprentice Year	Freedom Year
Sutherland, George	MK-10R	1816	
Sutherland, John	MT-7L	1723	
Sutherland, Patrick	HE-6R	1817	1839
Sutter, John	ZI-11R	1815	
Swan, Robert	HE-5L	1776	1786
Syme, John (1)	SY-2	1552	
Syme, John (2)	MO-4LT	1589	
Syme, Michael	SY-2	*c.* 1563	1575
Syme, Nicoll	SY-1	*c.* 1540	1552
Syme, William	MO-4LT	*c.* 1589	
Symontoun, James	ML-4; SM-4	1635	1645
Symour, John	FC-6	1680	
Tait, Adam	TA-7	1724	1740
Tait, Benjamin	AI-8	1747	1763
Tait, James (1)	YO-6; TA-6	1694	1704
Tait, James (2)	GE-7	1724	
Tait, Robert	MK-10L	1805	
Tansh, George	DA-8L	1747	
Tatton, Henry Roy	CT-14; TT-14	1938	1950
Taws, William	WT-9	1764	
Taylor, James	AI-8	1754	
Taylor, John (1)	GL-8	1743	1760
Taylor, John (2)	GL-9	1764	
Taylor, William	GL-8; WT-8	*c.* 1745	1753
Tennant, Francis	ML-3	1601	
Thom, Alexander	YO-7	1697	
Thomas, William	CF-2; CR-2	1620	
Thomson, Alexander (1)	WT-9	1759	
Thomson, Alexander (2)	CU-12L	1818	
Thomson, David	GO-8	1762	
Thomson, George	JP-7	1745	
Thomson, Henry	CO-2	1552	1561
Thomson, James (1)	DA-9R	1799	
Thomson, James (2)	MU-11R	1821	
Thomson, John Alexander	MK-11L	1826	
Thomson, Ninaine	DL-3L	1605	
Thomson, Oliver	DL-3L	1610	
Thomson, Robert (1)	DL-2L	1577	1589
Thomson, Robert (2)	NA-11R	1819	
Thomson, Thomas	GC-5R	1605/09	1617
Thomson, William	HE-5L	1766	
Threipland, John	CR-5L; TR-5	1667	1674
Todd, John	AI-8	1768	

Apprentice/Freeman	Map Position(s)	Apprentice Year	Freedom Year
Tournie, George	GI-2	1563	
Trail, John	JP-7	1736	
Traquair, James	GC-6L	1638	
Trotter, Nicoll	CR-3L&R	1627	1635
Troup, John	DL-3L	1600	
Turnbull, James	JP-7	1739	
Turnbull, Patrick	TR-6	1681	1689
Tweedie, Walter	WL-7	1762	
Umphra, Lawrence	JL-5	1671	
Ure, Archibald	ME-3; UR-3	1709	1718
Ure, James	UR-4	1734	
Ure, William	WL-6	1706	1715
Urie, William	EF		*c.* 1550-54
Urquhart, Leonard	FE-2	1815	1843
Urquhart, Thomas	ZI-10R	1815	
Veitch, Hamilton	DA-9R	*c.* 1796	
Veitch, Robert	TM-9	1810	
Vogel, John (2)	DI-4L	1746	
Walker, Daniel	RO-10L	*c.* 1805	*c.* 1815
Walker, James	RA-8	1743	
Walkinshaw, James	MA-6	1702	
Wallace, David	DL-3L	1608	
Wallace, William	SC-6	1668	1681
Wardlaw, John	GC-6R	1630	1642
Wardlope, John	GC-7L	1635	
Watson, Andrew	TM-7	1719	
Watson, George	RD-5	1653	
Watson, James (1)	JL-6	1688	
Watson, James (2)	MI-8	1760	
Watson, Joseph	MO-5LT	1656	
Watson, William	HE-6R	1799	
Watt, Alexander Hamilton	NA-11L	1814	1823
Watt, James	FO-3	1734	
Watt, James Haldane	MU-11L	1814	
Watt, John	PE-5R	1696/97	
Watt, Thomas (1)	ME-3	1698	
Watt, Thomas (2)	GM-9	1720	
Weddell, Hercules	BA-2	1592	1608
Weddell, John	BA-3	1622	
Weems, James (1)	AY-8R	1727	1738
Weems, James (2)	AY-9R	1770	
Weir, Alexander McKenzie	RB-13	1866	1903
Weir, Andrew White	RB-13	1861	

Apprentice/Freeman	Map Position(s)	Apprentice Year	Freedom Year
Weir, George	BL-7	1717	
Weir, Samuel	HE-6R	1817	1847
Welsh, James	IN-7	1736	1746
Welsh, John	MY-8; WE-8	1726	1742
White, John	DA-8L	1754	
Wilkie, Andrew	ZI-10L	1805	1813
Wilkie, David	ZI-10L	1805	
Williamson, Archibald	GO-8	1765	
Williamson, John	JM-10R	1812	
Williamson, Thomas	DE-5	1765	
Wilson, Adam	MO-4LT	1589	1599
Wilson, Alexander	KE-7R	1761	
Wilson, David	CA-7	1720	
Wilson, George	DL-2R	1589	
Wilson, Gideon	ZI-11L	1813	
Wilson, James	NA-12	1856	
Wilson, John (1)	GO-8	1759	
Wilson, John (2)	CU-11L	1807	1817
Wilson, Robert	AI-8	1758	
Wilson, William	DI-4L	1739	
Wingate, John	FC-7	1703	
Winter, Robert	DA-9R	1808	
Wood, George	PE-6C	1706	
Wynraham, Alexander	HT-4L	1608	
Yetts, John	HE-6L	1789	
Yorstoun, George (1)	CY-5L; YO-5	1674	1684
Yorstoun, George (2)	MI-7	1702	1715
Yorstoun, George (3)	TA-7	1715	
Yorstoun, James (1)	GM-8	1697	
Yorstoun, James (2)	YO-7	1701	1710
Yorstoun, John	YO-6	1688	1697
Yorstoun, Mungo	SE-6L; MY-6	1691	1702
Yorstoun, Thomas	CY-4L	1663	1673
Young, Adam	GO-8	1754	
Young, George	CF-3	1617	
Young, Henry	EF		*c.* 1540-1550
Young, John	CU-12L	1818	
Young, Richard	EF		*c.* 1535
Young, Thomas	AY-9R	1767	
Young, William	PE-5L	1683	
Younger, James	MU-11L	1818	
Ziegler, Alexander (1)	JI-8	1747	1791
Ziegler, Alexander (2)	JI-10	1811	
Ziegler, John	JI-9; ZI-9L&R	1792	1798

Apprentice/Freeman	Map Position(s)	Apprentice Year	Freedom Year
Ziegler, William (1)	JI-9	1792	1800
Ziegler, William (2)	ZI-10R	1812	

Training Maps Including Maker's Marks

Overall Maps – Interconnections of the Trees and Branches

The following two pages show the interconnections among the 88 trees and branches spanning approximately 450 years. The first overall diagram begins with Daniel Crawford and the Crawford Tree (CF) in the 16th century. There are a total of 53 trees and branches that are interconnected. Several training lines exceed 400 years in duration. These include the longest continuous line that runs from Daniel Crawford through Alexander Reid – John Seaton – Mungo Yorstoun – James McKenzie (1) – James Nasmyth – the Crichtons to Henry Tatton and his apprentices. Other major lineages flow from Daniel Crawford via:

1) Thomas Cleghorne (1) – Edward Cleghorne (1) – Thomas Yorstoun – Robert Inglis - William Ged – William Aytoun – Alexander Gardner – James McKay – Walker Crichton and his apprentices.

2) Thomas Cleghorne (1) – Edward Cleghorne (1) – Thomas Yorstoun - Robert Inglis – David Mitchell – Edward Lothian – Patrick Robertson – the Cunninghams – the Robbs and their apprentices.

3) Thomas Cleghorne (1) – Edward Cleghorne (1) – Thomas Yorstoun – George Yorstoun (1) - James Tait – William Gilchrist – William Taylor – James Douglas and his apprentices or alternatively from William Gilchrist to William Marshall and his apprentices.

The second overall diagram contains 35 trees and branches. These include prominent early trees of the Cokies, Heriots, Dennistouns, Stalkers, Rynds, Symes, Mosmans, Allanes as well as the Foulis and Kirkwood families. Later 19th century trees started by George Fenwick, George McHattie and Richard Sheldon are also on this diagram. Finally, the second diagram has two trees with branches begun by freemen who came to Edinburgh with some training in hand. These are the trees of Alexander Forbes (1) and Zaccharias Mellinus.

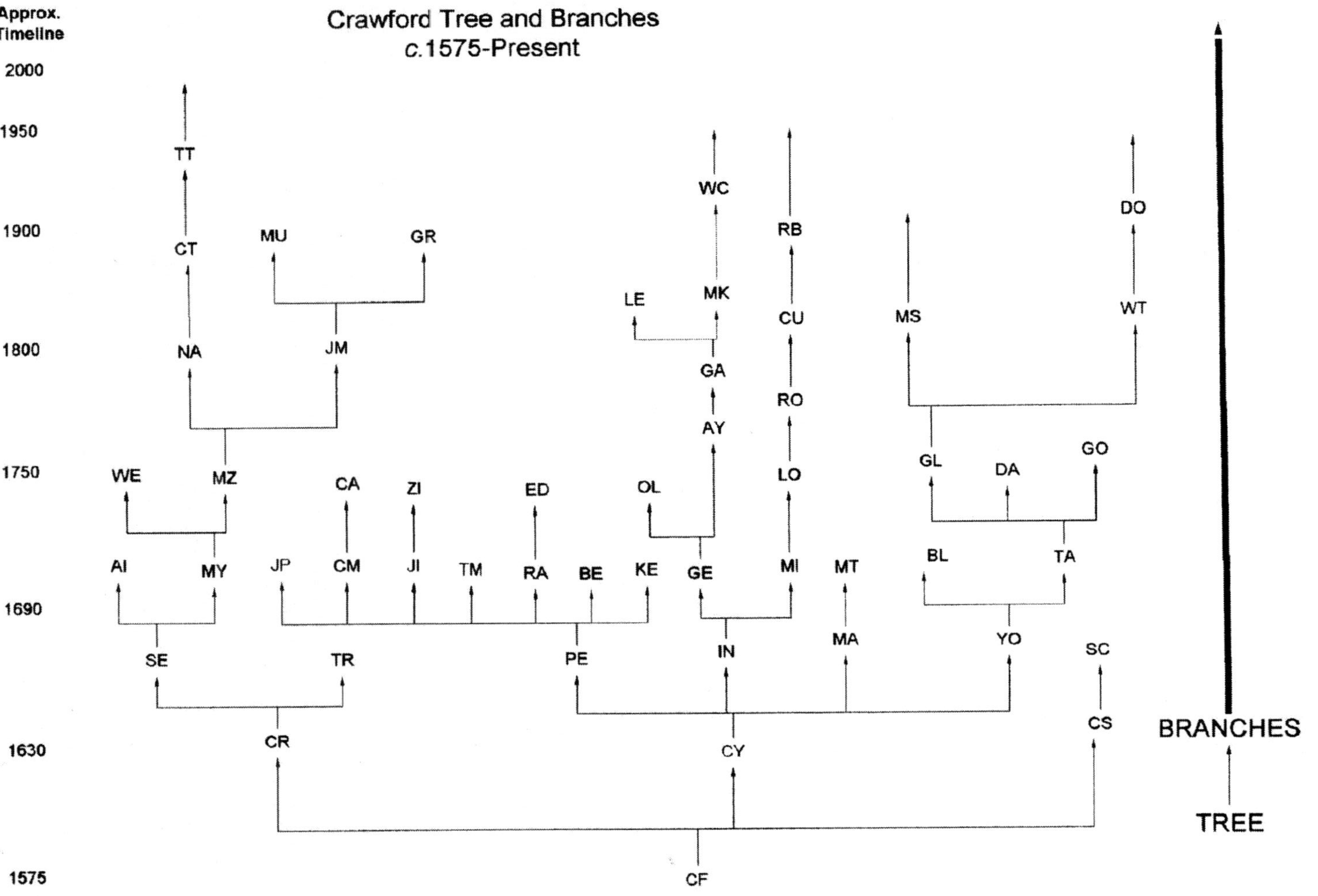
Crawford Tree and Branches
c.1575-Present
Approx. Timeline
2000
1950
1900
1800
1750
1690
1630
1575
TT
CT
NA
MU
GR
JM
WE
MZ
AI
MY
SE
TR
CR
JP
CM
CA
JI
ZI
TM
RA
ED
BE
KE
PE
OL
GE
AY
GA
MK
LE
WC
MI
LO
RO
CU
RB
IN
MT
MA
CY
MS
WT
DO
GL
DA
GO
BL
TA
YO
SC
CS
CF
BRANCHES
TREE

Additional Trees and Branches
APPROX. YEAR
1900
1850
1800
1750
1700
1650
1600
1550
1500
HE
DE
DI
FO
FK
EF
CG
UR
ME
BO
GC
AN
GI
AL
MH
FE
SH
GM
BR
FC
RD
DL
David Dennistoun
SY
GH
HT
SM
JL
WL
ML
RY
ST
MO
LD
CO
BA

Training Maps Including Maker's Marks

The Trees and Branches

The following 110 pages display the 88 trees and branches in alphabetical order. When it was necessary for a branch to be divided into halves (or into thirds for Penman), the linked sections of the same branch appear on succeeding pages. Maker's marks are displayed to the left of the entry when they are available. When the name appears in all-caps, the individual was admitted as a freeman goldsmith of Edinburgh. The alphabetical index of apprentices can be used to locate a specific individual. Likewise, the overall maps of the trees and branches can be used to aid navigation among inter-connected branches.

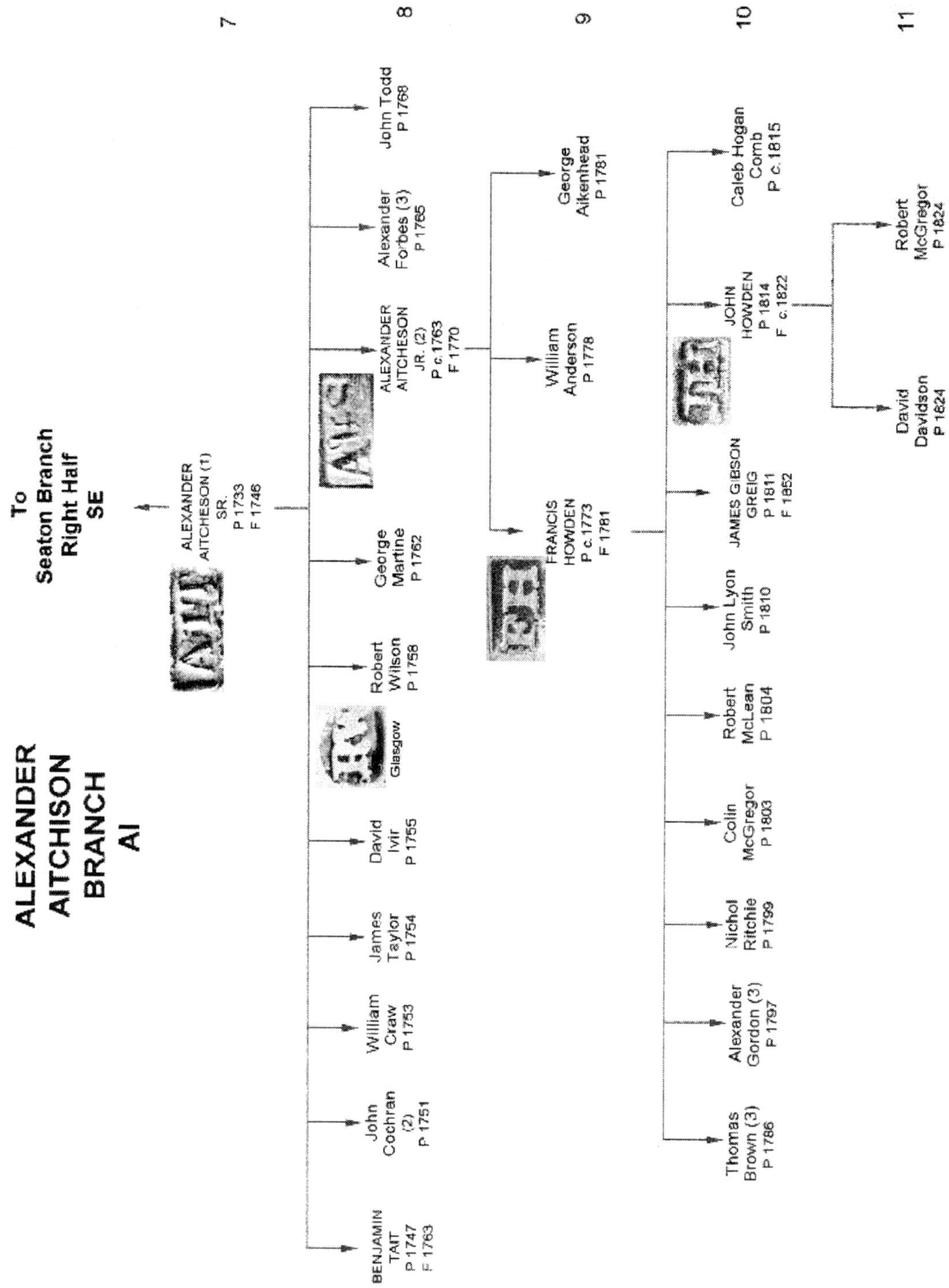
ALEXANDER
AITCHISON
BRANCH
AI
To
Seaton Branch
Right Half
SE
ALEXANDER AITCHESON (1) SR. P 1733 F 1746
7
BENJAMIN TAIT P 1747 F 1763
John Cochran (2) P 1751
William Craw P 1753
James Taylor P 1754
David Ivir P 1755
Glasgow
Robert Wilson P 1758
George Martine P 1762
ALEXANDER AITCHESON JR. (2) P c.1763 F 1770
Alexander Forbes (3) P 1765
John Todd P 1768
8
FRANCIS HOWDEN P c.1773 F 1781
William Anderson P 1778
George Aikenhead P 1781
9
Thomas Brown (3) P 1786
Alexander Gordon (3) P 1797
Nichol Ritchie P 1799
Colin McGregor P 1803
Robert McLean P 1804
John Lyon Smith P 1810
JAMES GIBSON GREIG P 1811 F 1852
JOHN HOWDEN P 1814 F c.1822
Caleb Hogan Comb P c.1815
10
David Davidson P 1824
Robert McGregor P 1824
11

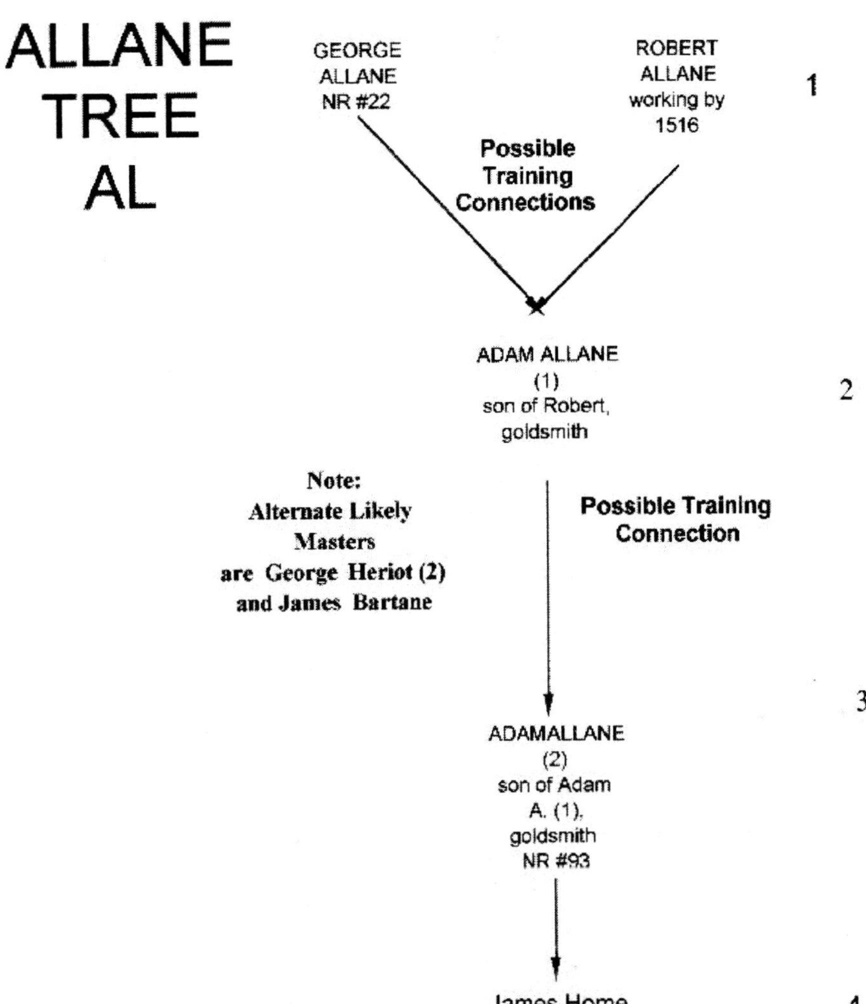
ALLANE
TREE
AL
GEORGE
ALLANE
NR #22
ROBERT
ALLANE
working by
1516
1
Possible
Training
Connections
ADAM ALLANE
(1)
son of Robert,
goldsmith
2
Note:
Alternate Likely
Masters
are George Heriot (2)
and James Bartane
Possible Training
Connection
3
ADAMALLANE
(2)
son of Adam
A. (1),
goldsmith
NR #93
James Home
P 1596
4

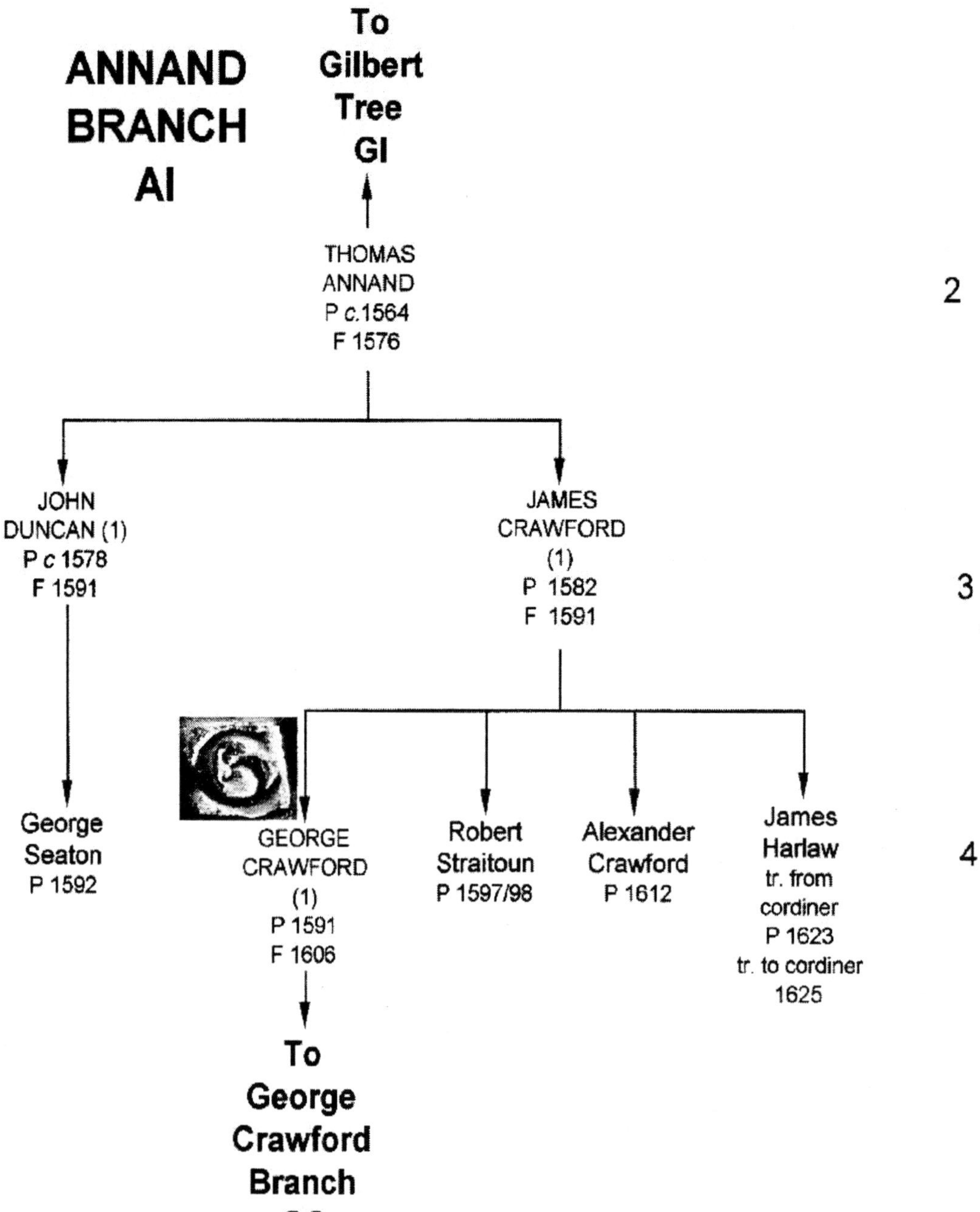
ANNAND
BRANCH
AI
To
Gilbert
Tree
GI
THOMAS
ANNAND
P c.1564
F 1576
2
JOHN
DUNCAN (1)
P c 1578
F 1591
JAMES
CRAWFORD
(1)
P 1582
F 1591
3
George
Seaton
P 1592
GEORGE
CRAWFORD
(1)
P 1591
F 1606
Robert
Straitoun
P 1597/98
Alexander
Crawford
P 1612
James
Harlaw
tr. from
cordiner
P 1623
tr. to cordiner
1625
4
To
George
Crawford
Branch
GC

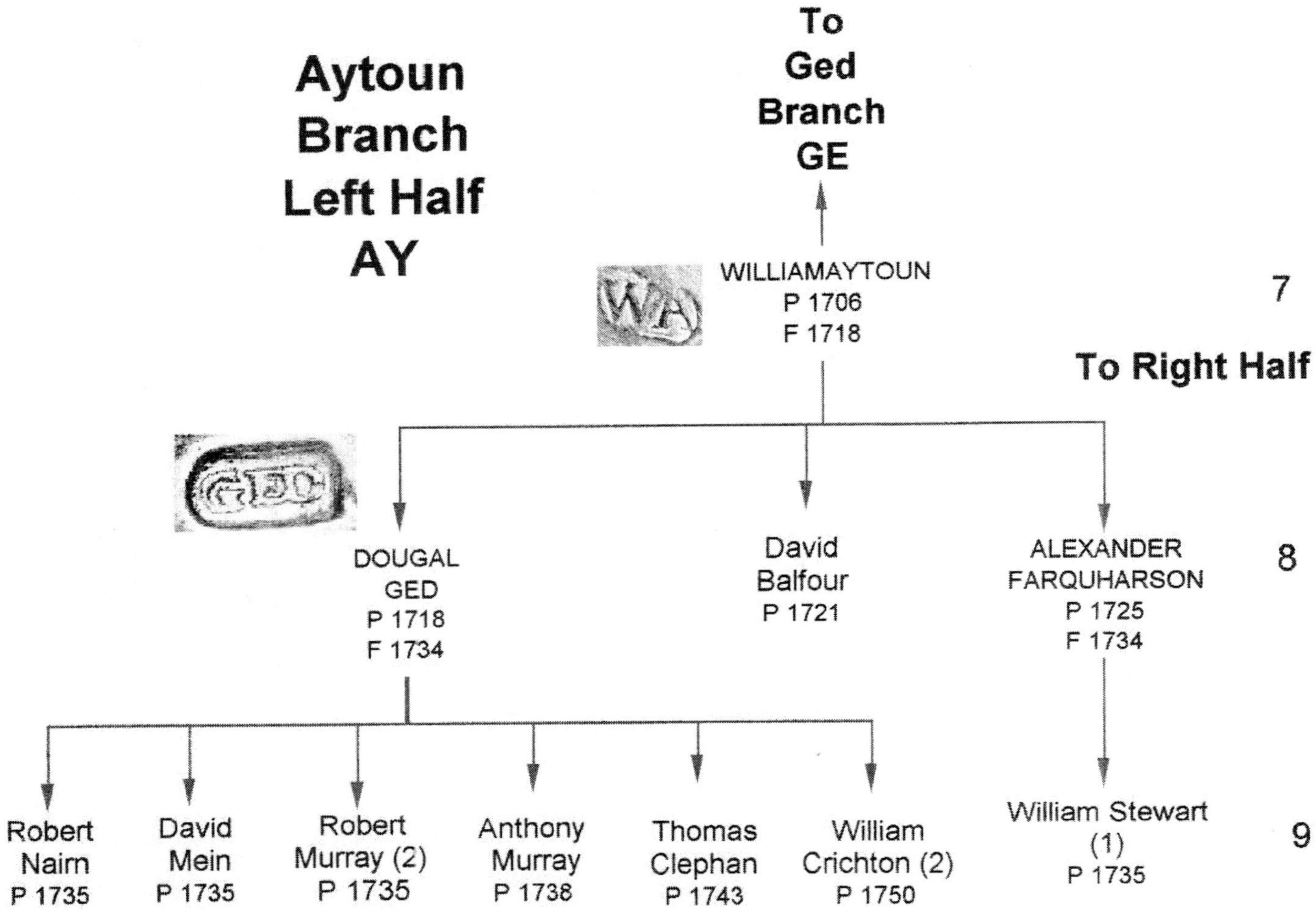

Aytoun
Branch
Left Half
AY
To
Ged
Branch
GE
WA
WILLIAMAYTOUN
P 1706
F 1718
7
To Right Half
GED
DOUGAL
GED
P 1718
F 1734
David
Balfour
P 1721
ALEXANDER
FARQUHARSON
P 1725
F 1734
8
Robert
Naim
P 1735
David
Mein
P 1735
Robert
Murray (2)
P 1735
Anthony
Murray
P 1738
Thomas
Clephan
P 1743
William
Crichton (2)
P 1750
William Stewart
(1)
P 1735
9

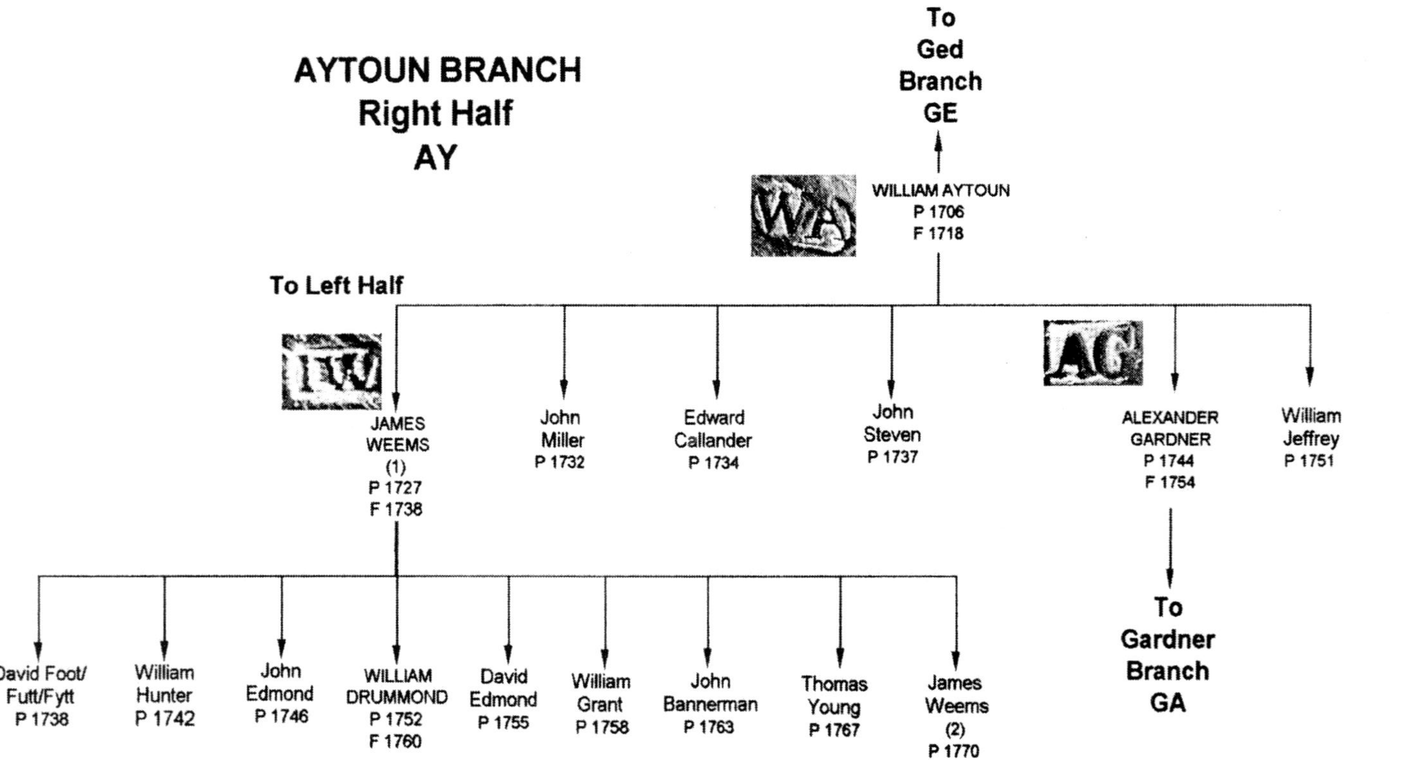
AYTOUN BRANCH
Right Half
AY
To Ged Branch GE
WILLIAM AYTOUN
P 1706
F 1718
7
To Left Half
JAMES WEEMS (1) P 1727 F 1738
John Miller P 1732
Edward Callander P 1734
John Steven P 1737
ALEXANDER GARDNER P 1744 F 1754
William Jeffrey P 1751
8
To Gardner Branch GA
David Foot/ Futt/Fytt P 1738
William Hunter P 1742
John Edmond P 1746
WILLIAM DRUMMOND P 1752 F 1760
David Edmond P 1755
William Grant P 1758
John Bannerman P 1763
Thomas Young P 1767
James Weems (2) P 1770
9

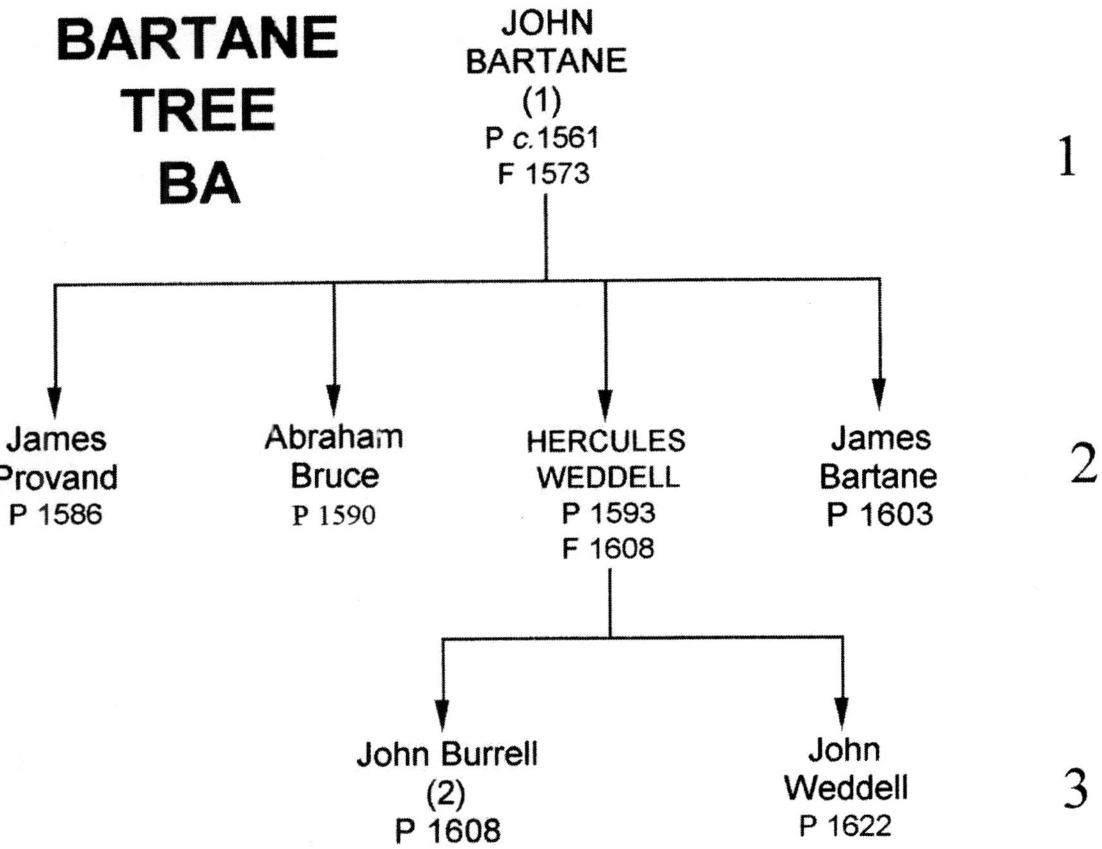
BARTANE
TREE
BA
JOHN
BARTANE
(1)
P c.1561
F 1573
1
James
Provand
P 1586
Abraham
Bruce
P 1590
HERCULES
WEDDELL
P 1593
F 1608
James
Bartane
P 1603
2
John Burrell
(2)
P 1608
John
Weddell
P 1622
3

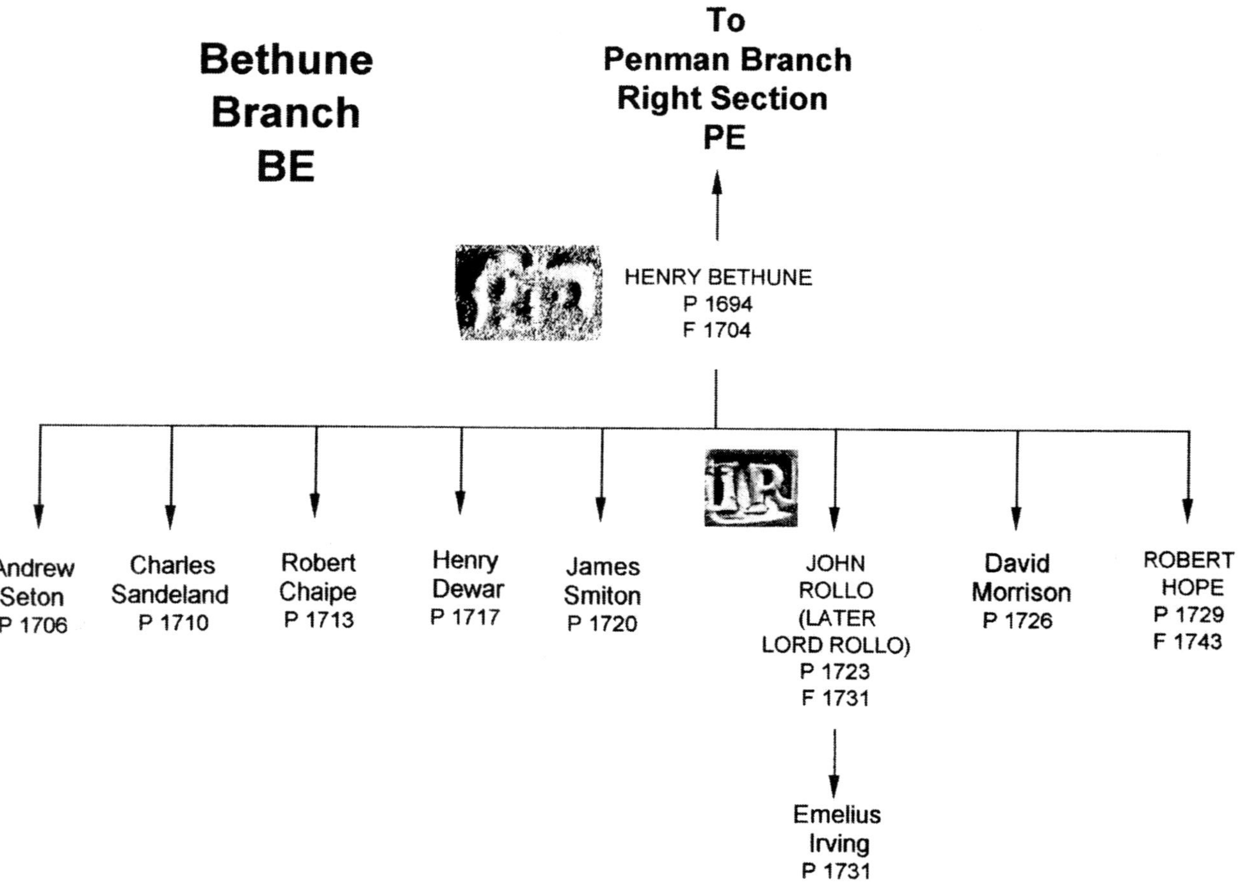
Bethune Branch BE
To Penman Branch Right Section PE
HENRY BETHUNE P 1694 F 1704
5
Andrew Seton P 1706
Charles Sandeland P 1710
Robert Chaipe P 1713
Henry Dewar P 1717
James Smiton P 1720
JOHN ROLLO (LATER LORD ROLLO) P 1723 F 1731
David Morrison P 1726
ROBERT HOPE P 1729 F 1743
6
Emelius Irving P 1731
7

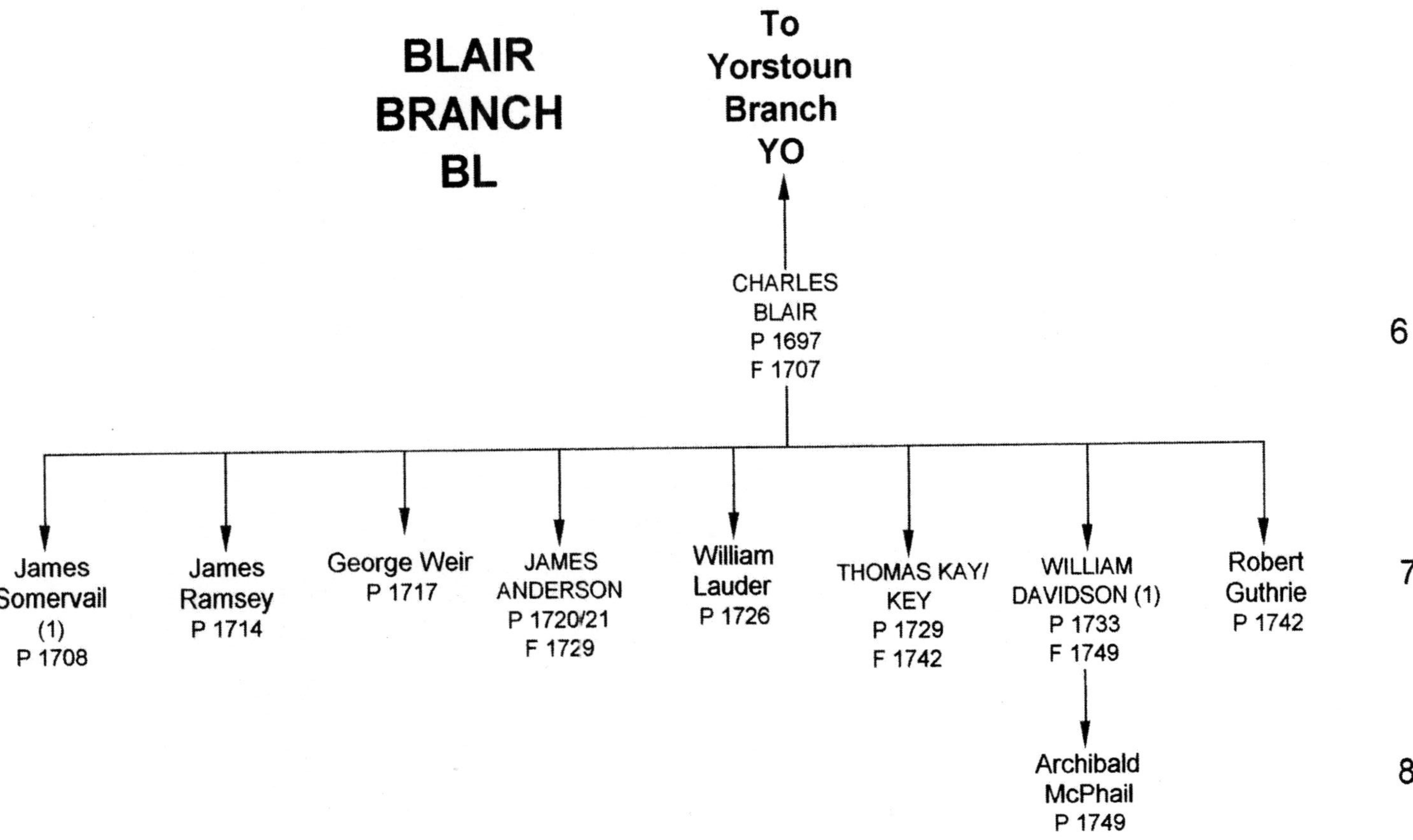
BLAIR
BRANCH
BL
To
Yorstoun
Branch
YO
CHARLES
BLAIR
P 1697
F 1707
6
James
Somervail
(1)
P 1708
James
Ramsey
P 1714
George Weir
P 1717
JAMES
ANDERSON
P 1720/21
F 1729
William
Lauder
P 1726
THOMAS KAY/
KEY
P 1729
F 1742
WILLIAM
DAVIDSON (1)
P 1733
F 1749
Robert
Guthrie
P 1742
7
Archibald
McPhail
P 1749
8

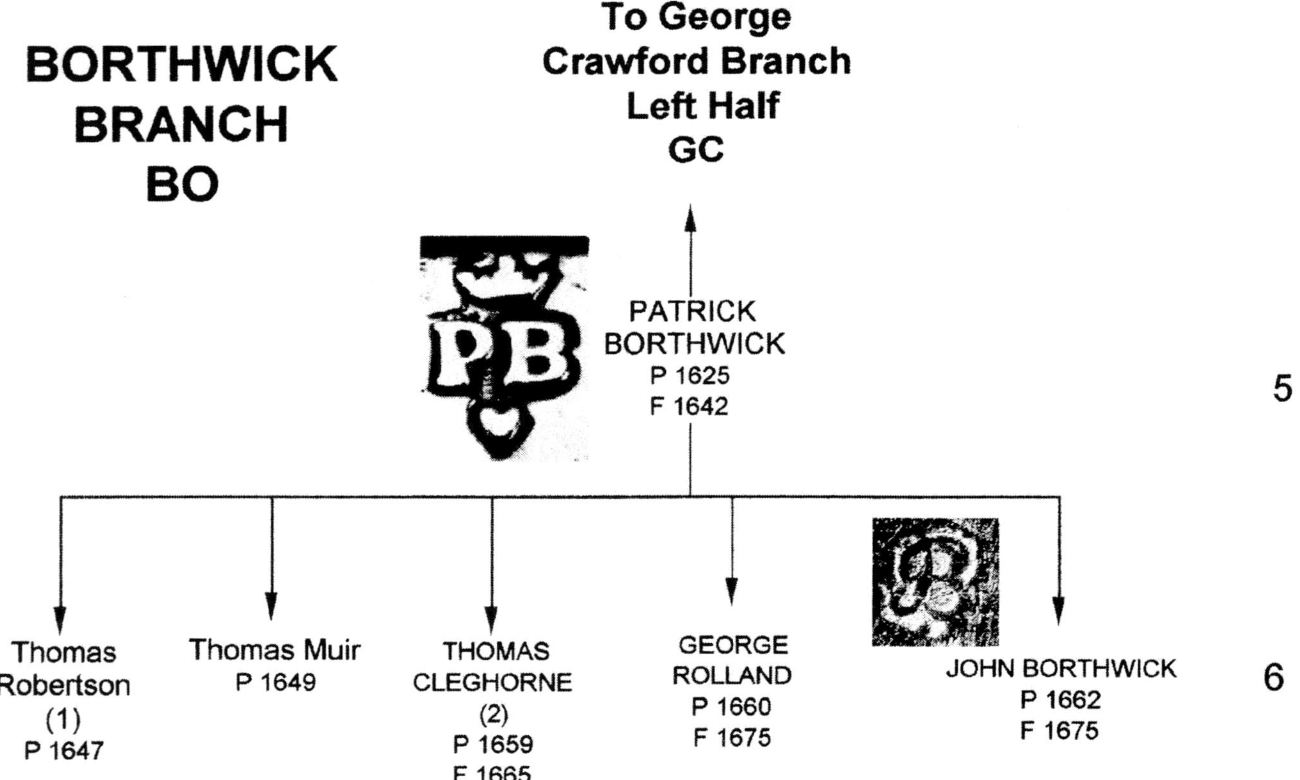
BORTHWICK
BRANCH
BO
To George
Crawford Branch
Left Half
GC
PB
PATRICK
BORTHWICK
P 1625
F 1642
5
Thomas
Robertson
(1)
P 1647
Thomas Muir
P 1649
THOMAS
CLEGHORNE
(2)
P 1659
F 1665
GEORGE
ROLLAND
P 1660
F 1675
JOHN BORTHWICK
P 1662
F 1675
6

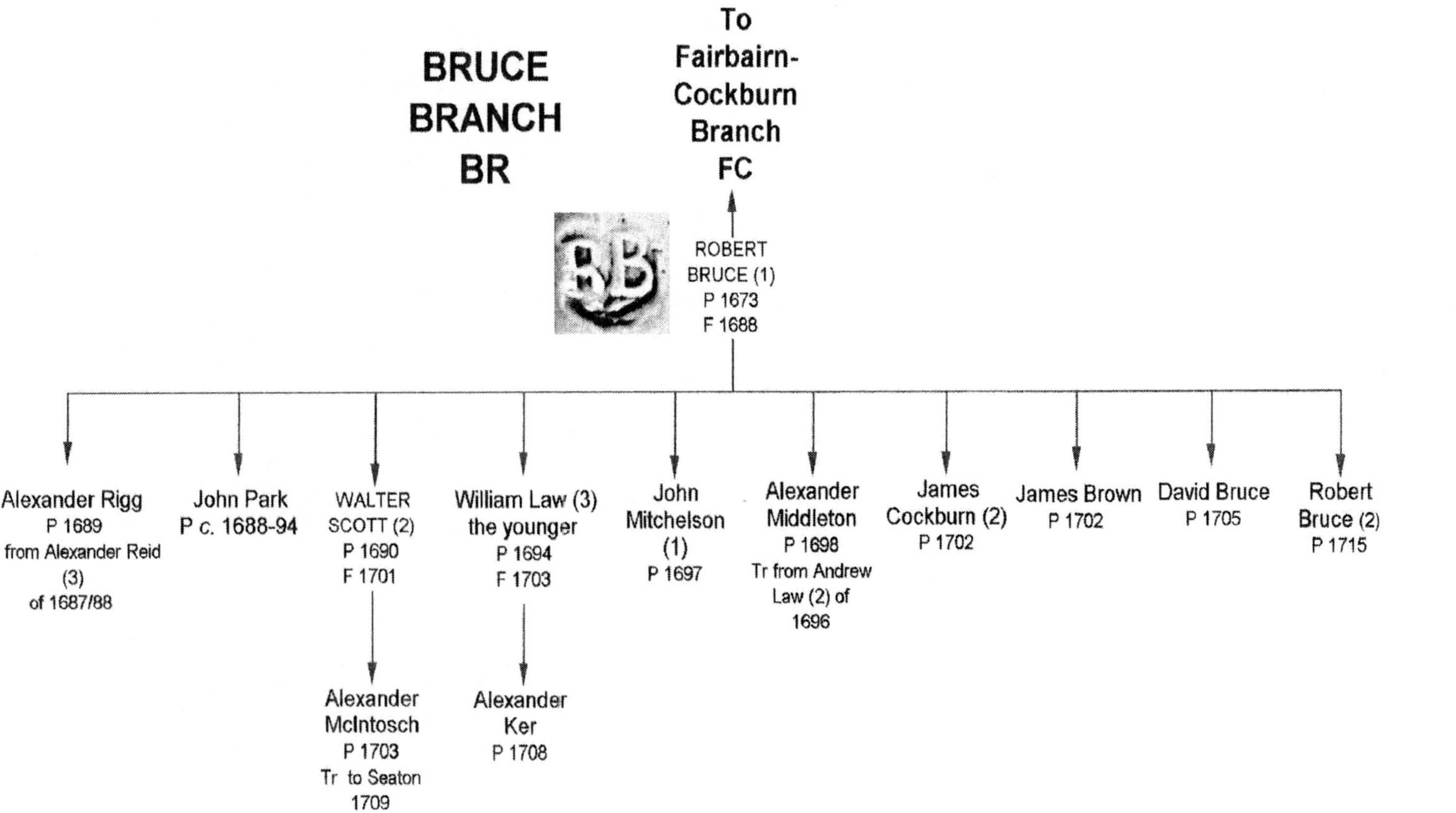
BRUCE
BRANCH
BR
To
Fairbairn-
Cockburn
Branch
FC
ROBERT
BRUCE (1)
P 1673
F 1688
6
Alexander Rigg
P 1689
Tr from Alexander Reid
(3)
of 1687/88
John Park
P c. 1688-94
WALTER
SCOTT (2)
P 1690
F 1701
William Law (3)
the younger
P 1694
F 1703
John
Mitchelson
(1)
P 1697
Alexander
Middleton
P 1698
Tr from Andrew
Law (2) of
1696
James
Cockburn (2)
P 1702
James Brown
P 1702
David Bruce
P 1705
Robert
Bruce (2)
P 1715
7
Alexander
McIntosch
P 1703
Tr to Seaton
1709
Alexander
Ker
P 1708
8

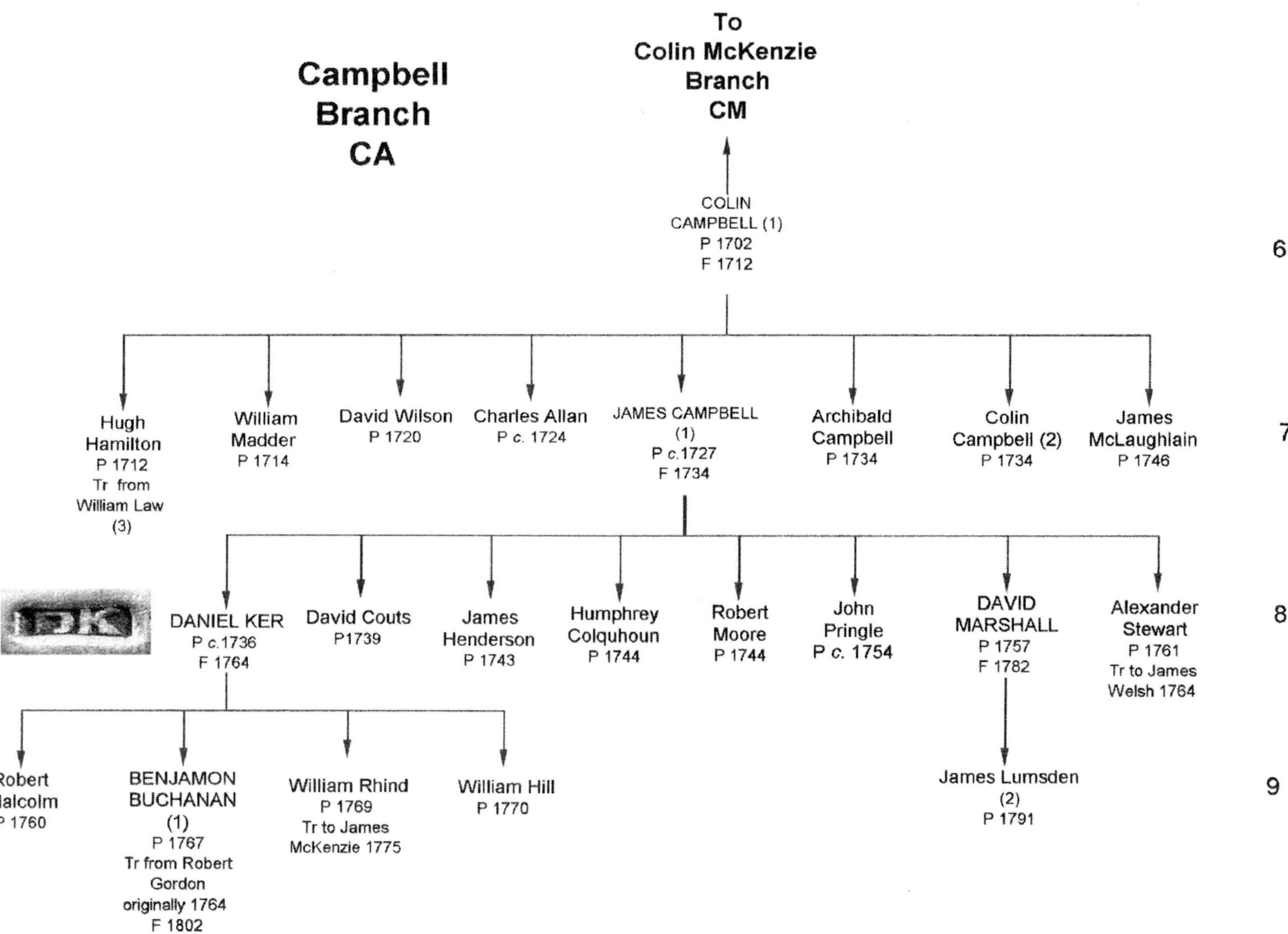

Campbell Branch CA
To Colin McKenzie Branch CM
COLIN CAMPBELL (1) P 1702 F 1712
6
Hugh Hamilton P 1712 Tr from William Law (3)
William Madder P 1714
David Wilson P 1720
Charles Allan P c. 1724
JAMES CAMPBELL (1) P c.1727 F 1734
Archibald Campbell P 1734
Colin Campbell (2) P 1734
James McLaughlain P 1746
7
DK
DANIEL KER P c.1736 F 1764
David Couts P1739
James Henderson P 1743
Humphrey Colquhoun P 1744
Robert Moore P 1744
John Pringle P c. 1754
DAVID MARSHALL P 1757 F 1782
Alexander Stewart P 1761 Tr to James Welsh 1764
8
Robert Malcolm P 1760
BENJAMON BUCHANAN (1) P 1767 Tr from Robert Gordon originally 1764 F 1802
William Rhind P 1769 Tr to James McKenzie 1775
William Hill P 1770
James Lumsden (2) P 1791
9

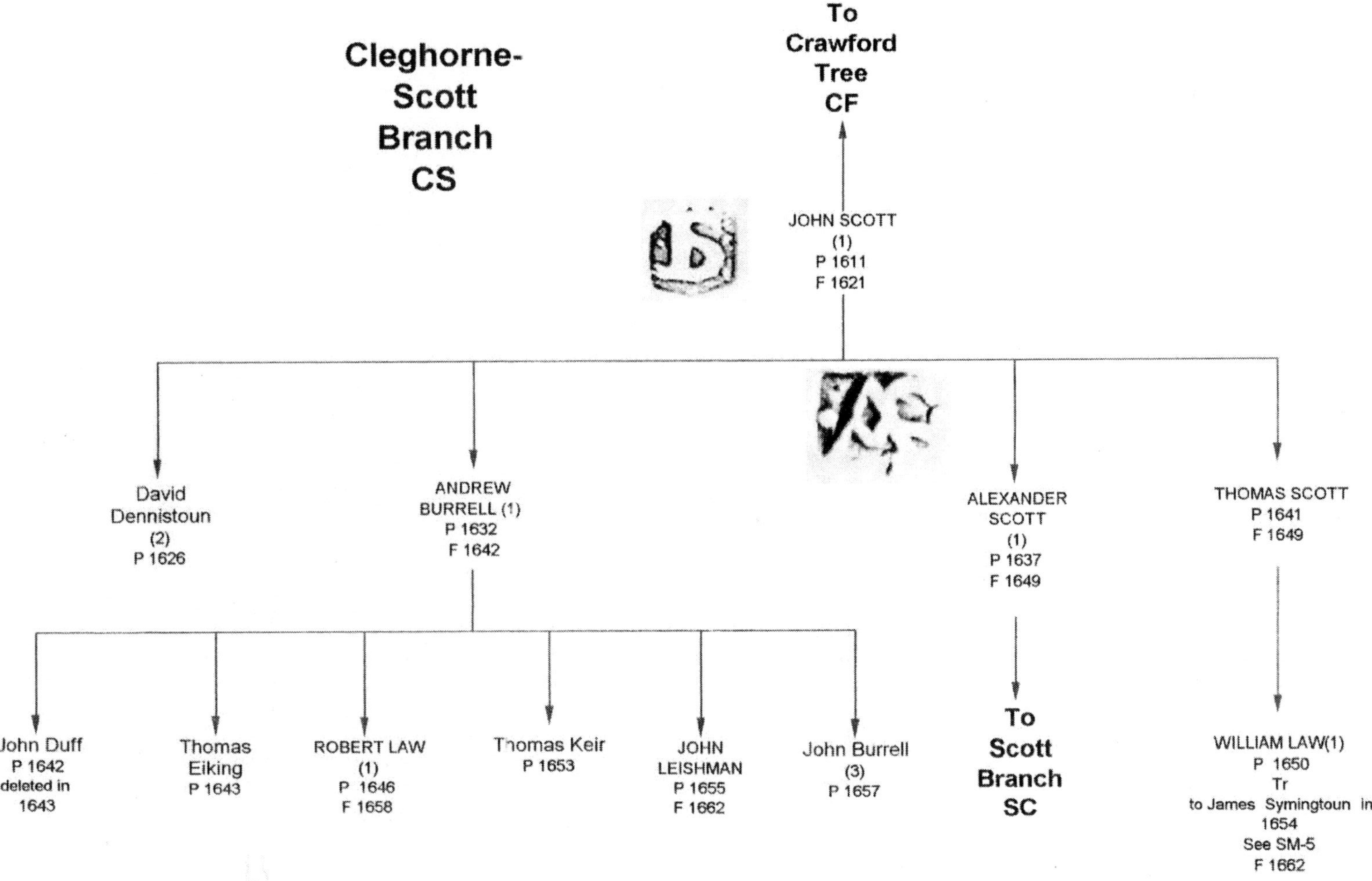
Cleghorne-Scott Branch CS
To Crawford Tree CF
JOHN SCOTT (1) P 1611 F 1621
David Dennistoun (2) P 1626
ANDREW BURRELL (1) P 1632 F 1642
ALEXANDER SCOTT (1) P 1637 F 1649
THOMAS SCOTT P 1641 F 1649
John Duff P 1642 deleted in 1643
Thomas Eiking P 1643
ROBERT LAW (1) P 1646 F 1658
Thomas Keir P 1653
JOHN LEISHMAN P 1655 F 1662
John Burrell (3) P 1657
To Scott Branch SC
WILLIAM LAW(1) P 1650 Tr to James Symingtoun in 1654 See SM-5 F 1662

CLEGHORNE-YORSTOUN Branch Left Half CY

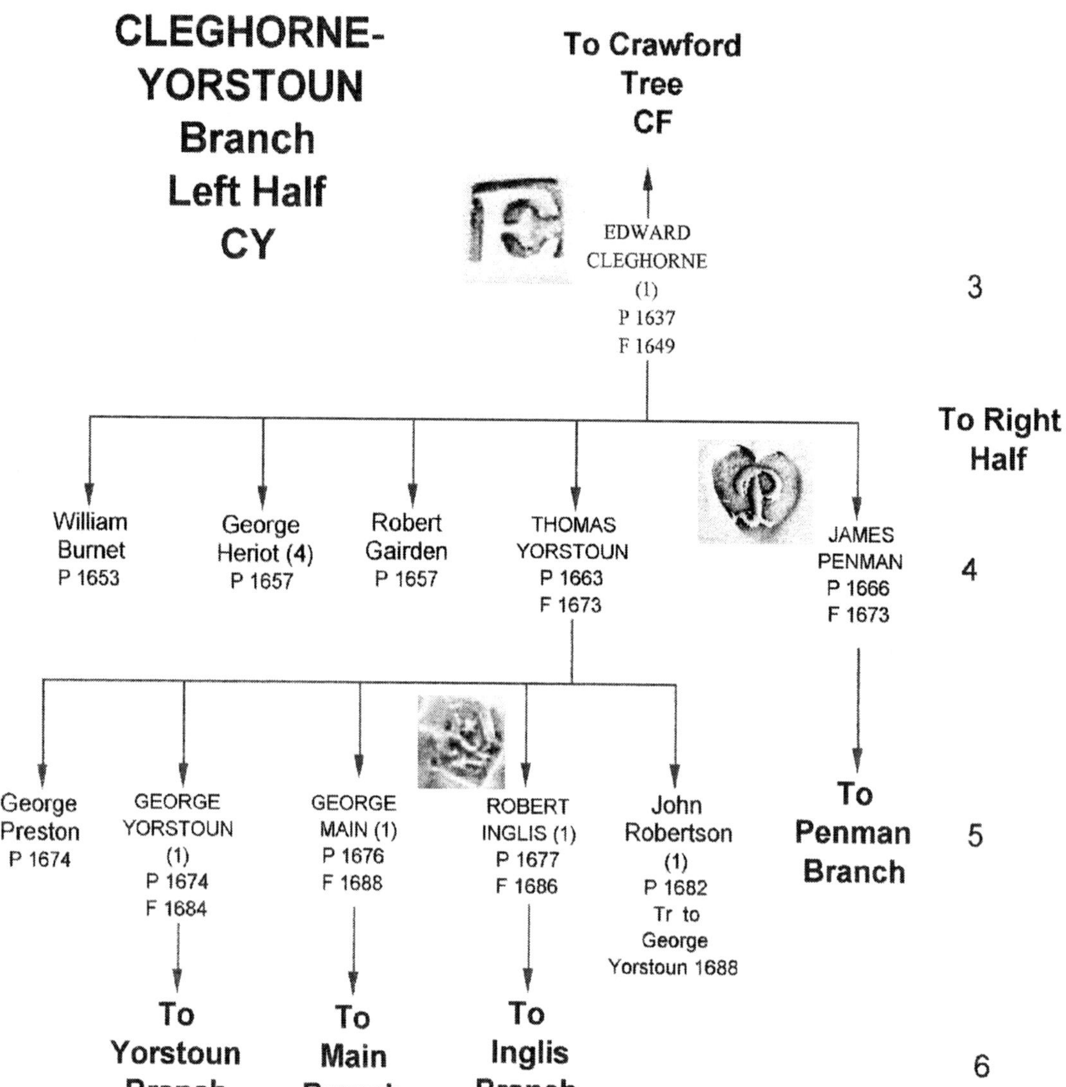

CLEGHORNE-YORSTOUN Branch Right Half CY

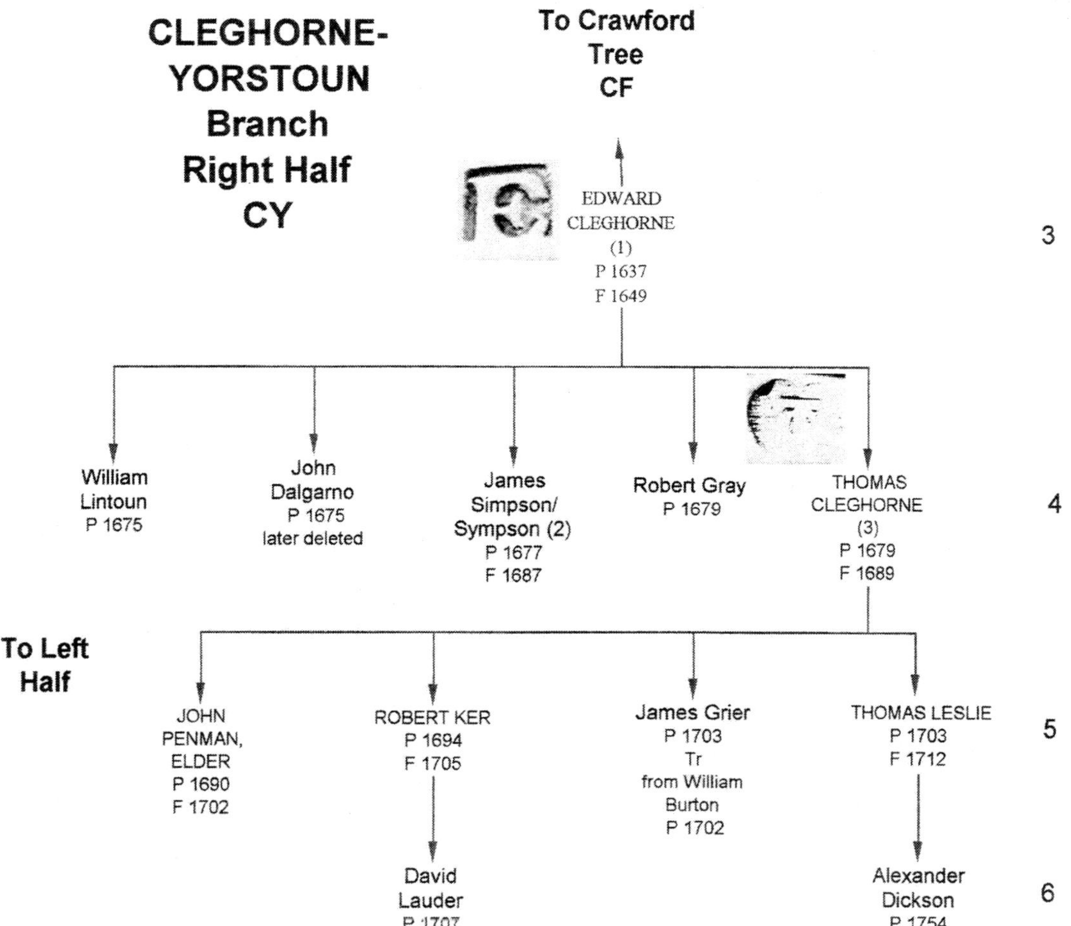

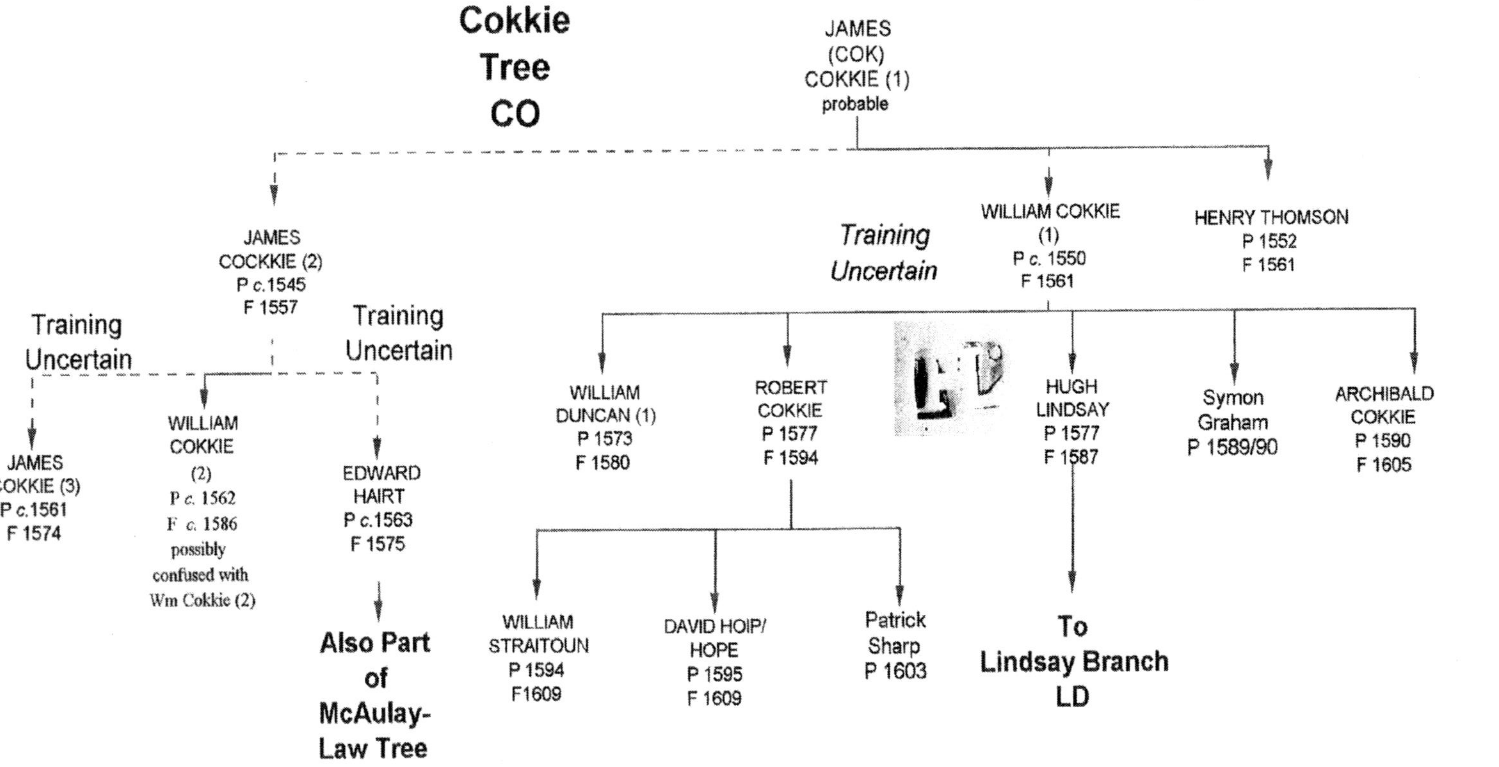
Cokkie
Tree
CO
JAMES
(COK)
COKKIE (1)
probable
1
JAMES
COCKKIE (2)
P c.1545
F 1557
Training
Uncertain
WILLIAM COKKIE
(1)
P c. 1550
F 1561
HENRY THOMSON
P 1552
F 1561
2
Training
Uncertain
Training
Uncertain
JAMES
COKKIE (3)
P c.1561
F 1574
WILLIAM
COKKIE
(2)
P c. 1562
F c. 1586
possibly
confused with
Wm Cokkie (2)
EDWARD
HAIRT
P c.1563
F 1575
WILLIAM
DUNCAN (1)
P 1573
F 1580
ROBERT
COKKIE
P 1577
F 1594
HUGH
LINDSAY
P 1577
F 1587
Symon
Graham
P 1589/90
ARCHIBALD
COKKIE
P 1590
F 1605
3
Also Part
of
McAulay-
Law Tree
WILLIAM
STRAITOUN
P 1594
F1609
DAVID HOIP/
HOPE
P 1595
F 1609
Patrick
Sharp
P 1603
To
Lindsay Branch
LD
4

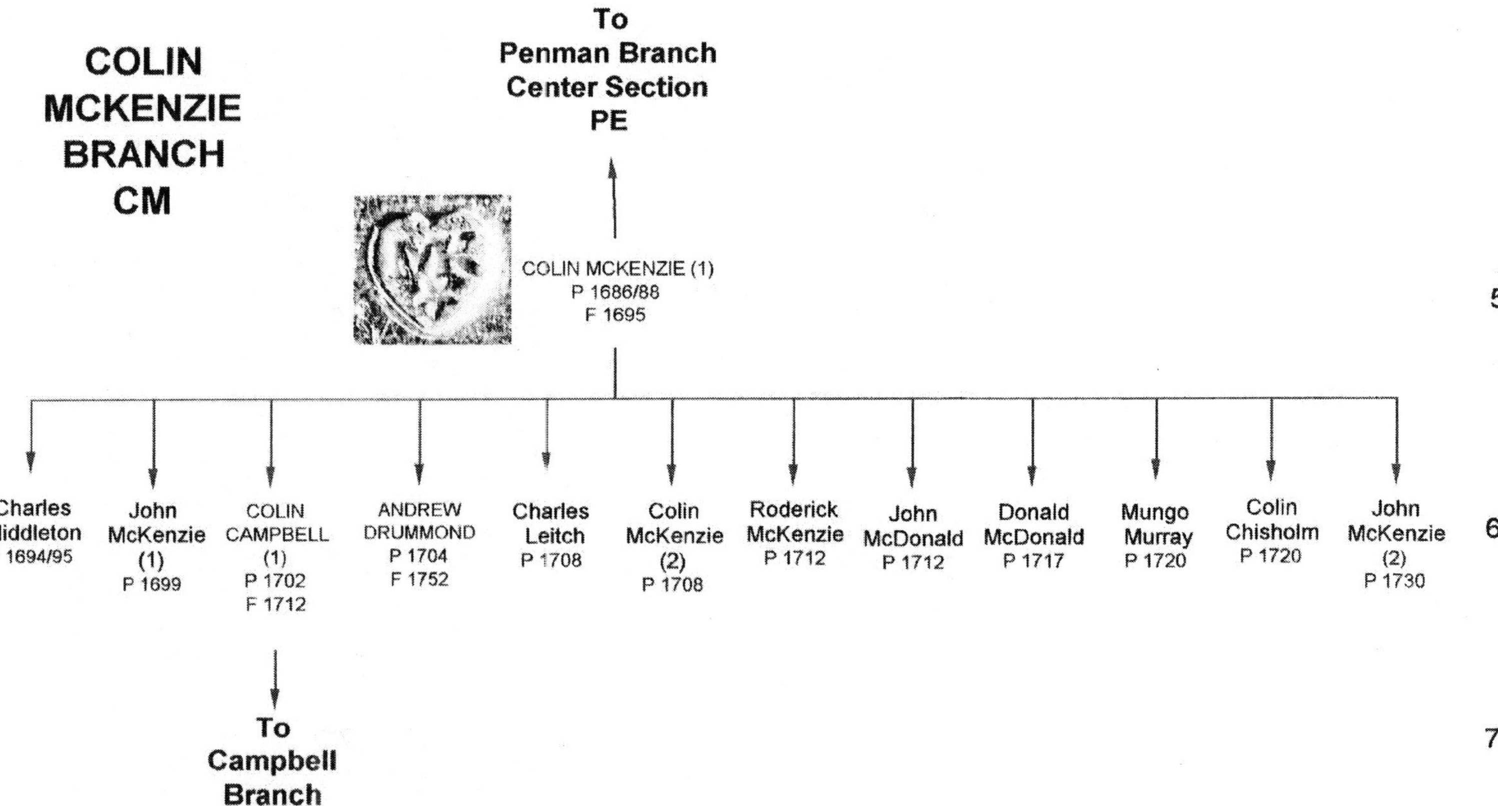
COLIN MCKENZIE BRANCH CM
To Penman Branch Center Section PE
COLIN MCKENZIE (1) P 1686/88 F 1695
5
Charles Middleton P 1694/95
John McKenzie (1) P 1699
COLIN CAMPBELL (1) P 1702 F 1712
ANDREW DRUMMOND P 1704 F 1752
Charles Leitch P 1708
Colin McKenzie (2) P 1708
Roderick McKenzie P 1712
John McDonald P 1712
Donald McDonald P 1717
Mungo Murray P 1720
Colin Chisholm P 1720
John McKenzie (2) P 1730
6
To Campbell Branch
7

CRAIG TREE CG

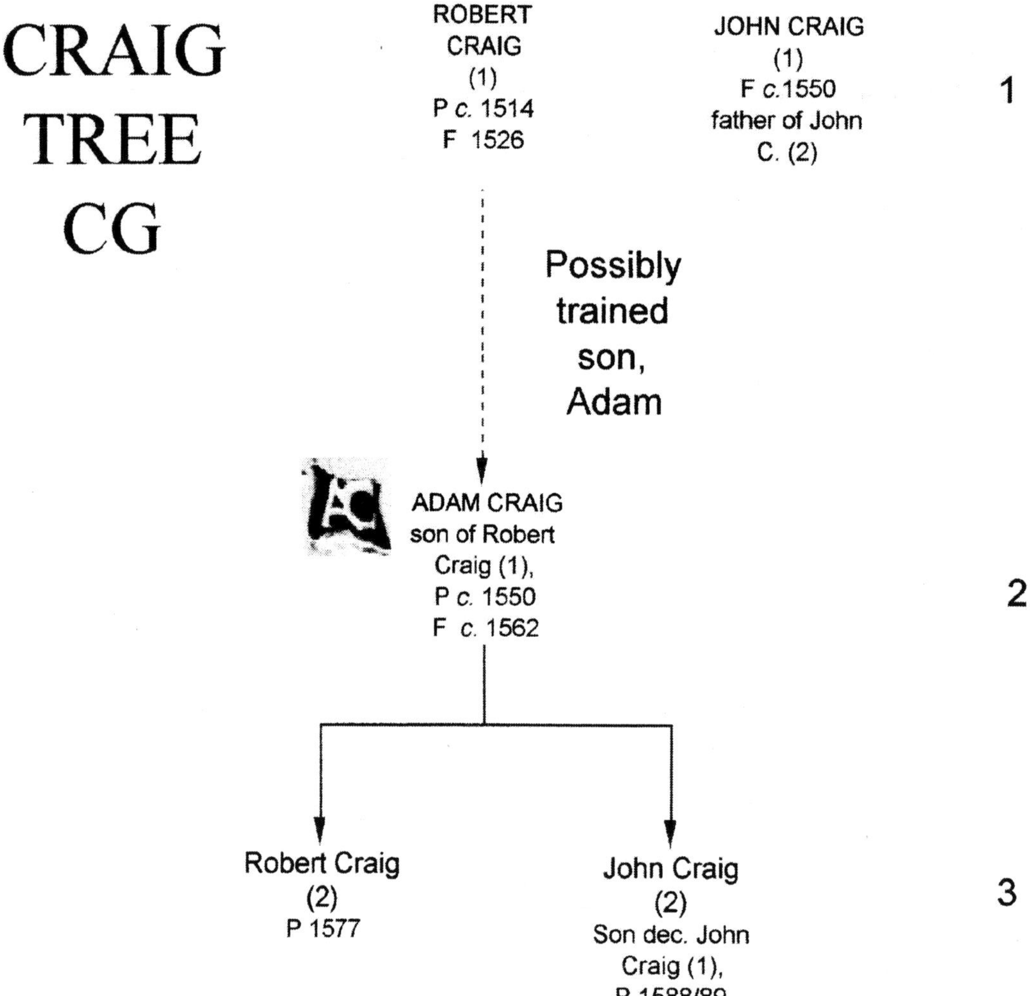

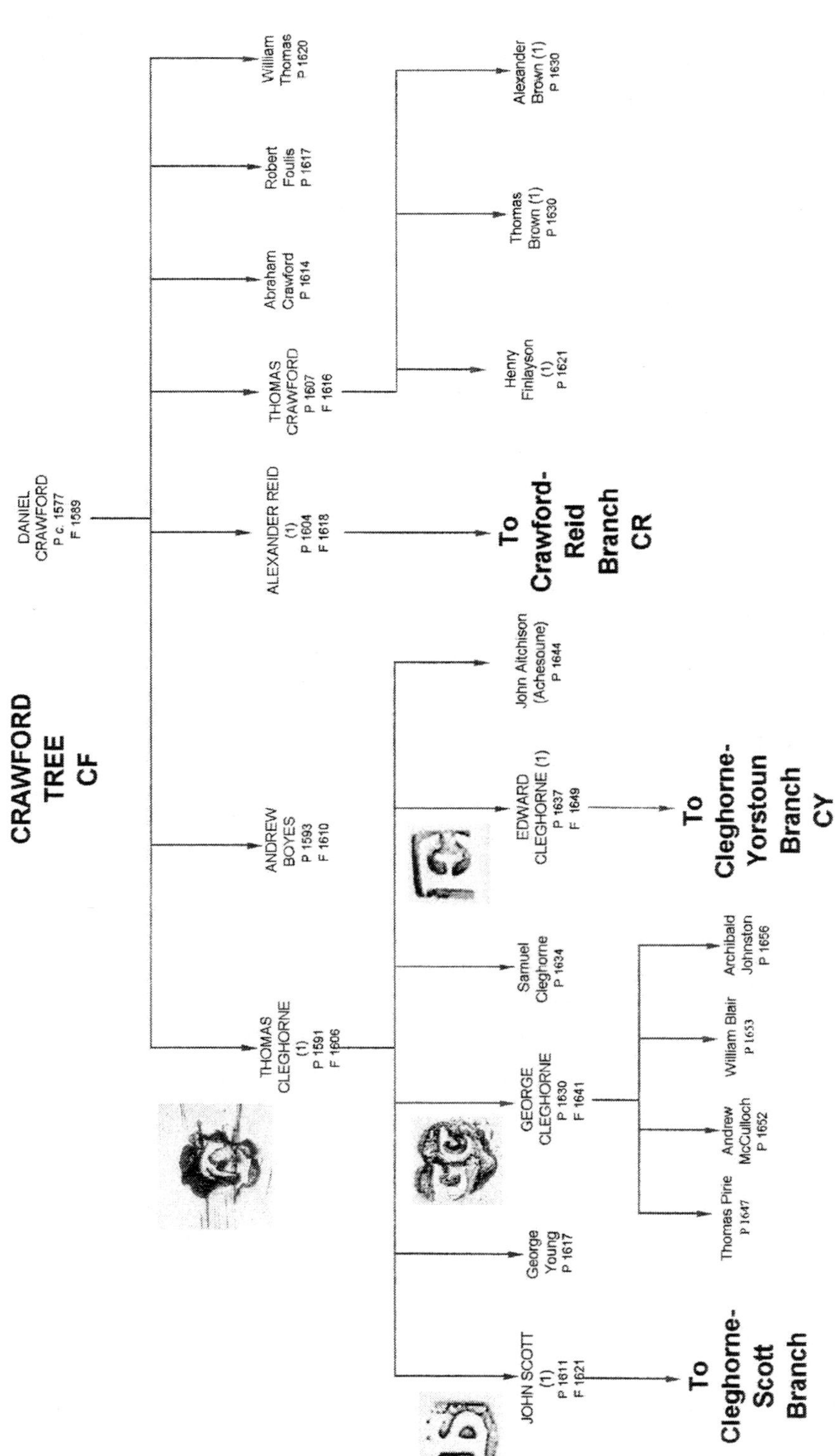

CRAWFORD TREE CF
1
2
3
4
DANIEL CRAWFORD P c. 1577 F 1589
THOMAS CLEGHORNE (1) P 1591 F 1606
ANDREW BOYES P 1593 F 1610
ALEXANDER REID (1) P 1604 F 1618
To Crawford-Reid Branch CR
THOMAS CRAWFORD P 1607 F 1616
Abraham Crawford P 1614
Robert Foulis P 1617
William Thomas P 1620
Henry Finlayson (1) P 1621
Thomas Brown (1) P 1630
Alexander Brown (1) P 1630
JOHN SCOTT (1) P 1611 F 1621
To Cleghorne-Scott Branch
George Young P 1617
GEORGE CLEGHORNE P 1630 F 1641
Samuel Cleghorne P 1634
EDWARD CLEGHORNE (1) P 1637 F 1649
To Cleghorne-Yorstoun Branch CY
John Aitchison (Achesoune) P 1644
Thomas Pine P 1647
Andrew McCulloch P 1652
William Blair P 1653
Archibald Johnston P 1656

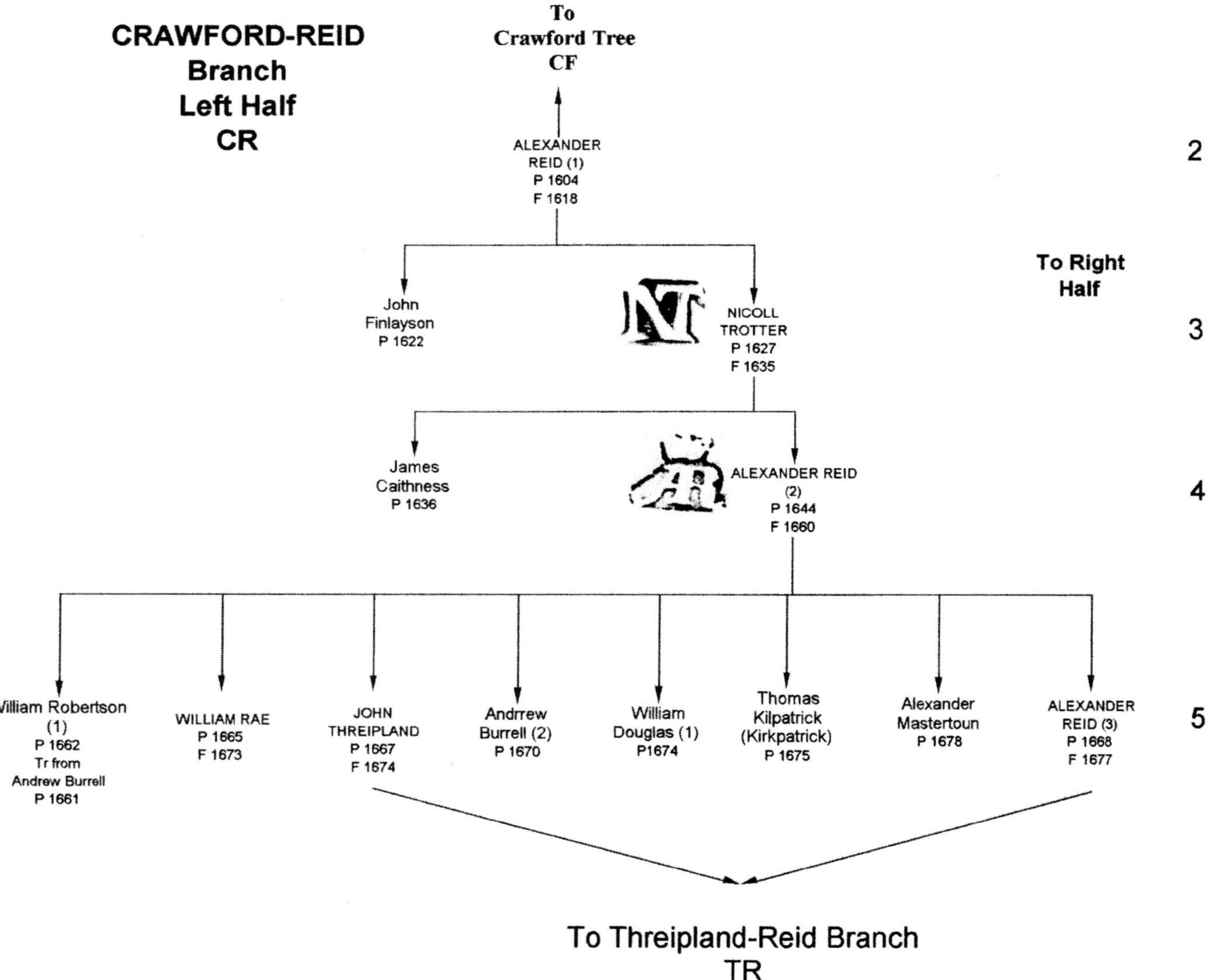
CRAWFORD-REID
Branch
Left Half
CR
To
Crawford Tree
CF
ALEXANDER
REID (1)
P 1604
F 1618
2
To Right
Half
John
Finlayson
P 1622
NICOLL
TROTTER
P 1627
F 1635
3
James
Caithness
P 1636
ALEXANDER REID
(2)
P 1644
F 1660
4
William Robertson
(1)
P 1662
Tr from
Andrew Burrell
P 1661
WILLIAM RAE
P 1665
F 1673
JOHN
THREIPLAND
P 1667
F 1674
Andrrew
Burrell (2)
P 1670
William
Douglas (1)
P1674
Thomas
Kilpatrick
(Kirkpatrick)
P 1675
Alexander
Mastertoun
P 1678
ALEXANDER
REID (3)
P 1668
F 1677
5
To Threipland-Reid Branch
TR

CRAWFORD-REID Branch Right Half CR

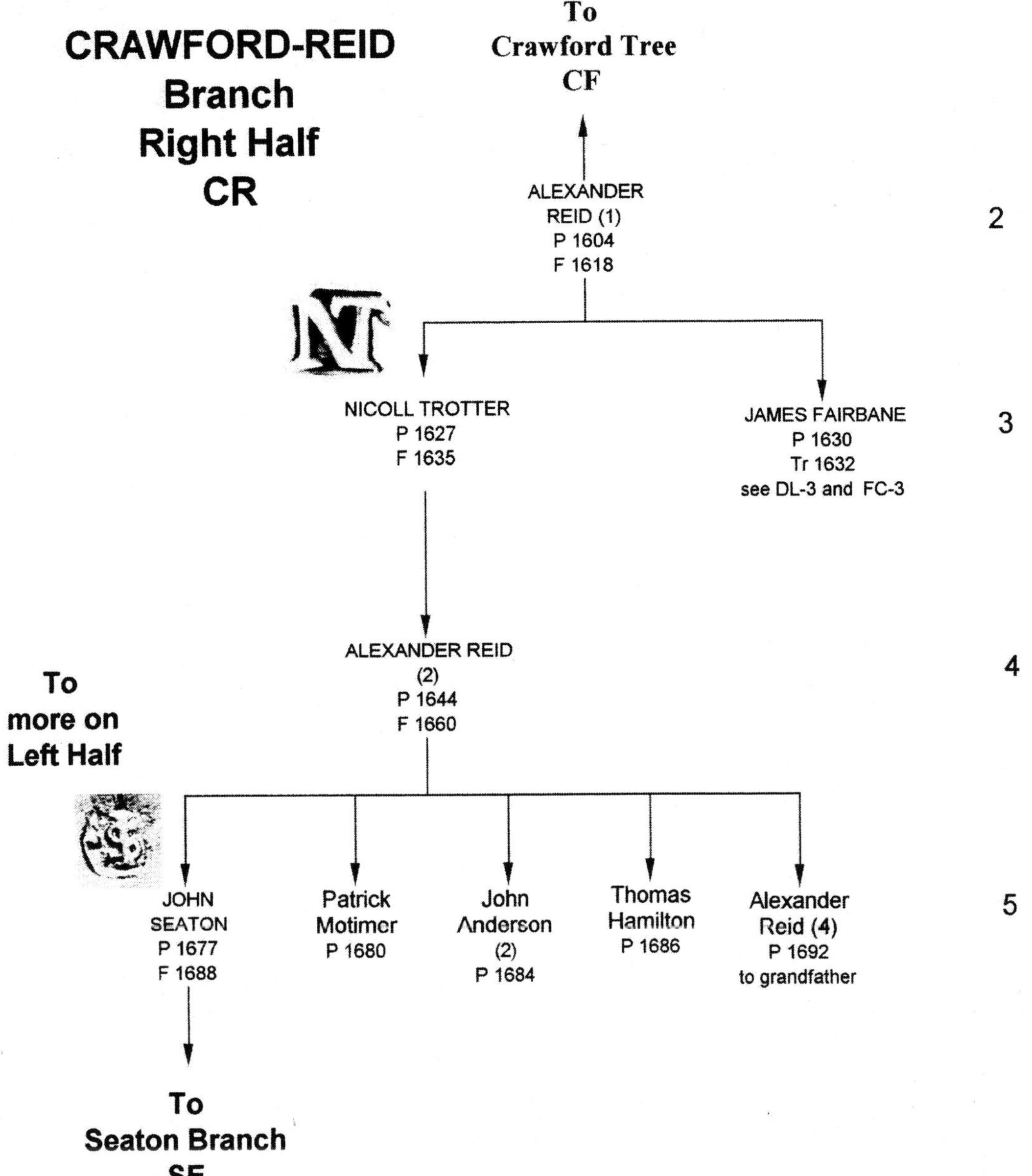

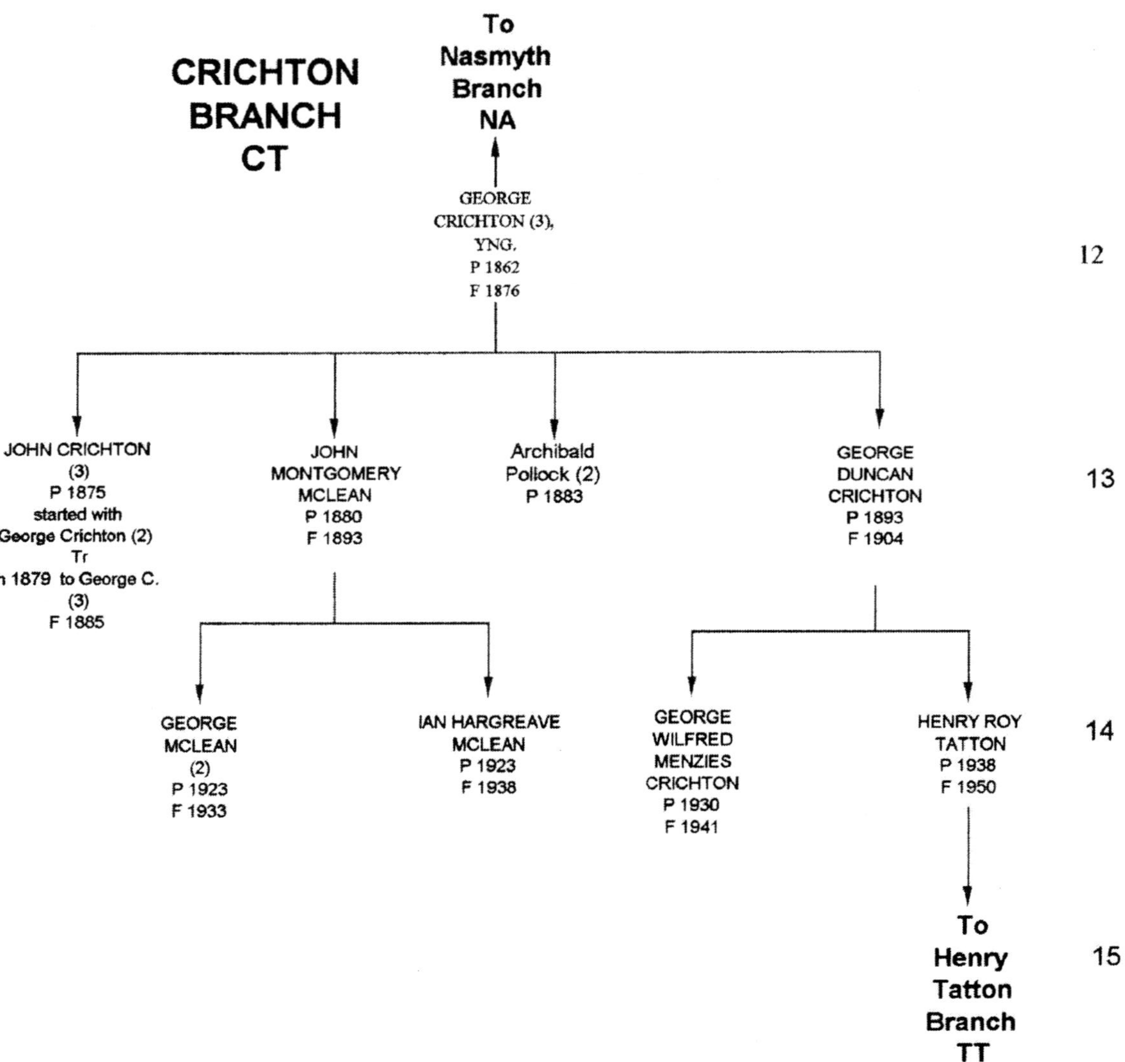
CRICHTON BRANCH CT
To Nasmyth Branch NA
GEORGE CRICHTON (3), YNG. P 1862 F 1876
12
JOHN CRICHTON (3) P 1875 started with George Crichton (2) Tr in 1879 to George C. (3) F 1885
JOHN MONTGOMERY MCLEAN P 1880 F 1893
Archibald Pollock (2) P 1883
GEORGE DUNCAN CRICHTON P 1893 F 1904
13
GEORGE MCLEAN (2) P 1923 F 1933
IAN HARGREAVE MCLEAN P 1923 F 1938
GEORGE WILFRED MENZIES CRICHTON P 1930 F 1941
HENRY ROY TATTON P 1938 F 1950
14
To Henry Tatton Branch TT
15

CUNNINGHAM BRANCH- Left Half CU

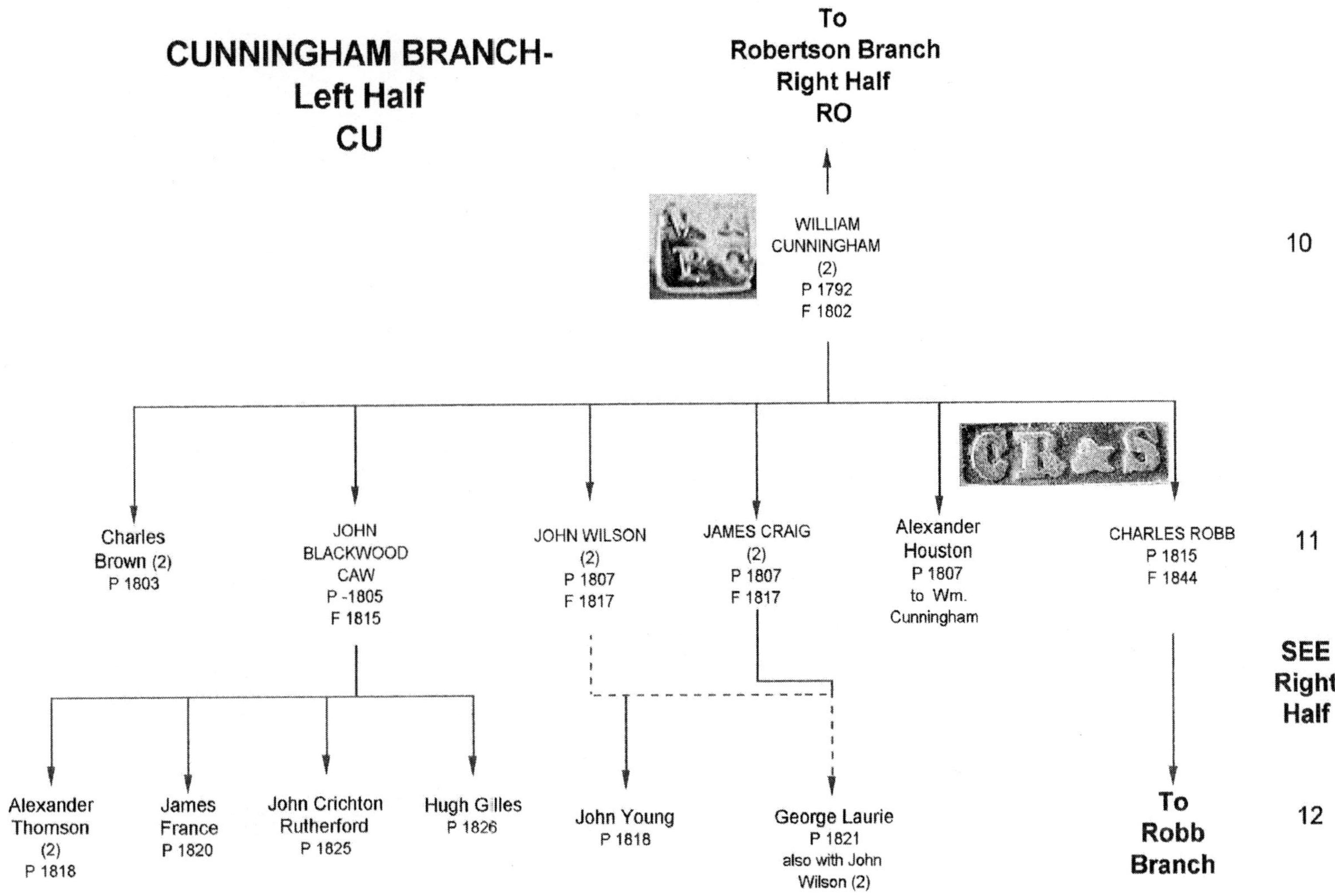

CUNNINGHAM BRANCH-Right Half CU

To Robertson Branch RO

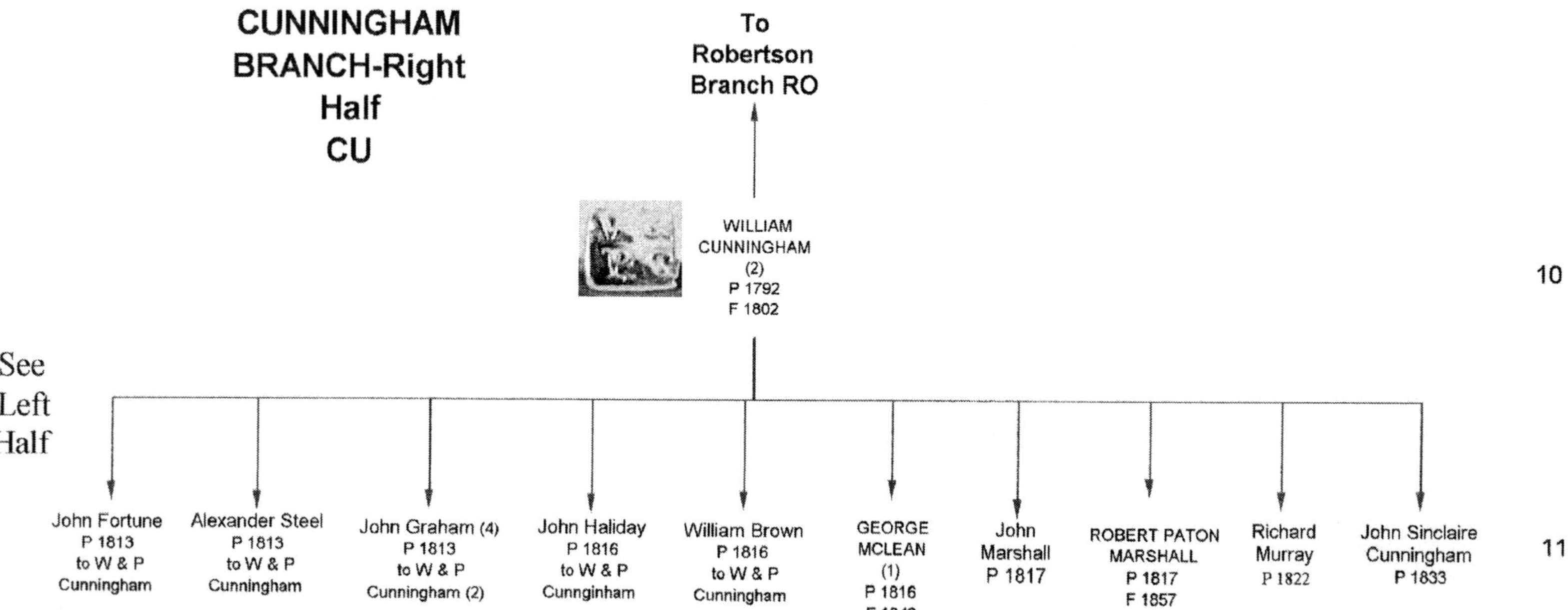

WILLIAM CUNNINGHAM (2)
P 1792
F 1802

10

See Left Half

John Fortune
P 1813
to W & P
Cunningham

Alexander Steel
P 1813
to W & P
Cunningham

John Graham (4)
P 1813
to W & P
Cunningham (2)

John Haliday
P 1816
to W & P
Cunnginham

William Brown
P 1816
to W & P
Cunningham

GEORGE MCLEAN (1)
P 1816
F 1849

John Marshall
P 1817

ROBERT PATON MARSHALL
P 1817
F 1857

Richard Murray
P 1822

John Sinclaire Cunningham
P 1833

11

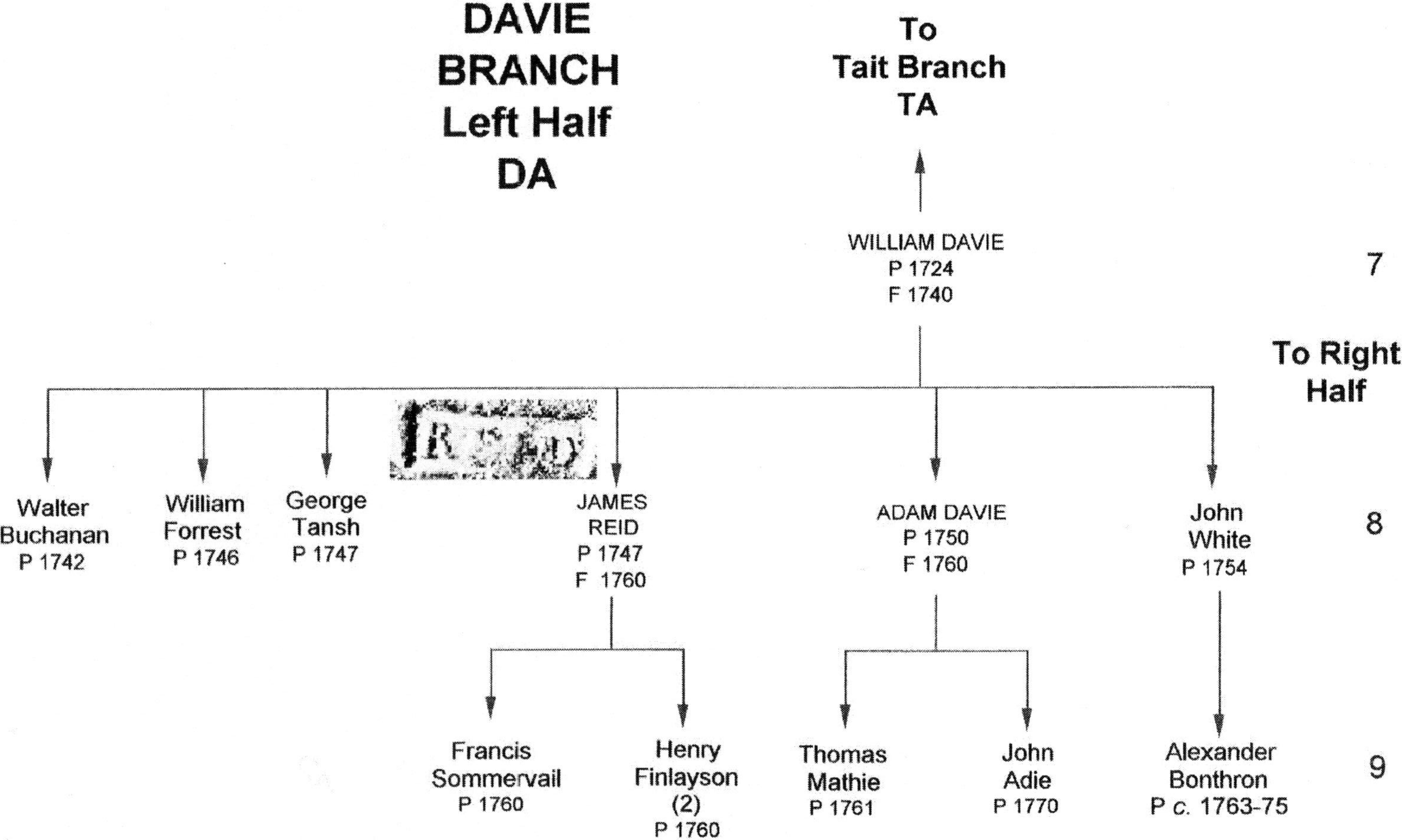

DAVIE
BRANCH
Left Half
DA
To
Tait Branch
TA
WILLIAM DAVIE
P 1724
F 1740
7
To Right
Half
Walter
Buchanan
P 1742
William
Forrest
P 1746
George
Tansh
P 1747
JAMES
REID
P 1747
F 1760
ADAM DAVIE
P 1750
F 1760
John
White
P 1754
8
Francis
Sommervail
P 1760
Henry
Finlayson
(2)
P 1760
Thomas
Mathie
P 1761
John
Adie
P 1770
Alexander
Bonthron
P c. 1763-75
9

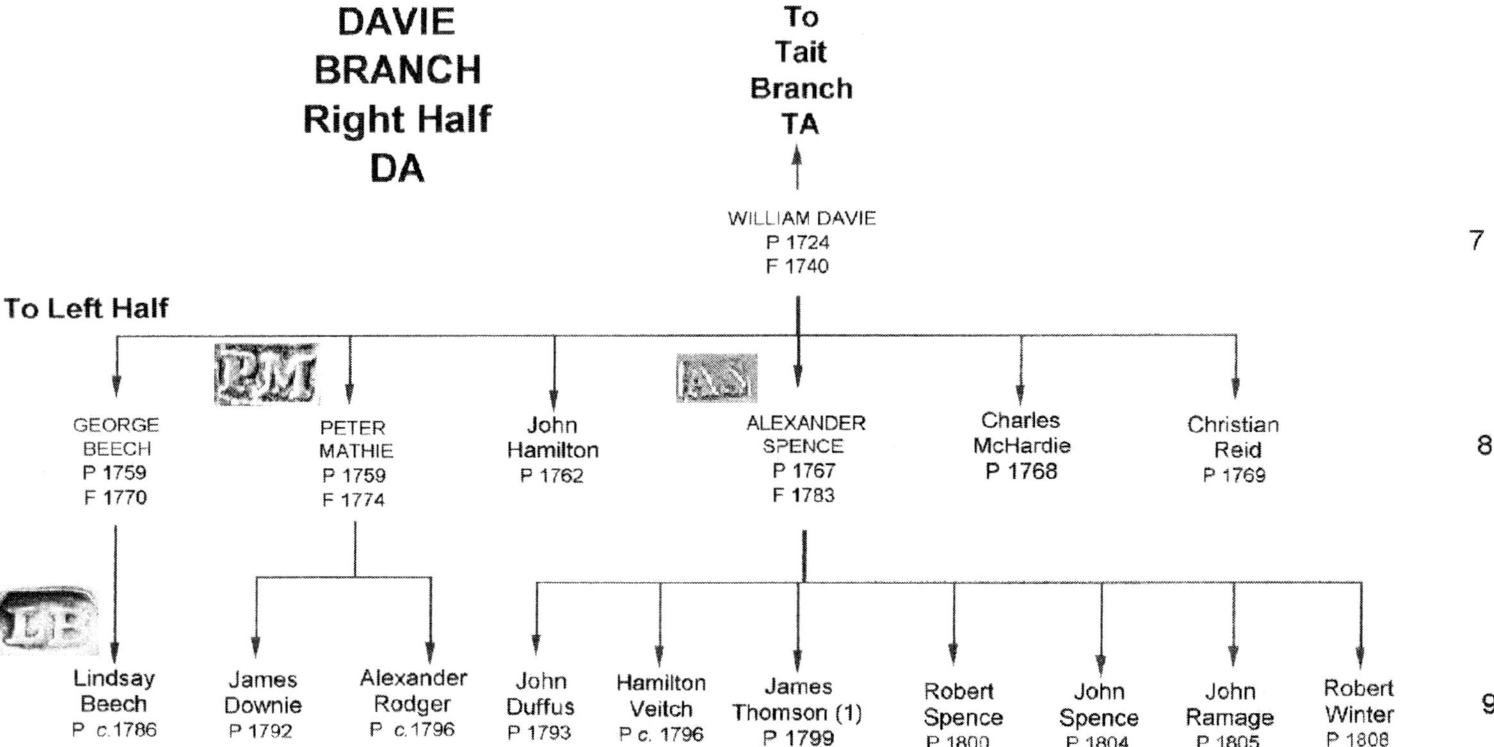
DAVIE
BRANCH
Right Half
DA
To
Tait
Branch
TA
WILLIAM DAVIE
P 1724
F 1740
7
To Left Half
PM
AS
GEORGE
BEECH
P 1759
F 1770
PETER
MATHIE
P 1759
F 1774
John
Hamilton
P 1762
ALEXANDER
SPENCE
P 1767
F 1783
Charles
McHardie
P 1768
Christian
Reid
P 1769
8
LB
Lindsay
Beech
P c.1786
James
Downie
P 1792
Alexander
Rodger
P c.1796
John
Duffus
P 1793
Hamilton
Veitch
P c. 1796
James
Thomson (1)
P 1799
Robert
Spence
P 1800
John
Spence
P 1804
John
Ramage
P 1805
Robert
Winter
P 1808
9

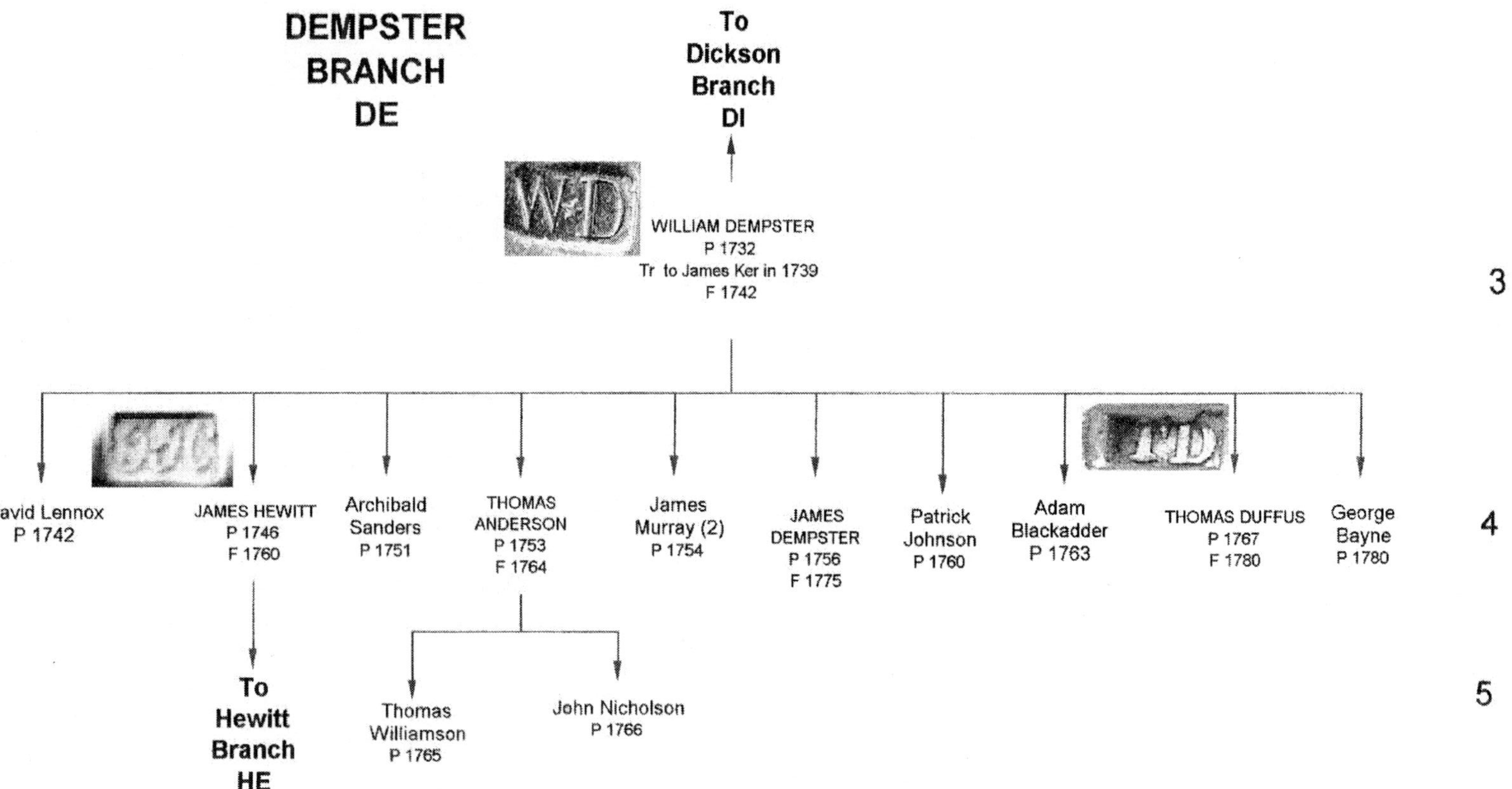
DEMPSTER
BRANCH
DE
To
Dickson
Branch
DI
WILLIAM DEMPSTER
P 1732
Tr to James Ker in 1739
F 1742
3
David Lennox
P 1742
JAMES HEWITT
P 1746
F 1760
Archibald
Sanders
P 1751
THOMAS
ANDERSON
P 1753
F 1764
James
Murray (2)
P 1754
JAMES
DEMPSTER
P 1756
F 1775
Patrick
Johnson
P 1760
Adam
Blackadder
P 1763
THOMAS DUFFUS
P 1767
F 1780
George
Bayne
P 1780
4
To
Hewitt
Branch
HE
Thomas
Williamson
P 1765
John Nicholson
P 1766
5

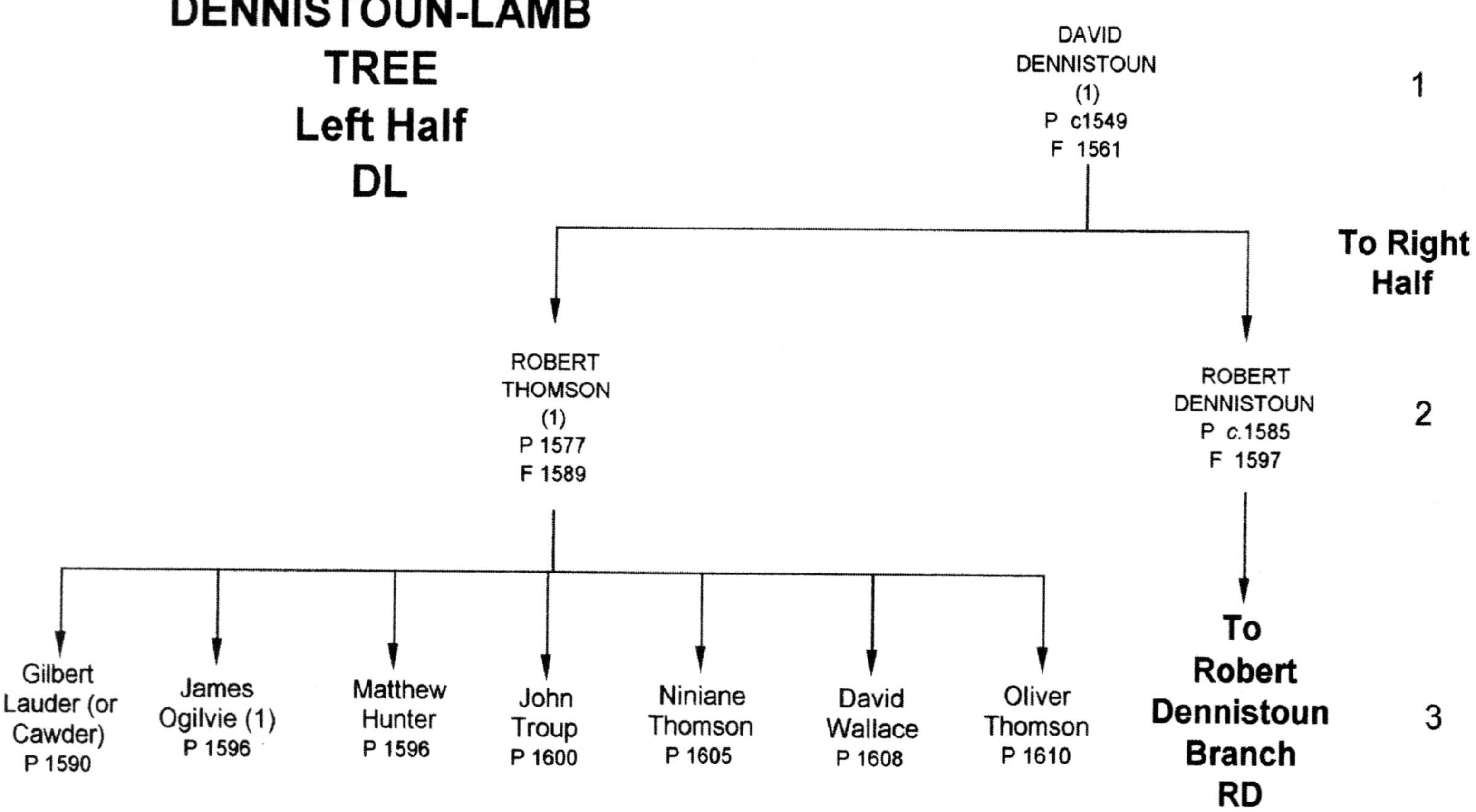
DENNISTOUN-LAMB
TREE
Left Half
DL
DAVID
DENNISTOUN
(1)
P c1549
F 1561
1
To Right
Half
ROBERT
THOMSON
(1)
P 1577
F 1589
ROBERT
DENNISTOUN
P c.1585
F 1597
2
Gilbert
Lauder (or
Cawder)
P 1590
James
Ogilvie (1)
P 1596
Matthew
Hunter
P 1596
John
Troup
P 1600
Niniane
Thomson
P 1605
David
Wallace
P 1608
Oliver
Thomson
P 1610
To
Robert
Dennistoun
Branch
RD
3

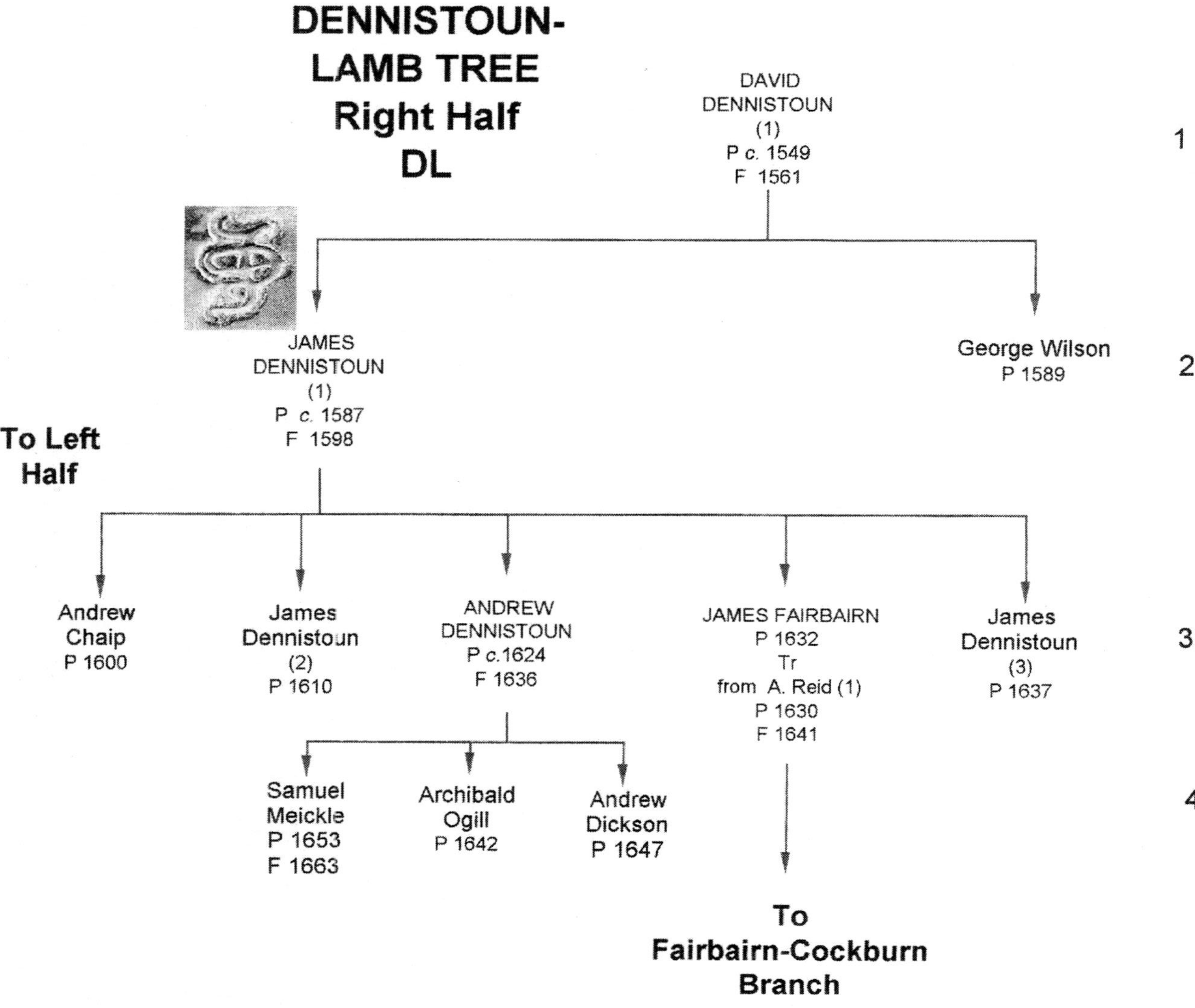

DENNISTOUN-
LAMB TREE
Right Half
DL
DAVID
DENNISTOUN
(1)
P c. 1549
F 1561
1
JAMES
DENNISTOUN
(1)
P c. 1587
F 1598
George Wilson
P 1589
2
To Left
Half
Andrew
Chaip
P 1600
James
Dennistoun
(2)
P 1610
ANDREW
DENNISTOUN
P c.1624
F 1636
JAMES FAIRBAIRN
P 1632
Tr
from A. Reid (1)
P 1630
F 1641
James
Dennistoun
(3)
P 1637
3
Samuel
Meickle
P 1653
F 1663
Archibald
Ogill
P 1642
Andrew
Dickson
P 1647
4
To
Fairbairn-Cockburn
Branch

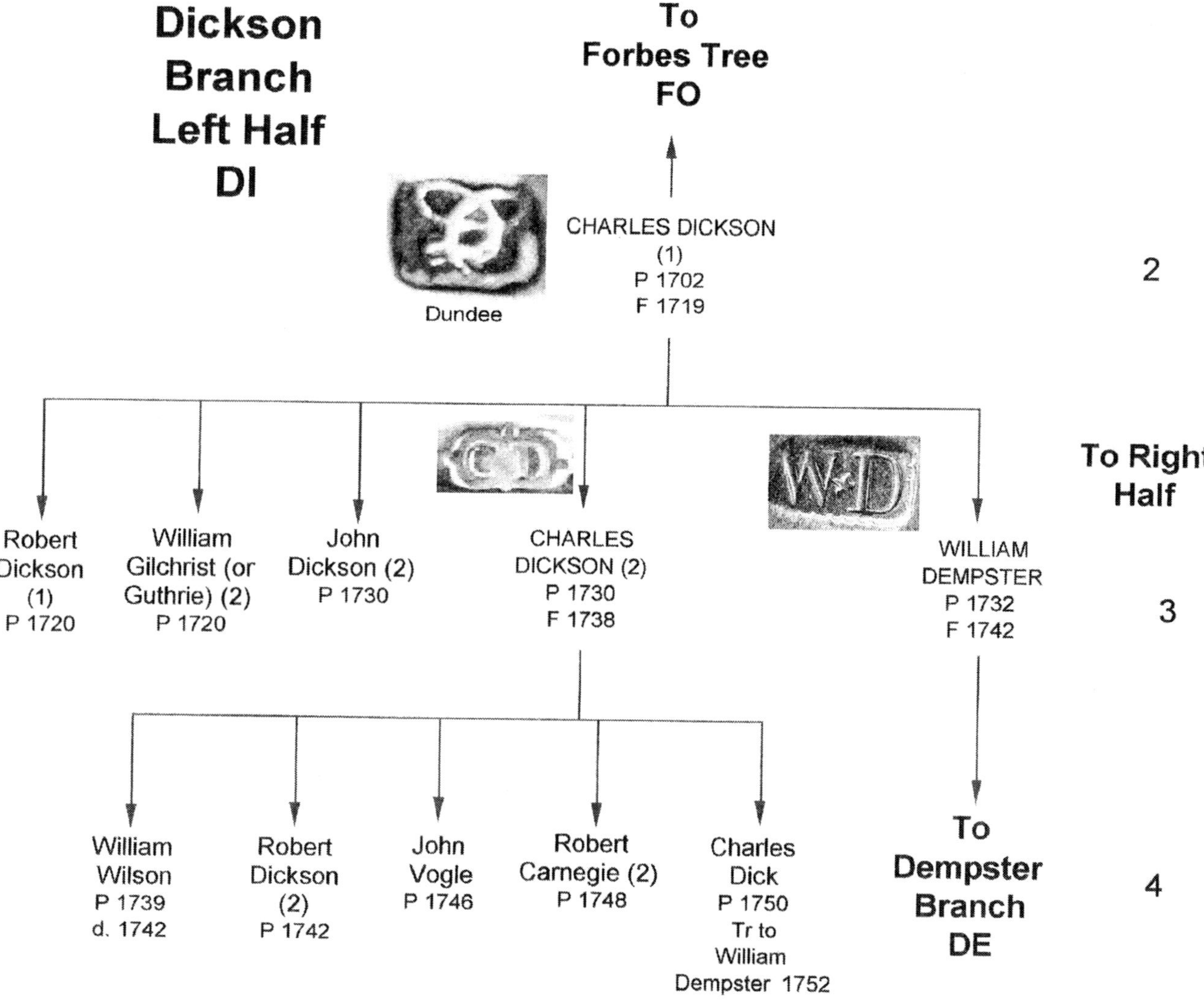

Dickson Branch Left Half DI
To Forbes Tree FO
Dundee
CHARLES DICKSON (1) P 1702 F 1719
2
Robert Dickson (1) P 1720
William Gilchrist (or Guthrie) (2) P 1720
John Dickson (2) P 1730
CHARLES DICKSON (2) P 1730 F 1738
WILLIAM DEMPSTER P 1732 F 1742
To Right Half
3
William Wilson P 1739 d. 1742
Robert Dickson (2) P 1742
John Vogle P 1746
Robert Carnegie (2) P 1748
Charles Dick P 1750 Tr to William Dempster 1752
To Dempster Branch DE
4

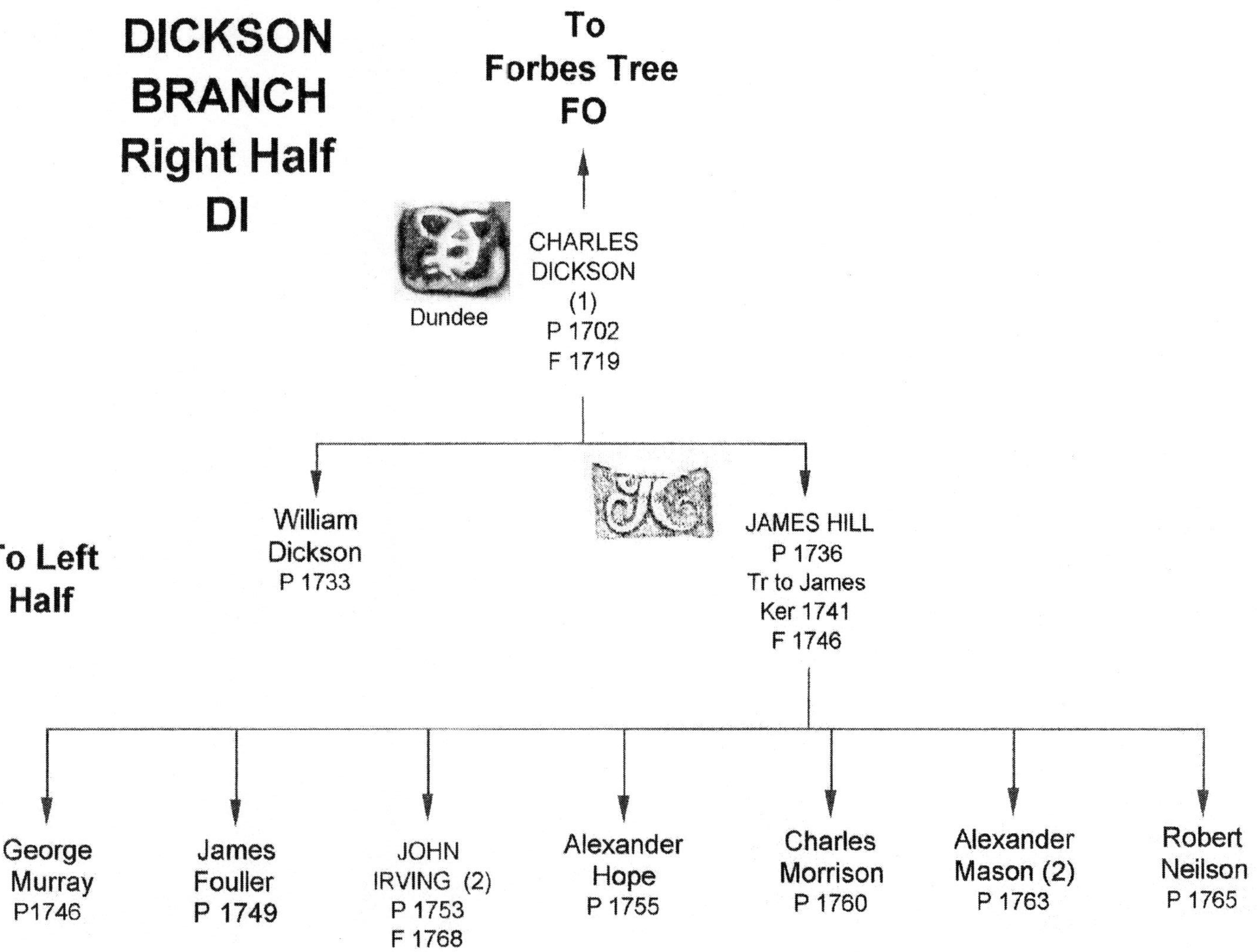
DICKSON
BRANCH
Right Half
DI
To
Forbes Tree
FO
Dundee
CHARLES
DICKSON
(1)
P 1702
F 1719
2
William
Dickson
P 1733
JAMES HILL
P 1736
Tr to James
Ker 1741
F 1746
To Left
Half
3
George
Murray
P1746
James
Fouller
P 1749
JOHN
IRVING (2)
P 1753
F 1768
Alexander
Hope
P 1755
Charles
Morrison
P 1760
Alexander
Mason (2)
P 1763
Robert
Neilson
P 1765
4

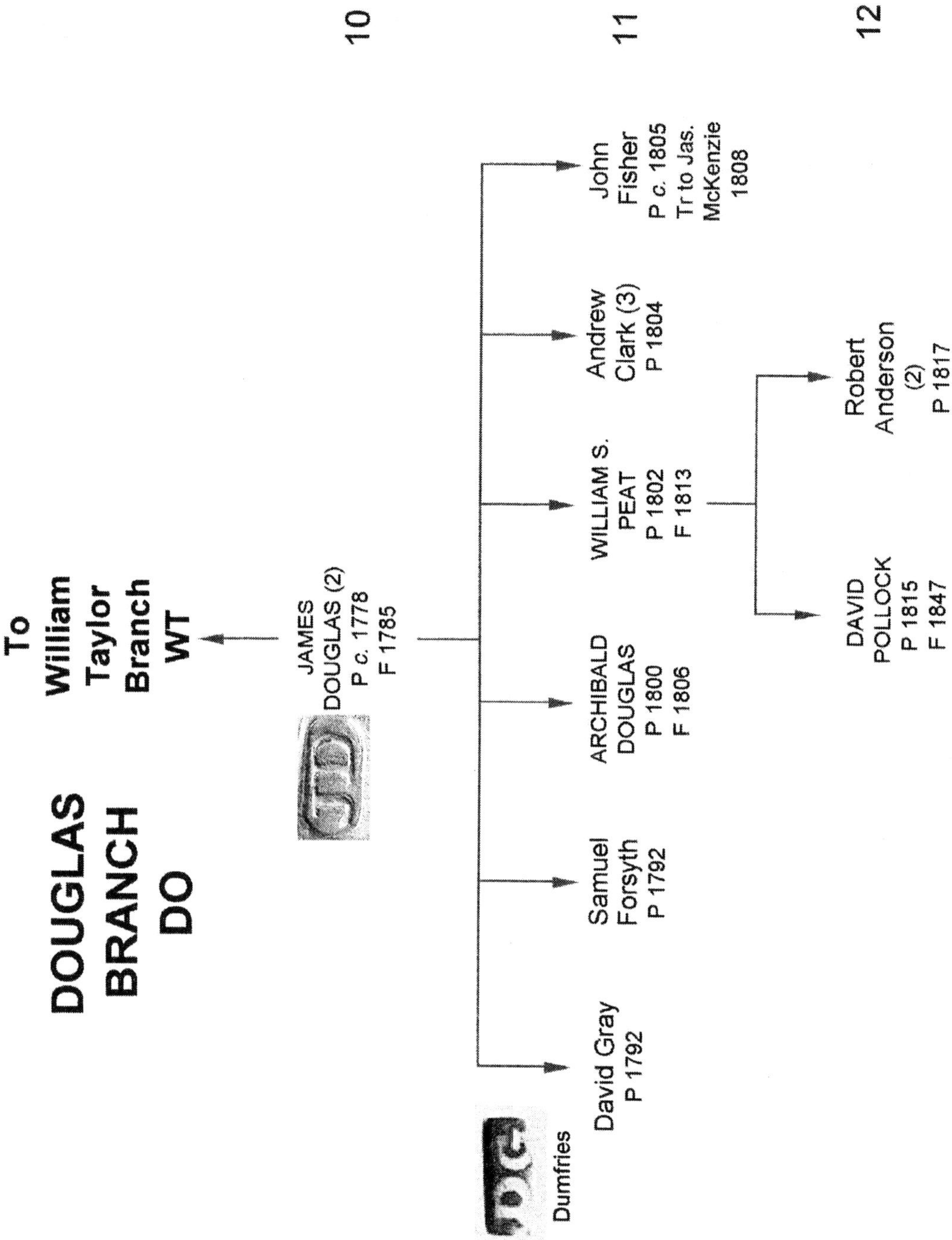
DOUGLAS BRANCH DO
To William Taylor Branch WT
JAMES DOUGLAS (2) P c. 1778 F 1785
Dumfries
10
David Gray P 1792
Samuel Forsyth P 1792
ARCHIBALD DOUGLAS P 1800 F 1806
WILLIAM S. PEAT P 1802 F 1813
Andrew Clark (3) P 1804
John Fisher P c. 1805 Tr to Jas. McKenzie 1808
11
DAVID POLLOCK P 1815 F 1847
Robert Anderson (2) P 1817
12

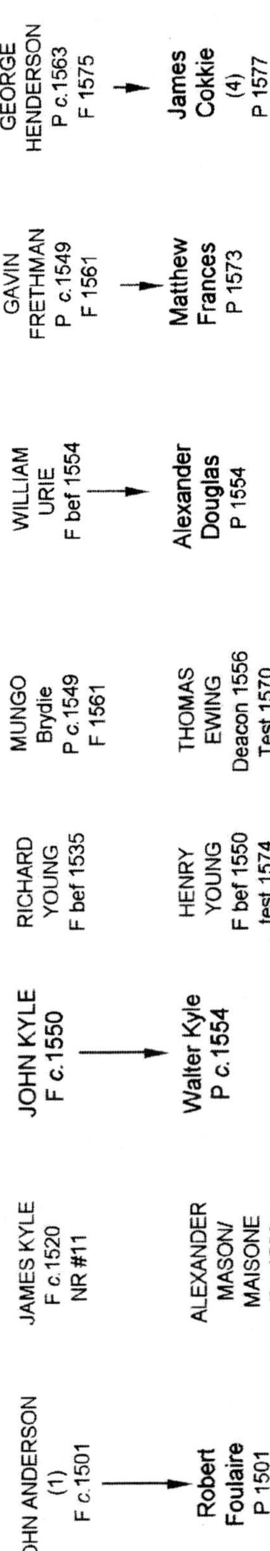
EARLY
FRAGMENTS
EF
JOHN ANDERSON
(1)
F c.1501
Robert
Foulaire
P 1501
JAMES KYLE
F c.1520
NR #11
ALEXANDER
MASON/
MAISONE
F c.1530
JOHN KYLE
F c.1550
Walter Kyle
P c.1554
RICHARD
YOUNG
F bef 1535
HENRY
YOUNG
F bef 1550
test 1574
MUNGO
Brydie
P c.1549
F 1561
THOMAS
EWING
Deacon 1556
Test 1570
WILLIAM
URIE
F bef 1554
Alexander
Douglas
P 1554
GAVIN
FRETHMAN
P c.1549
F 1561
Matthew
Frances
P 1573
GEORGE
HENDERSON
P c.1563
F 1575
James
Cokkie
(4)
P 1577

EDMONSTOUN BRANCH ED

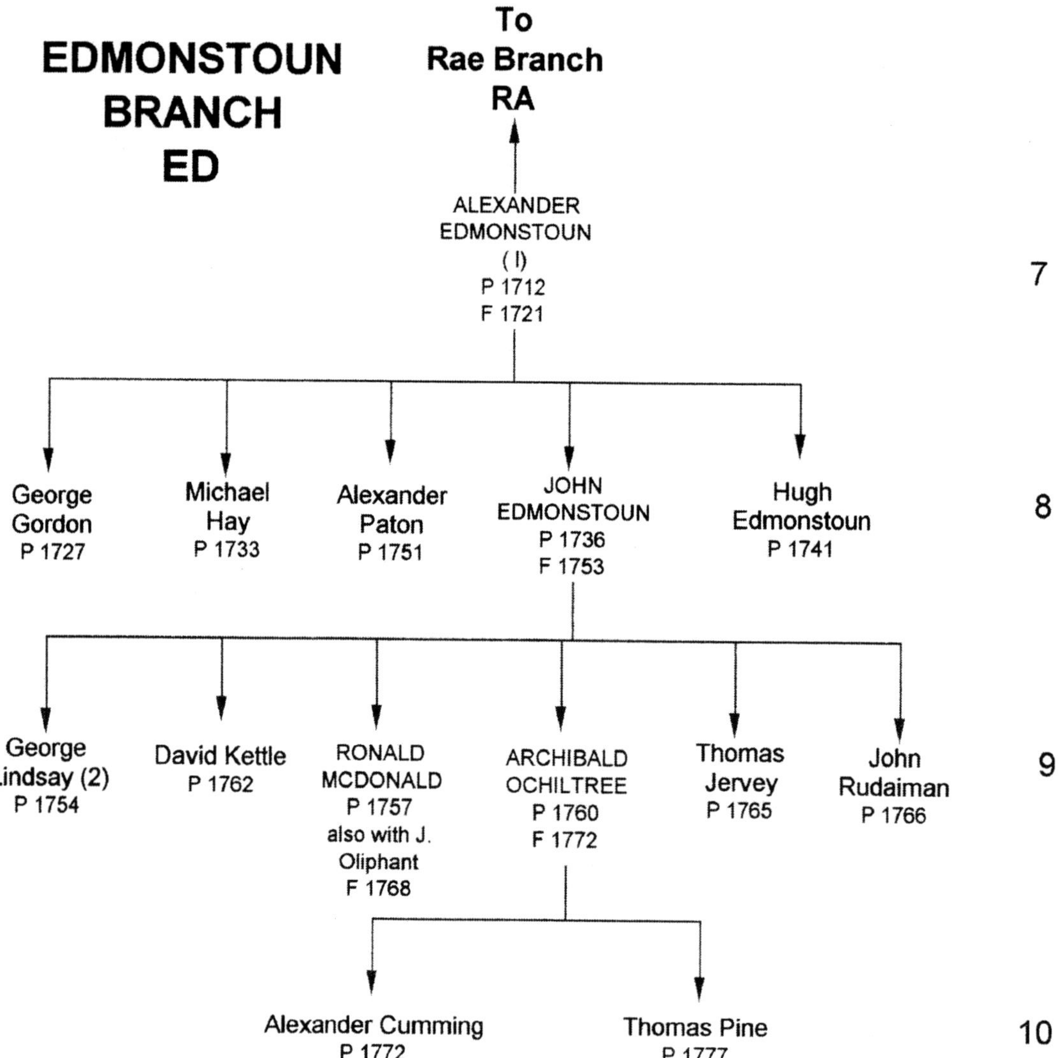

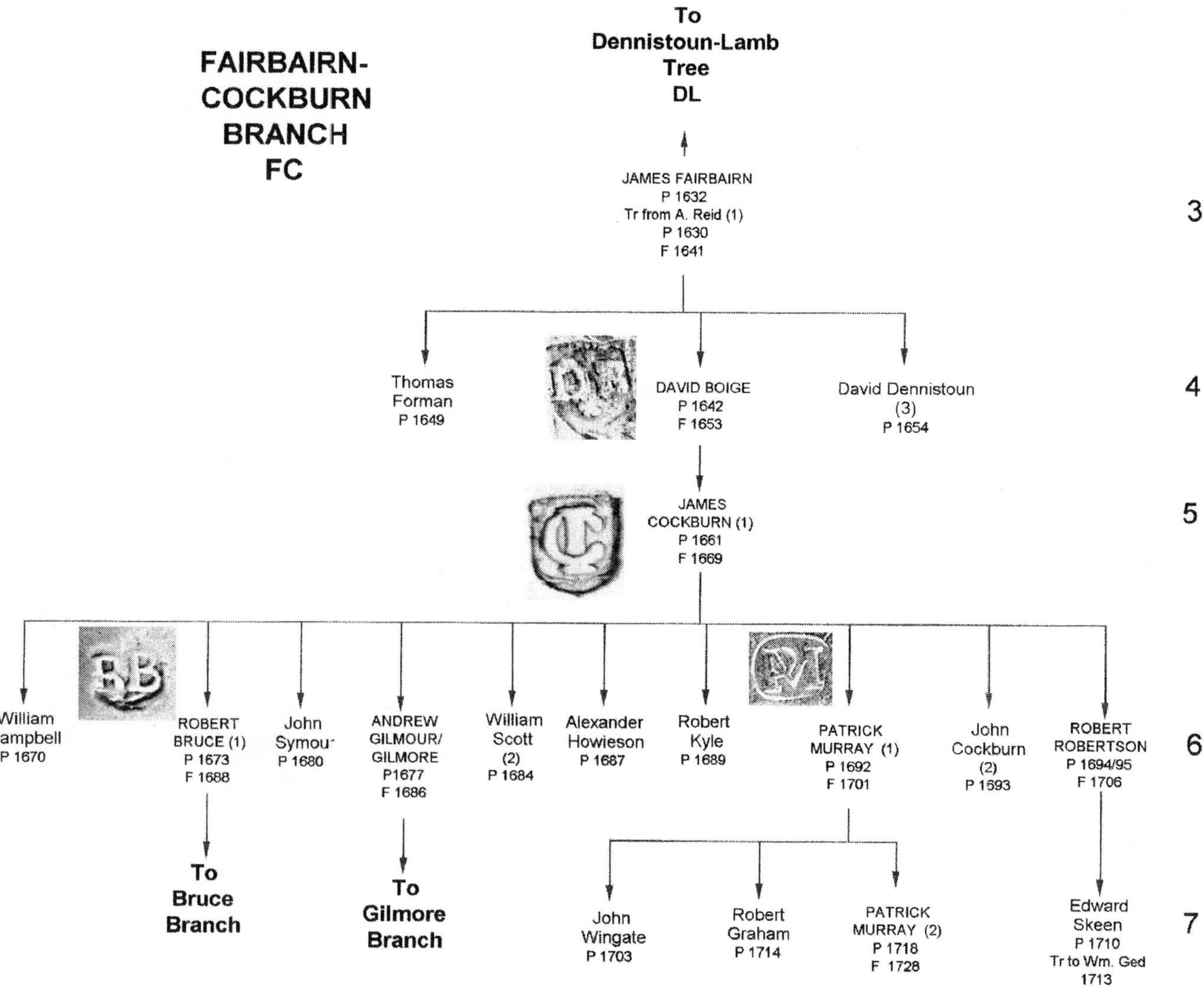
FAIRBAIRN-
COCKBURN
BRANCH
FC
To
Dennistoun-Lamb
Tree
DL
JAMES FAIRBAIRN
P 1632
Tr from A. Reid (1)
P 1630
F 1641
3
Thomas
Forman
P 1649
DAVID BOIGE
P 1642
F 1653
David Dennistoun
(3)
P 1654
4
JAMES
COCKBURN (1)
P 1661
F 1669
5
William
Campbell
P 1670
ROBERT
BRUCE (1)
P 1673
F 1688
John
Symou-
P 1680
ANDREW
GILMOUR/
GILMORE
P1677
F 1686
William
Scott
(2)
P 1684
Alexander
Howieson
P 1687
Robert
Kyle
P 1689
PATRICK
MURRAY (1)
P 1692
F 1701
John
Cockburn
(2)
P 1593
ROBERT
ROBERTSON
P 1694/95
F 1706
6
To
Bruce
Branch
To
Gilmore
Branch
John
Wingate
P 1703
Robert
Graham
P 1714
PATRICK
MURRAY (2)
P 1718
F 1728
Edward
Skeen
P 1710
Tr to Wm. Ged
1713
7

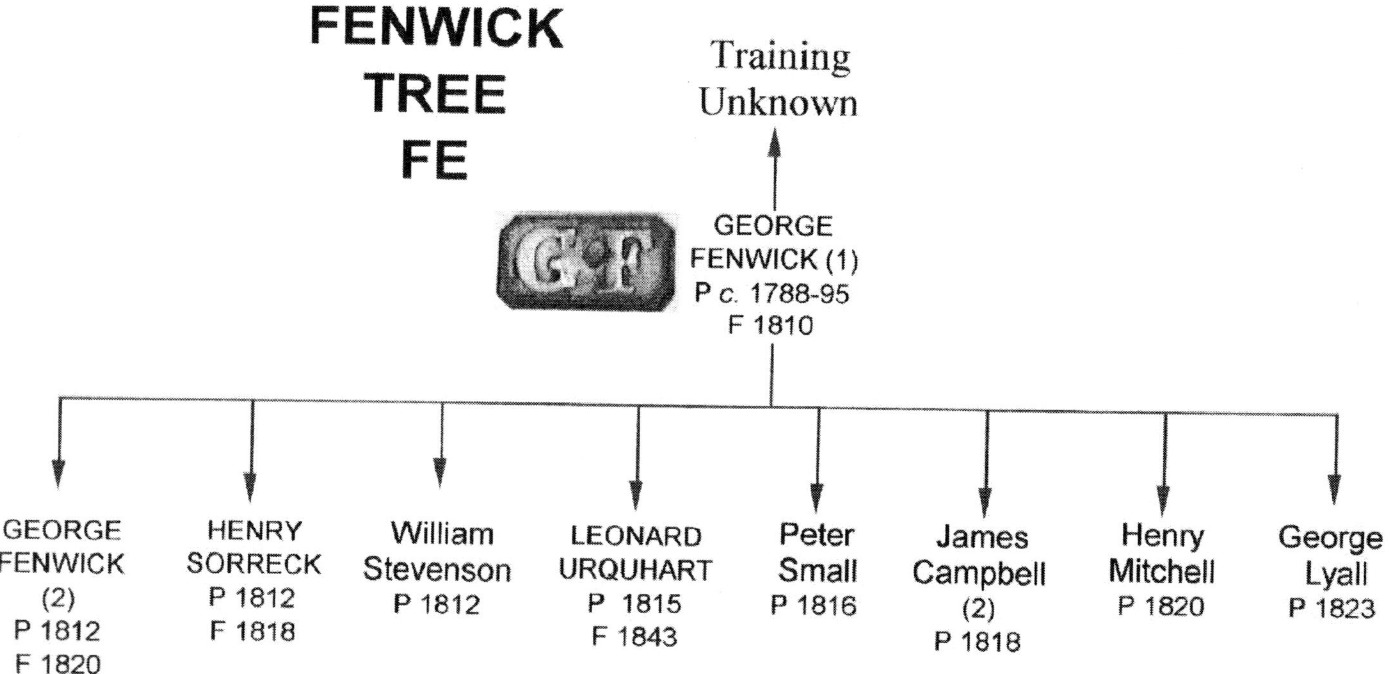
FENWICK
TREE
FE
Training
Unknown
GEORGE
FENWICK (1)
P c. 1788-95
F 1810
1
GEORGE
FENWICK
(2)
P 1812
F 1820
HENRY
SORRECK
P 1812
F 1818
William
Stevenson
P 1812
LEONARD
URQUHART
P 1815
F 1843
Peter
Small
P 1816
James
Campbell
(2)
P 1818
Henry
Mitchell
P 1820
George
Lyall
P 1823
2

FORBES TREE FO

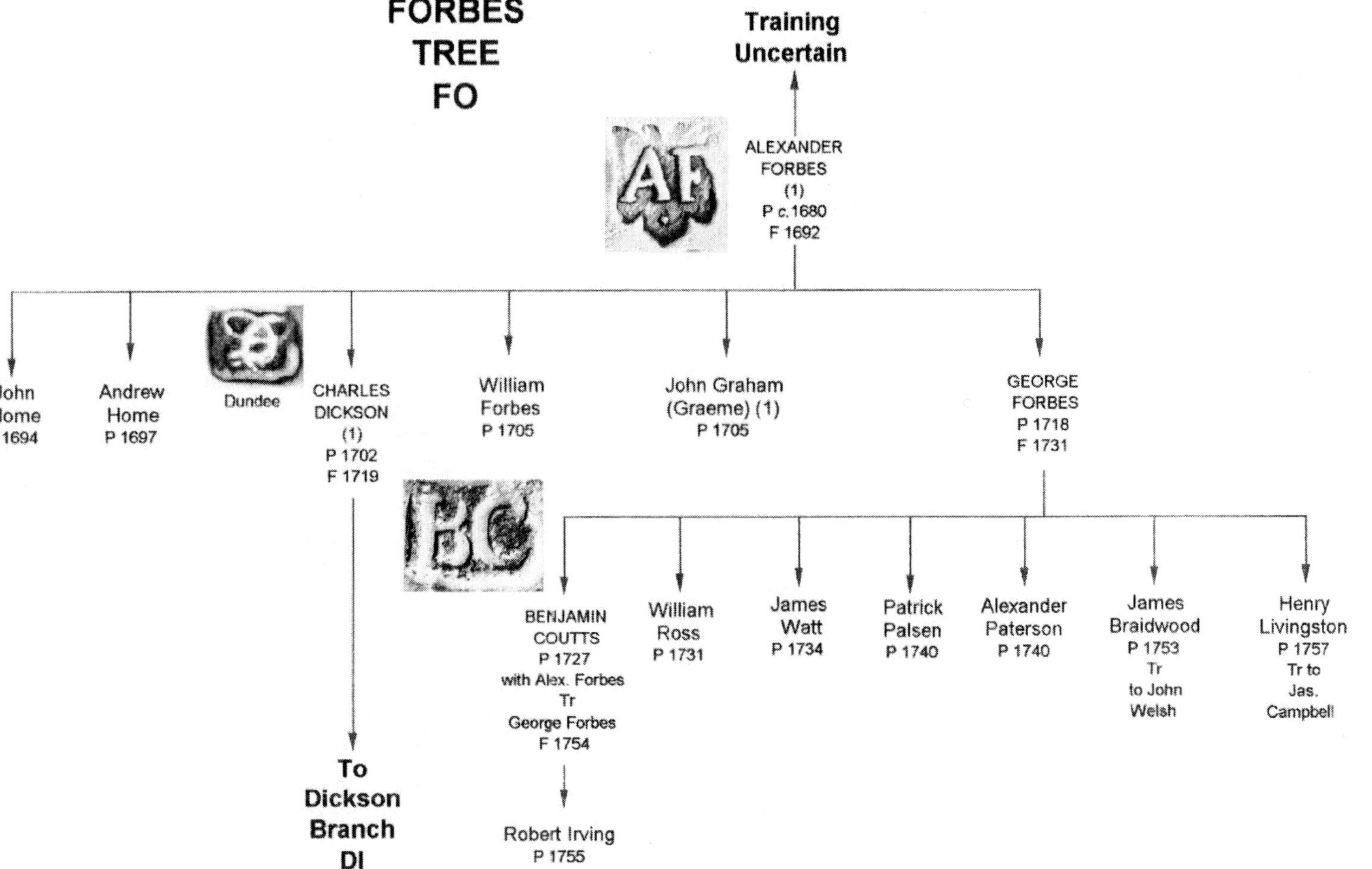

Foulis-Kirkwood Tree FK

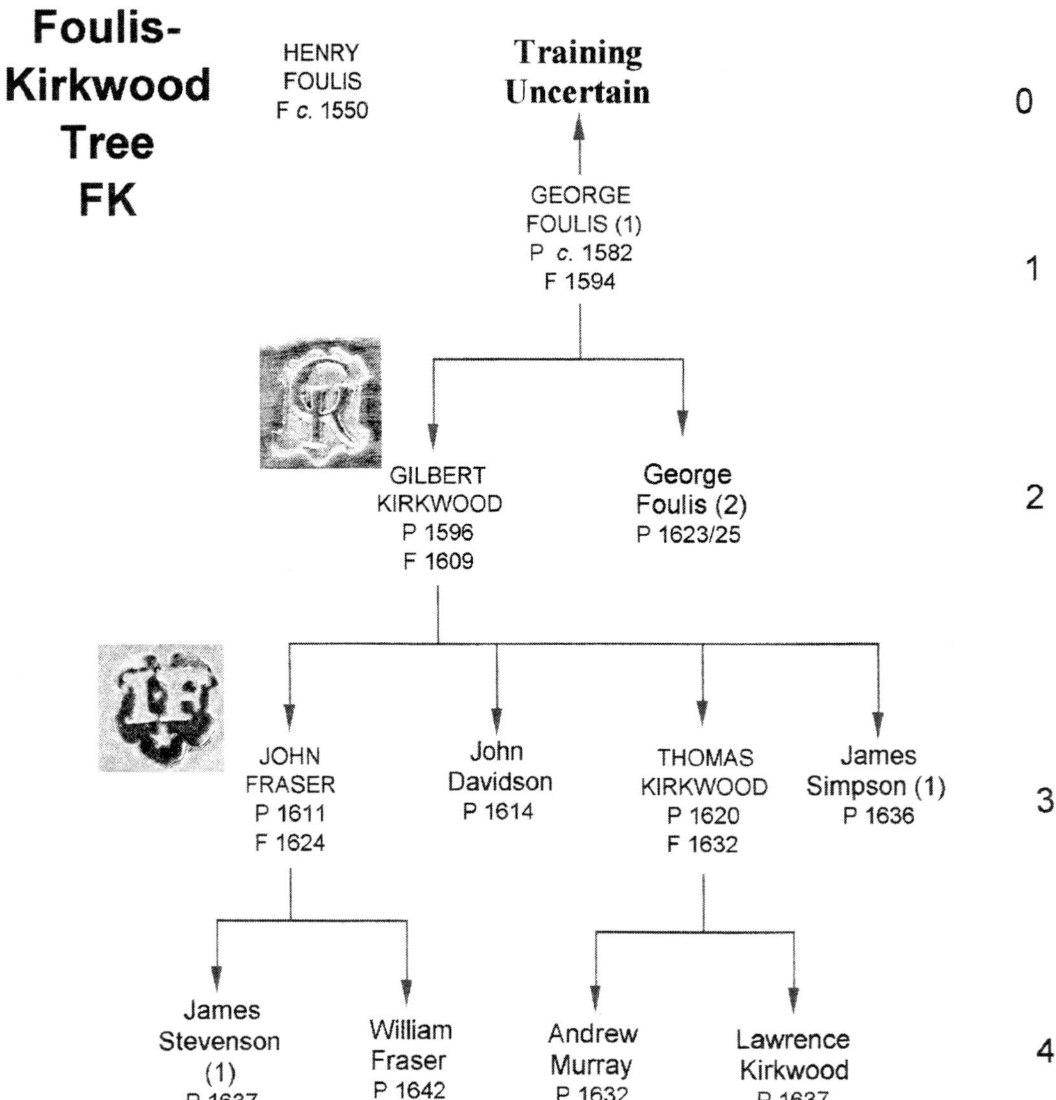

GARDNER BRANCH LEFT HALF GA

8

To Right Half

9

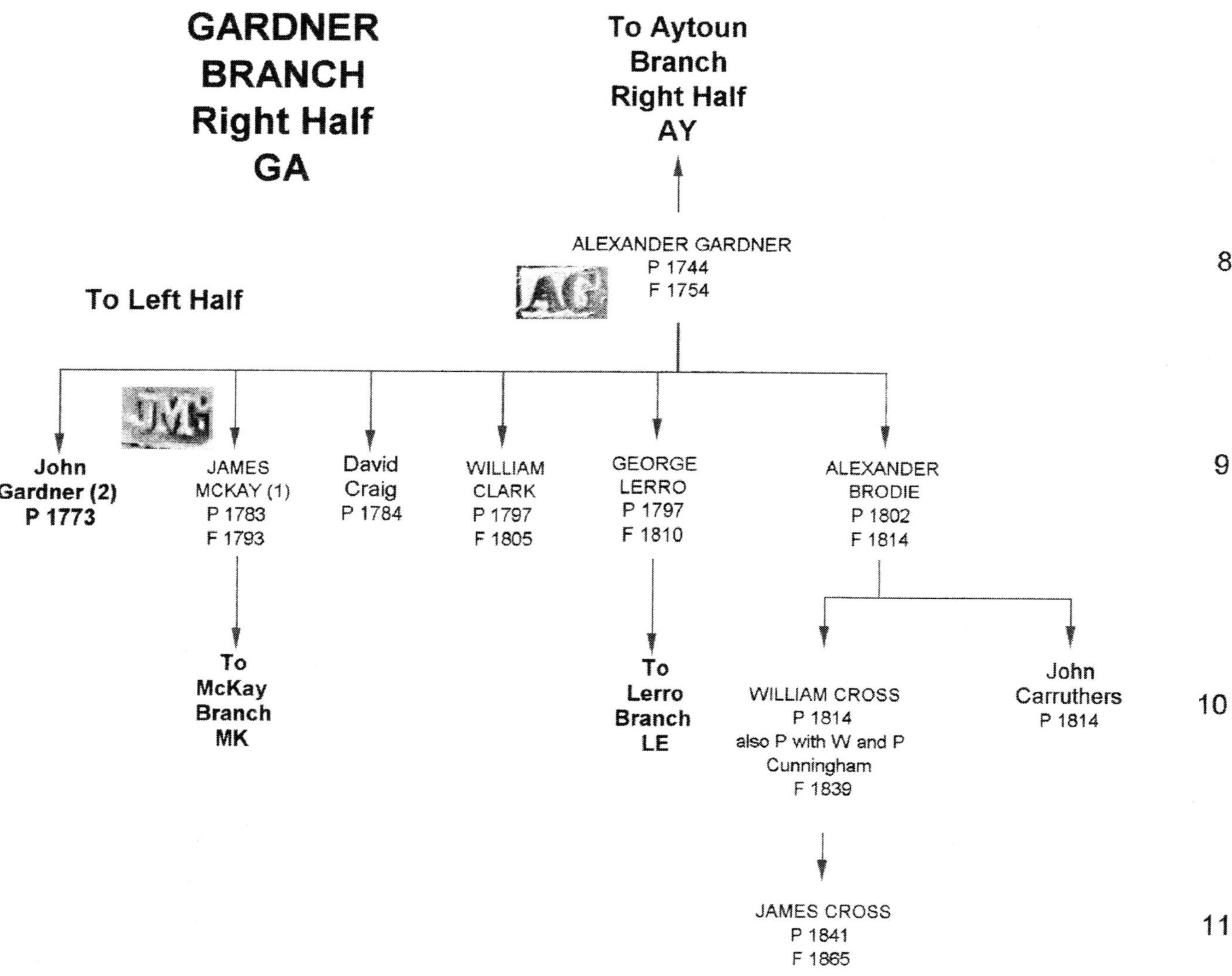
GARDNER
BRANCH
Right Half
GA
To Aytoun
Branch
Right Half
AY
ALEXANDER GARDNER
P 1744
F 1754
AG
8
To Left Half
JMG
John
Gardner (2)
P 1773
JAMES
MCKAY (1)
P 1783
F 1793
David
Craig
P 1784
WILLIAM
CLARK
P 1797
F 1805
GEORGE
LERRO
P 1797
F 1810
ALEXANDER
BRODIE
P 1802
F 1814
9
To
McKay
Branch
MK
To
Lerro
Branch
LE
WILLIAM CROSS
P 1814
also P with W and P
Cunningham
F 1839
John
Carruthers
P 1814
10
JAMES CROSS
P 1841
F 1865
11

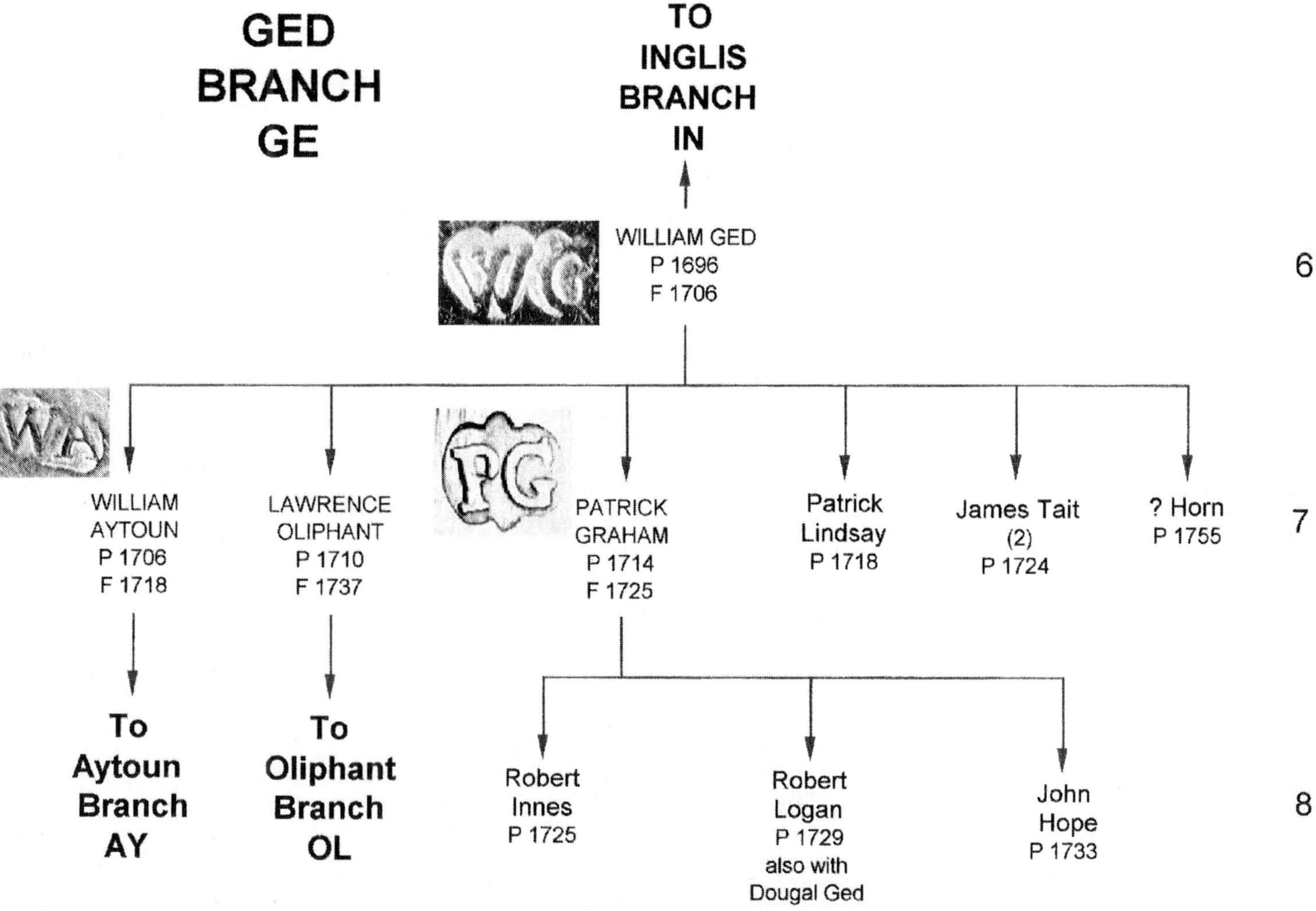
GED
BRANCH
GE
TO
INGLIS
BRANCH
IN
WILLIAM GED
P 1696
F 1706
6
WILLIAM
AYTOUN
P 1706
F 1718
LAWRENCE
OLIPHANT
P 1710
F 1737
PATRICK
GRAHAM
P 1714
F 1725
Patrick
Lindsay
P 1718
James Tait
(2)
P 1724
? Horn
P 1755
7
To
Aytoun
Branch
AY
To
Oliphant
Branch
OL
Robert
Innes
P 1725
Robert
Logan
P 1729
also with
Dougal Ged
John
Hope
P 1733
8

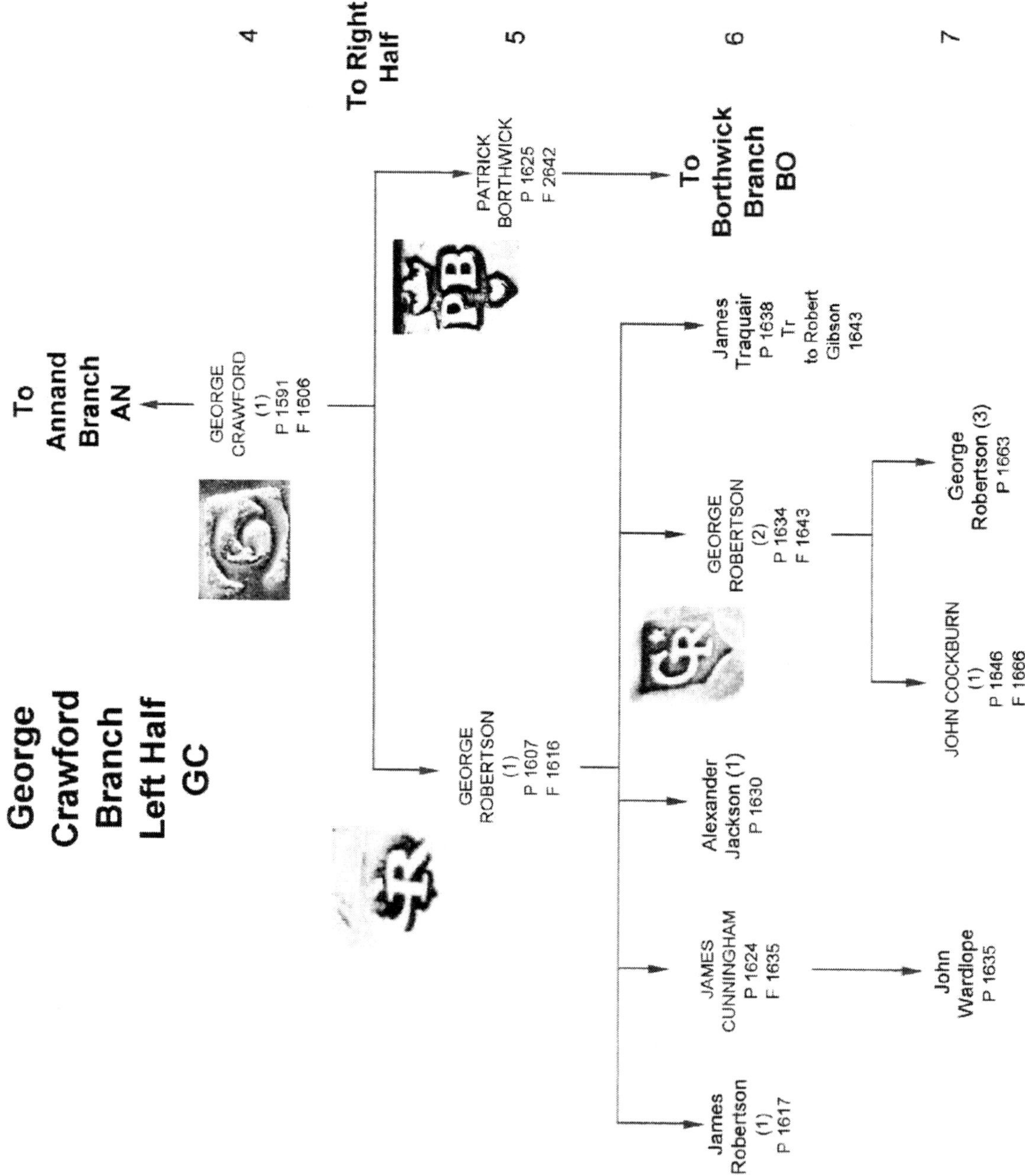
George Crawford Branch Left Half GC
To Annand Branch AN
GEORGE CRAWFORD (1) P 1591 F 1606
PATRICK BORTHWICK P 1625 F 2642
To Borthwick Branch BO
To Right Half
4
5
6
7
GEORGE ROBERTSON (1) P 1607 F 1616
James Robertson (1) P 1617
JAMES CUNNINGHAM P 1624 F 1635
John Wardlope P 1635
Alexander Jackson (1) P 1630
GEORGE ROBERTSON (2) P 1634 F 1643
JOHN COCKBURN (1) P 1646 F 1666
George Robertson (3) P 1663
James Traquair P 1638 Tr to Robert Gibson 1643

GEORGE CRAWFORD BRANCH Right Half GC

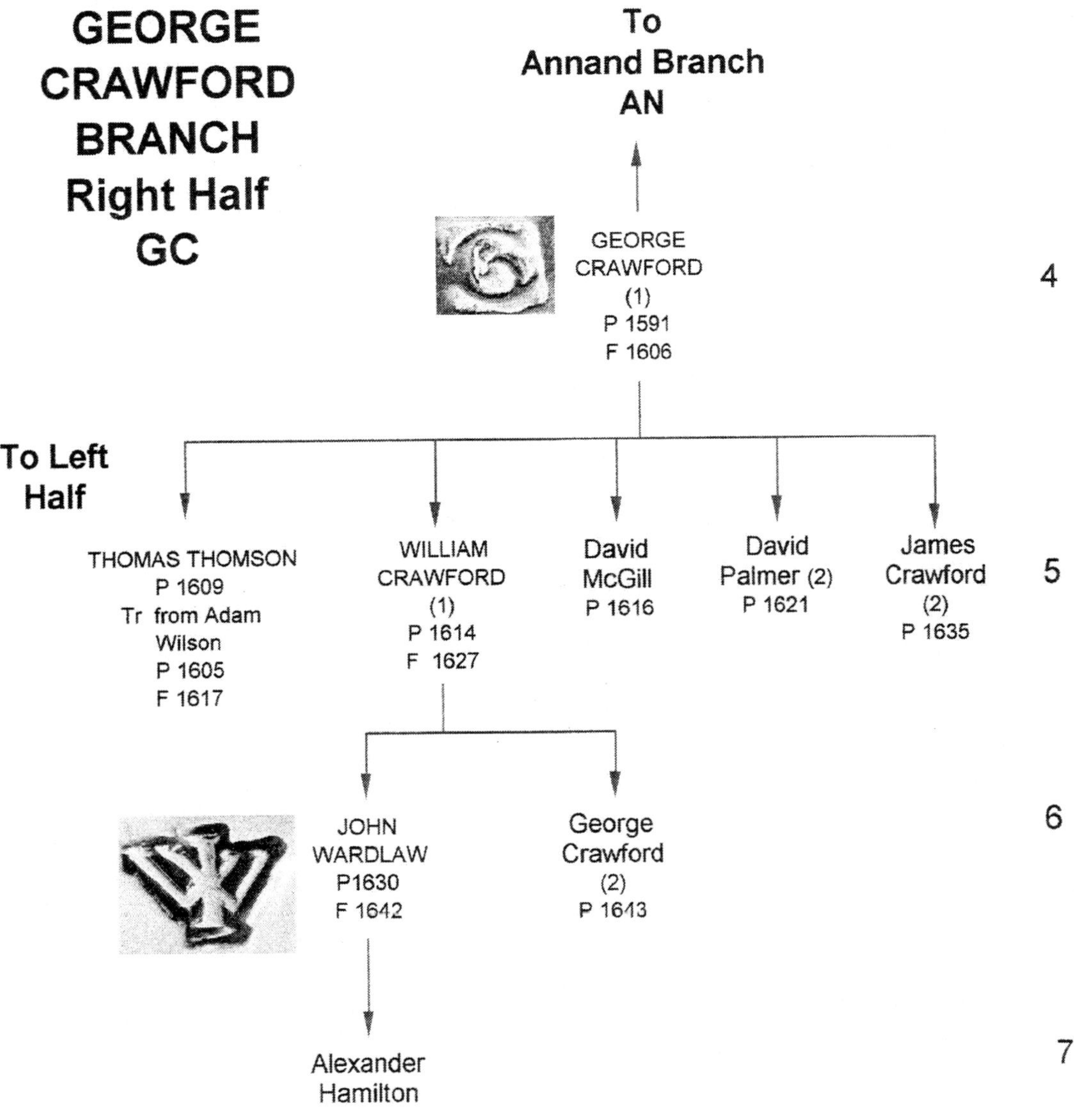

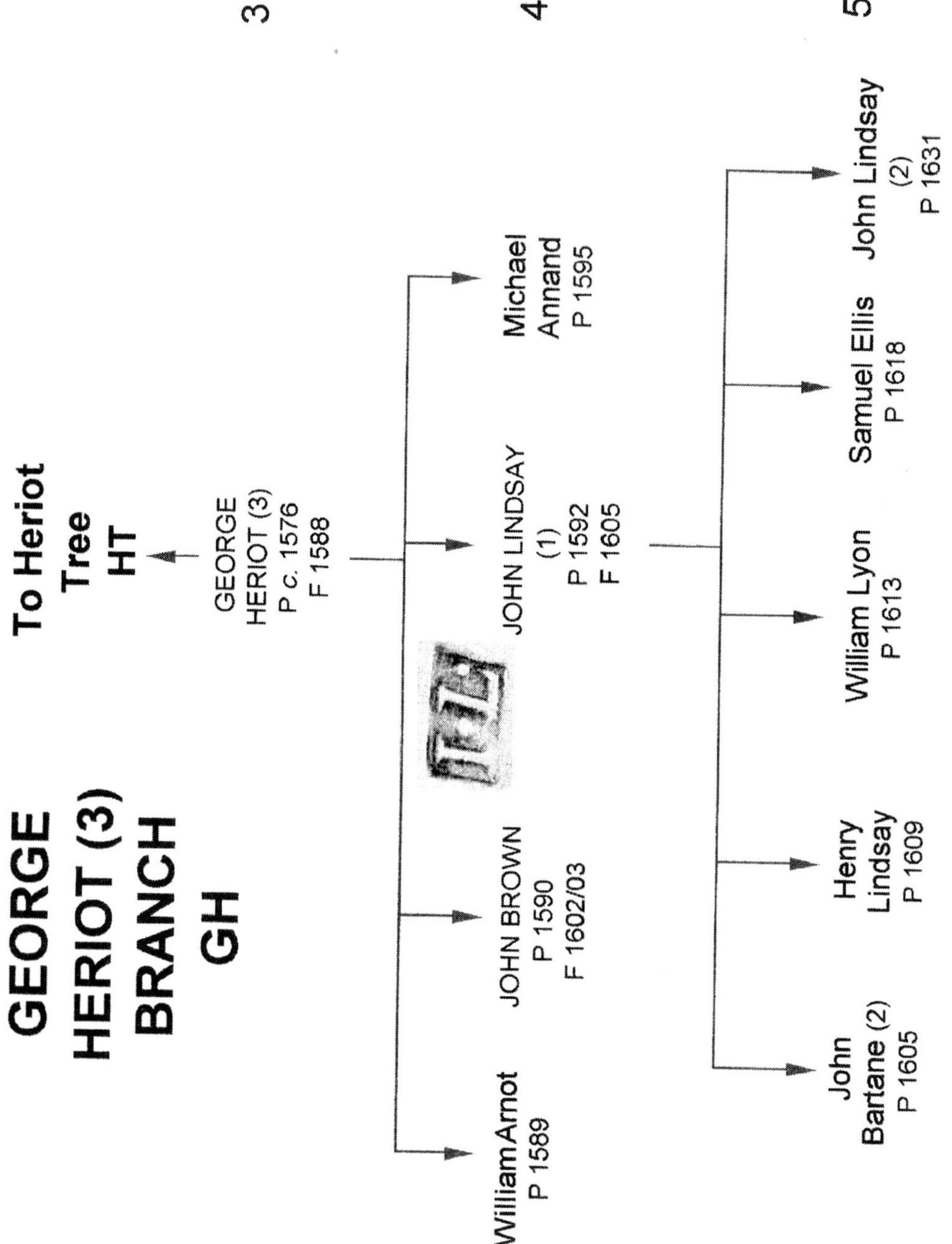
GEORGE HERIOT (3) BRANCH GH
To Heriot Tree HT
3
GEORGE HERIOT (3) P c. 1576 F 1588
4
William Arnot P 1589
JOHN BROWN P 1590 F 1602/03
JOHN LINDSAY (1) P 1592 F 1605
Michael Annand P 1595
5
John Bartane (2) P 1605
Henry Lindsay P 1609
William Lyon P 1613
Samuel Ellis P 1618
John Lindsay (2) P 1631

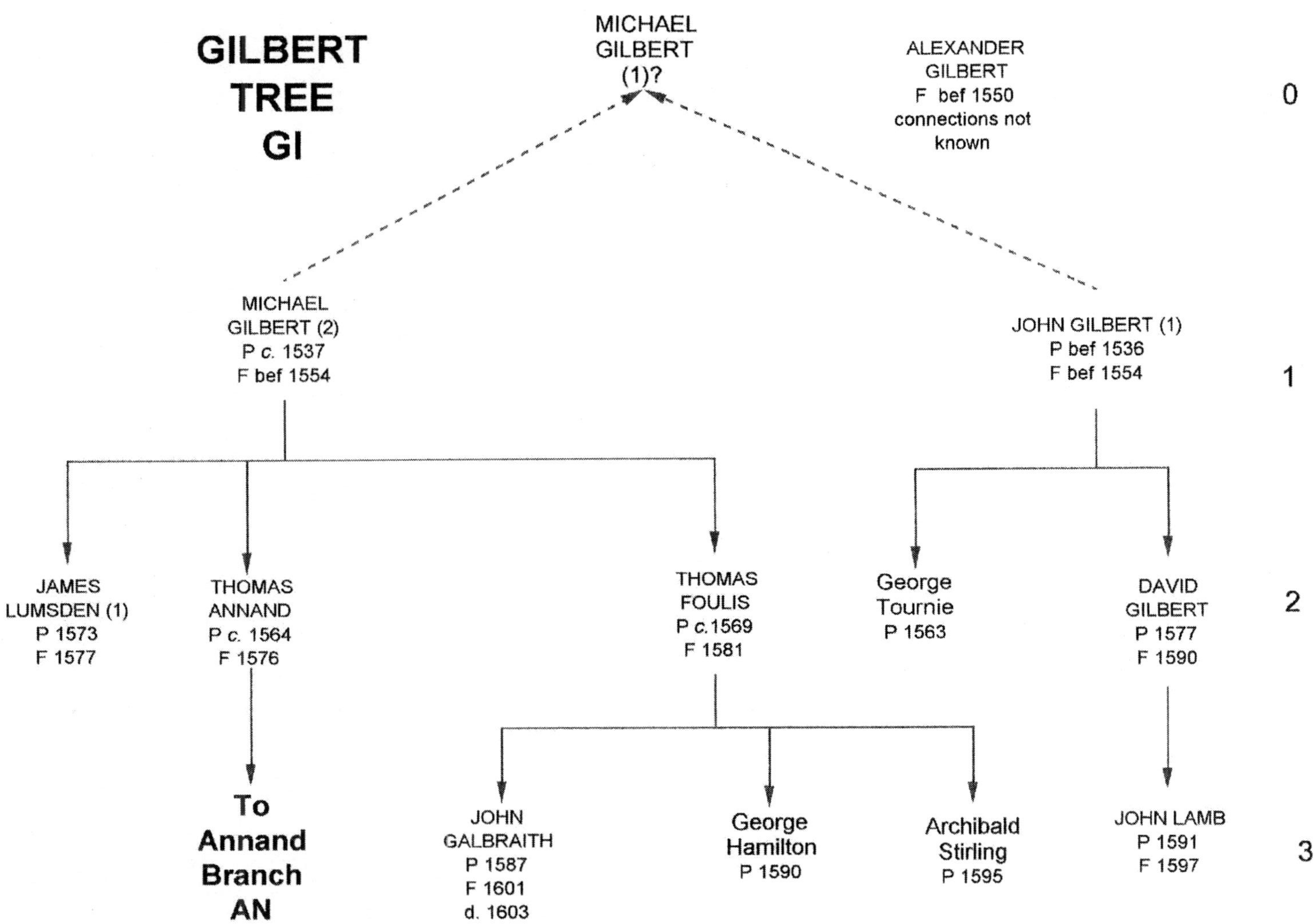

GILBERT
TREE
GI
MICHAEL
GILBERT
(1)?
ALEXANDER
GILBERT
F bef 1550
connections not
known
0
MICHAEL
GILBERT (2)
P c. 1537
F bef 1554
JOHN GILBERT (1)
P bef 1536
F bef 1554
1
JAMES
LUMSDEN (1)
P 1573
F 1577
THOMAS
ANNAND
P c. 1564
F 1576
THOMAS
FOULIS
P c.1569
F 1581
George
Tournie
P 1563
DAVID
GILBERT
P 1577
F 1590
2
To
Annand
Branch
AN
JOHN
GALBRAITH
P 1587
F 1601
d. 1603
George
Hamilton
P 1590
Archibald
Stirling
P 1595
JOHN LAMB
P 1591
F 1597
3

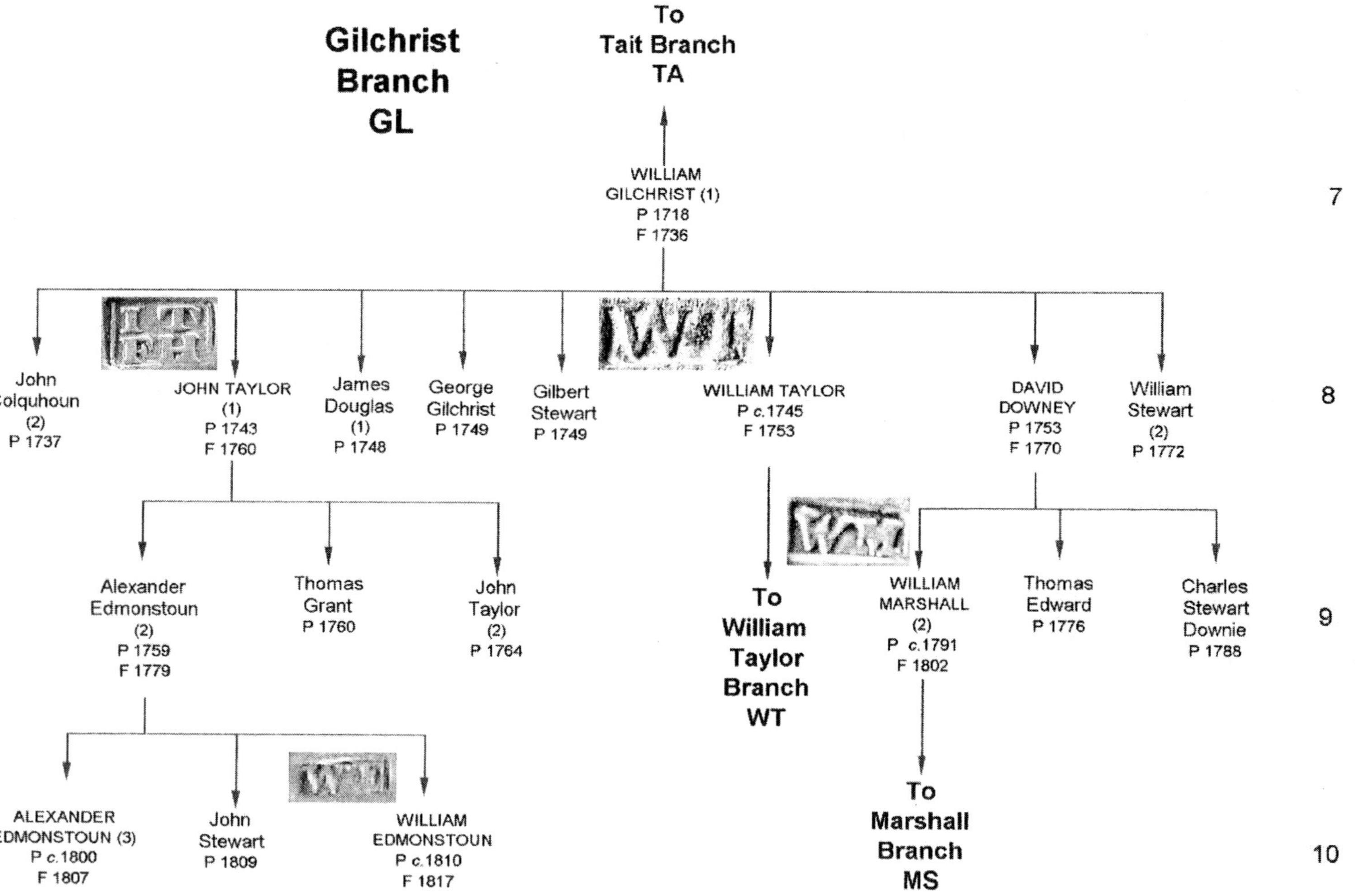
Gilchrist Branch GL
To Tait Branch TA
WILLIAM GILCHRIST (1) P 1718 F 1736
7
John Colquhoun (2) P 1737
JOHN TAYLOR (1) P 1743 F 1760
James Douglas (1) P 1748
George Gilchrist P 1749
Gilbert Stewart P 1749
WILLIAM TAYLOR P c.1745 F 1753
DAVID DOWNEY P 1753 F 1770
William Stewart (2) P 1772
8
Alexander Edmonstoun (2) P 1759 F 1779
Thomas Grant P 1760
John Taylor (2) P 1764
To William Taylor Branch WT
WILLIAM MARSHALL (2) P c.1791 F 1802
Thomas Edward P 1776
Charles Stewart Downie P 1788
9
ALEXANDER EDMONSTOUN (3) P c.1800 F 1807
John Stewart P 1809
WILLIAM EDMONSTOUN P c.1810 F 1817
To Marshall Branch MS
10

GILMORE BRANCH GM

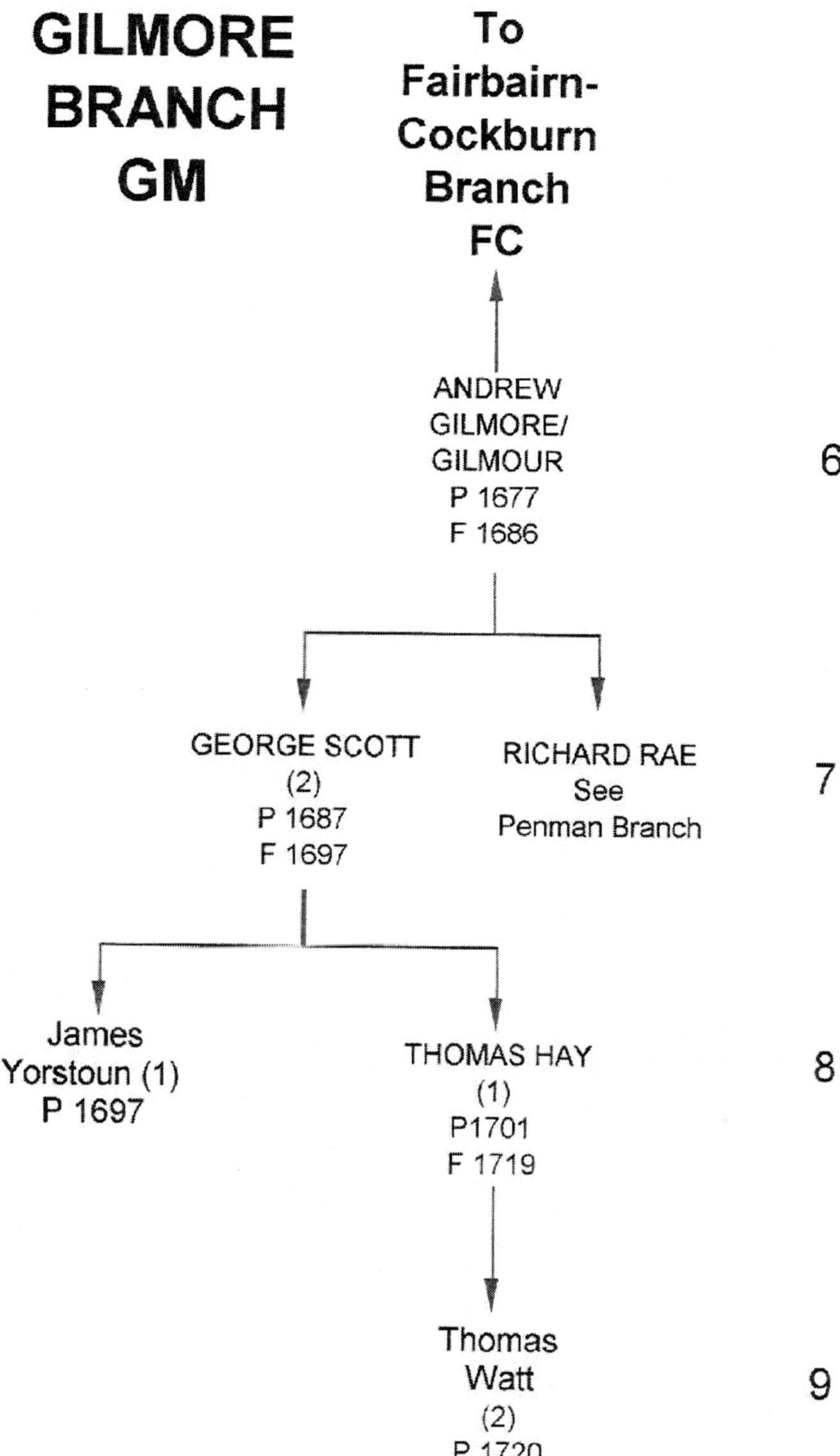

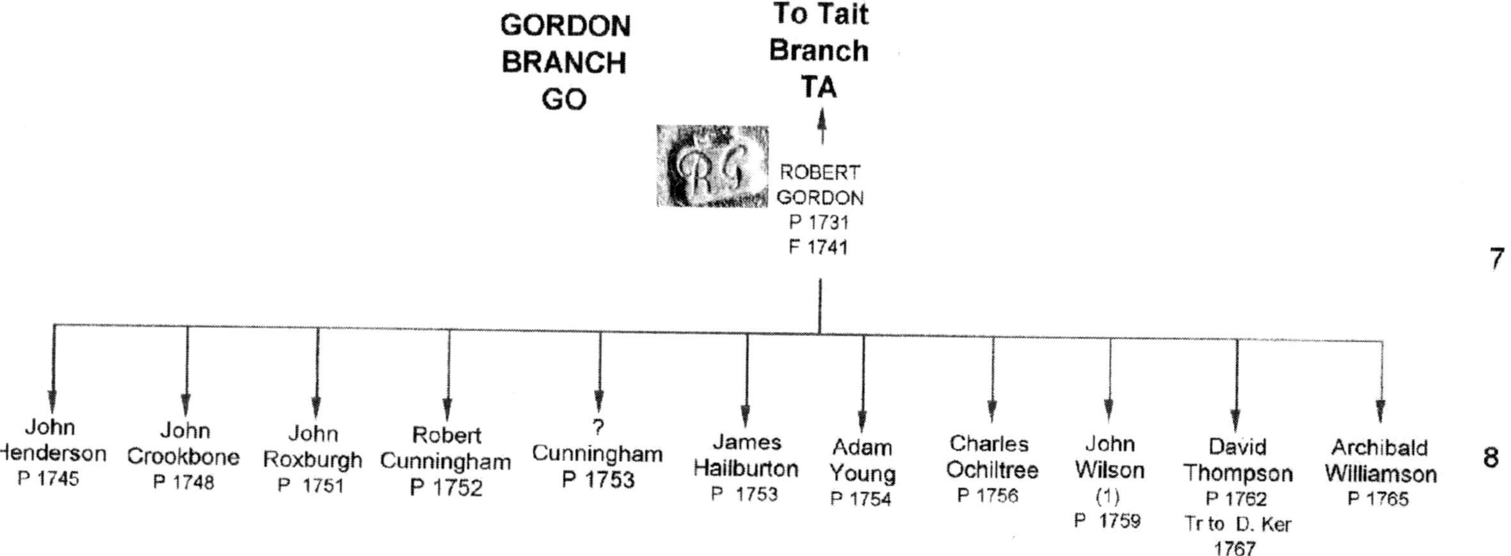
GORDON BRANCH GO
To Tait Branch TA
ROBERT GORDON P 1731 F 1741
7
John Henderson P 1745
John Crookbone P 1748
John Roxburgh P 1751
Robert Cunningham P 1752
? Cunningham P 1753
James Hailburton P 1753
Adam Young P 1754
Charles Ochiltree P 1756
John Wilson (1) P 1759
David Thompson P 1762 Tr to D. Ker 1767
Archibald Williamson P 1765
8

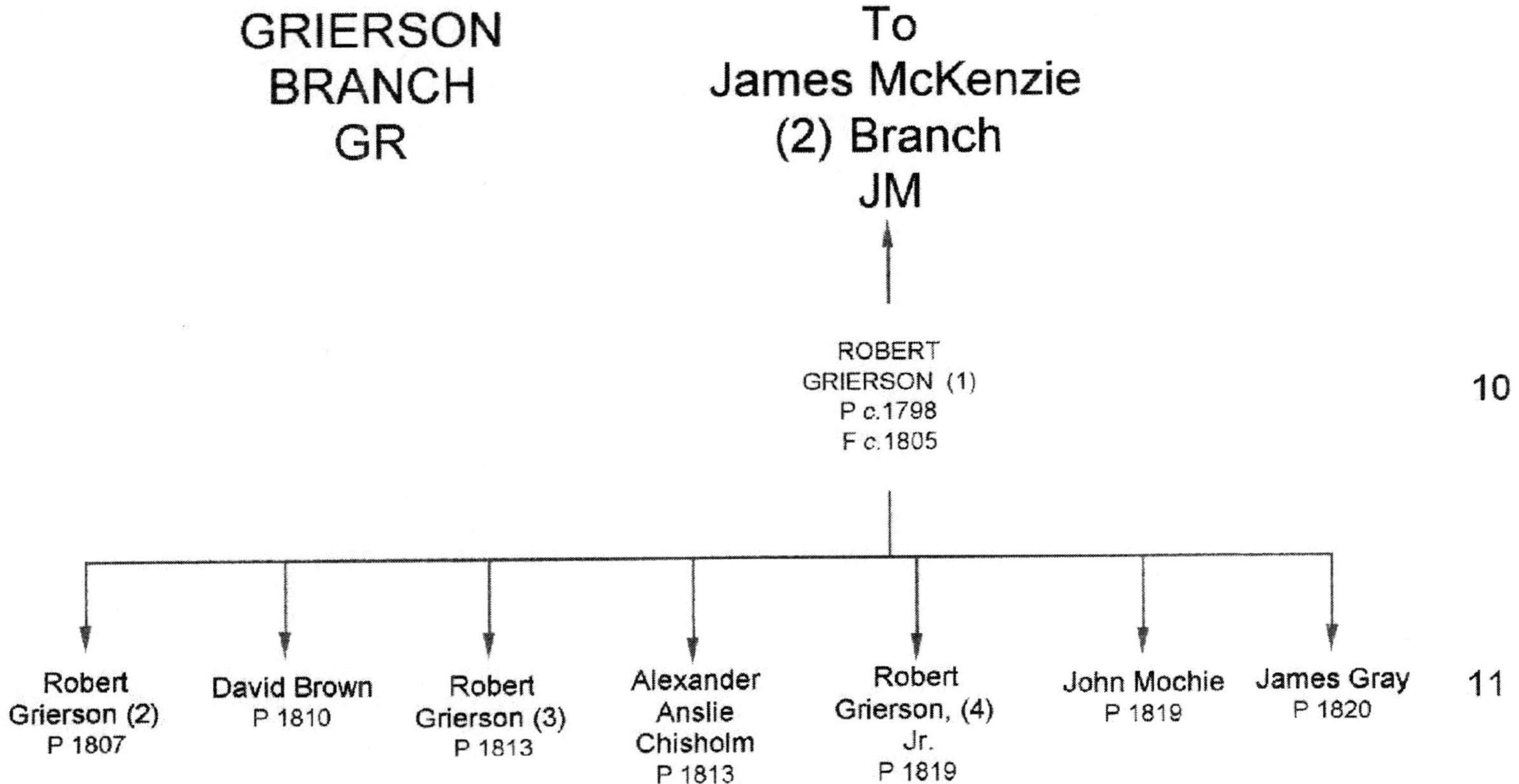
GRIERSON
BRANCH
GR
To
James McKenzie
(2) Branch
JM
ROBERT
GRIERSON (1)
P c.1798
F c.1805
10
Robert
Grierson (2)
P 1807
David Brown
P 1810
Robert
Grierson (3)
P 1813
Alexander
Anslie
Chisholm
P 1813
Robert
Grierson, (4)
Jr.
P 1819
John Mochie
P 1819
James Gray
P 1820
11

HENRY ROY TATTON BRANCH TT

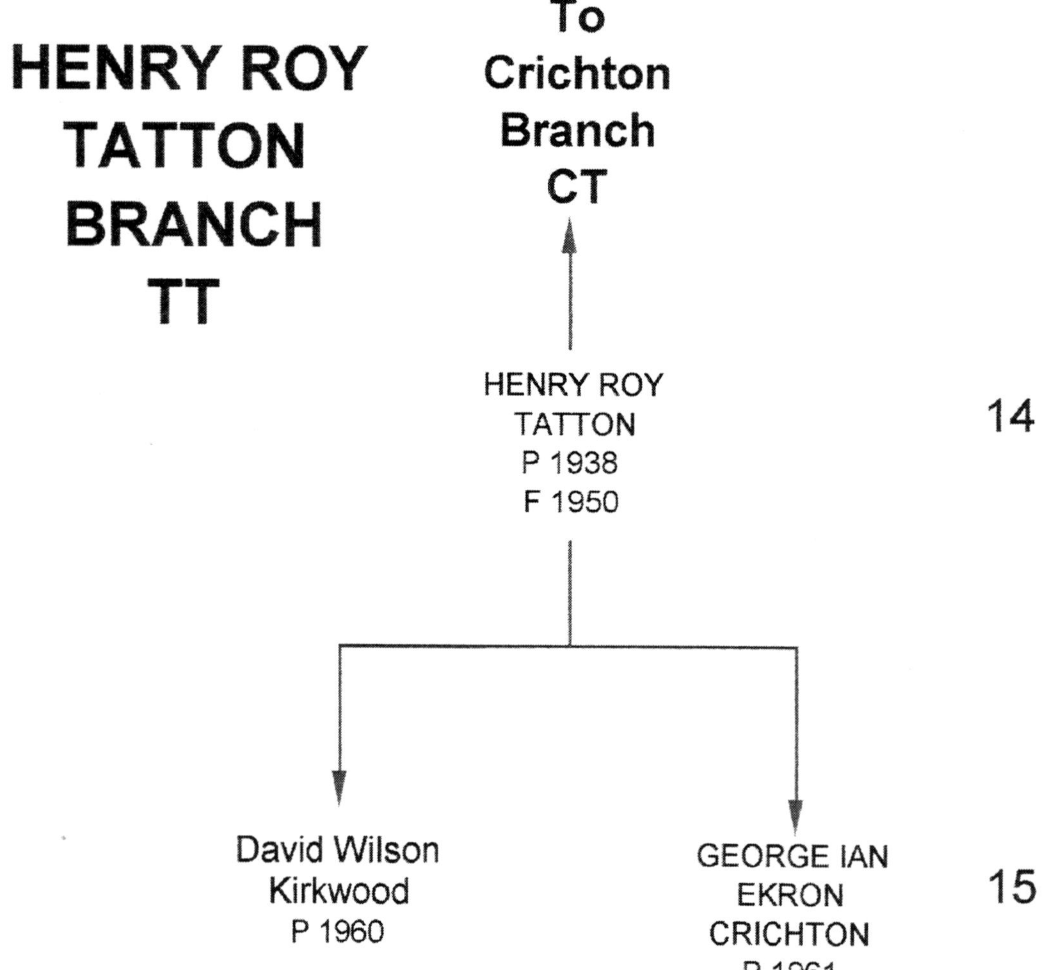

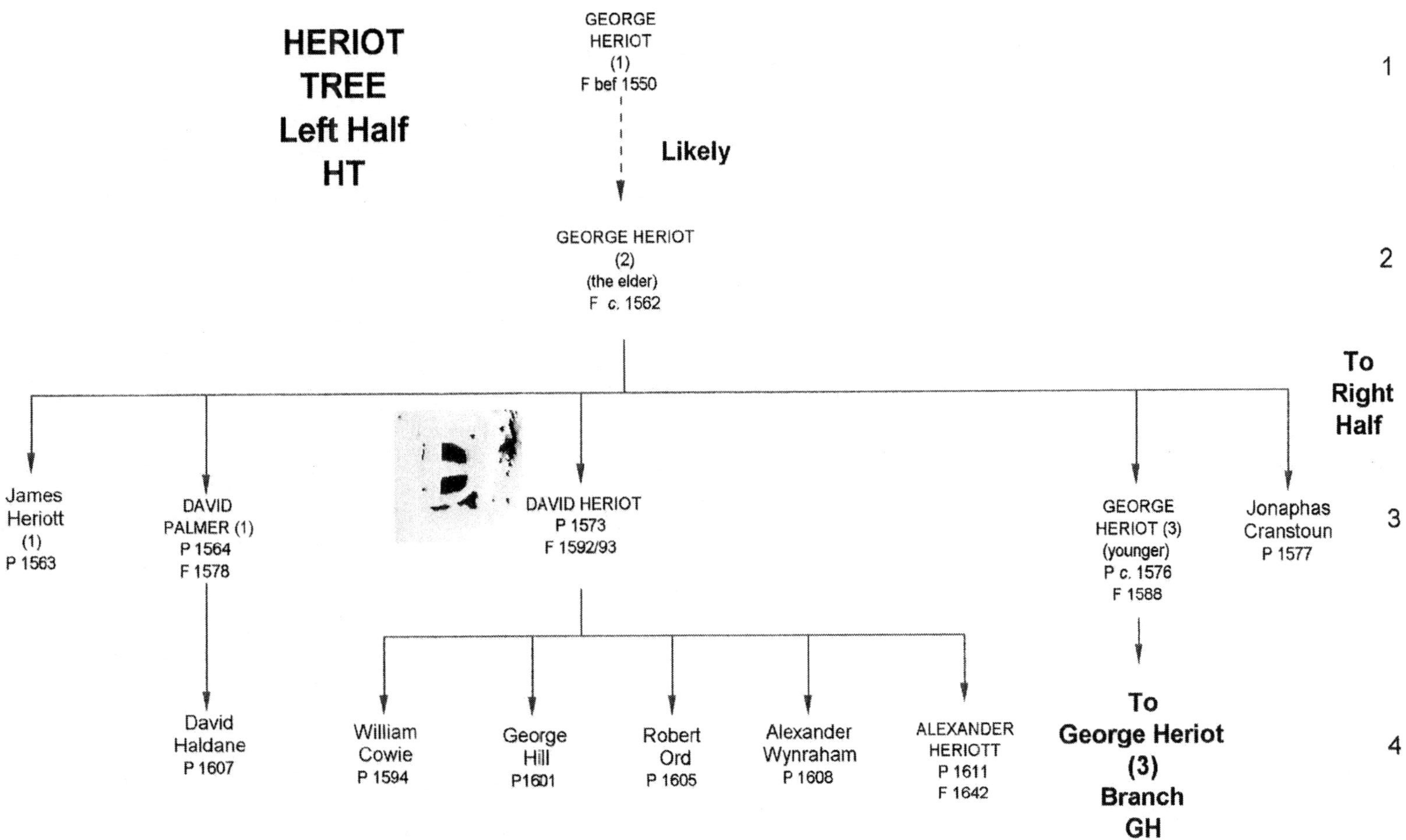
HERIOT
TREE
Left Half
HT
GEORGE
HERIOT
(1)
F bef 1550
Likely
GEORGE HERIOT
(2)
(the elder)
F c. 1562
To
Right
Half
James
Heriott
(1)
P 1563
DAVID
PALMER (1)
P 1564
F 1578
DAVID HERIOT
P 1573
F 1592/93
GEORGE
HERIOT (3)
(younger)
P c. 1576
F 1588
Jonaphas
Cranstoun
P 1577
David
Haldane
P 1607
William
Cowie
P 1594
George
Hill
P1601
Robert
Ord
P 1605
Alexander
Wynraham
P 1608
ALEXANDER
HERIOTT
P 1611
F 1642
To
George Heriot
(3)
Branch
GH
1
2
3
4

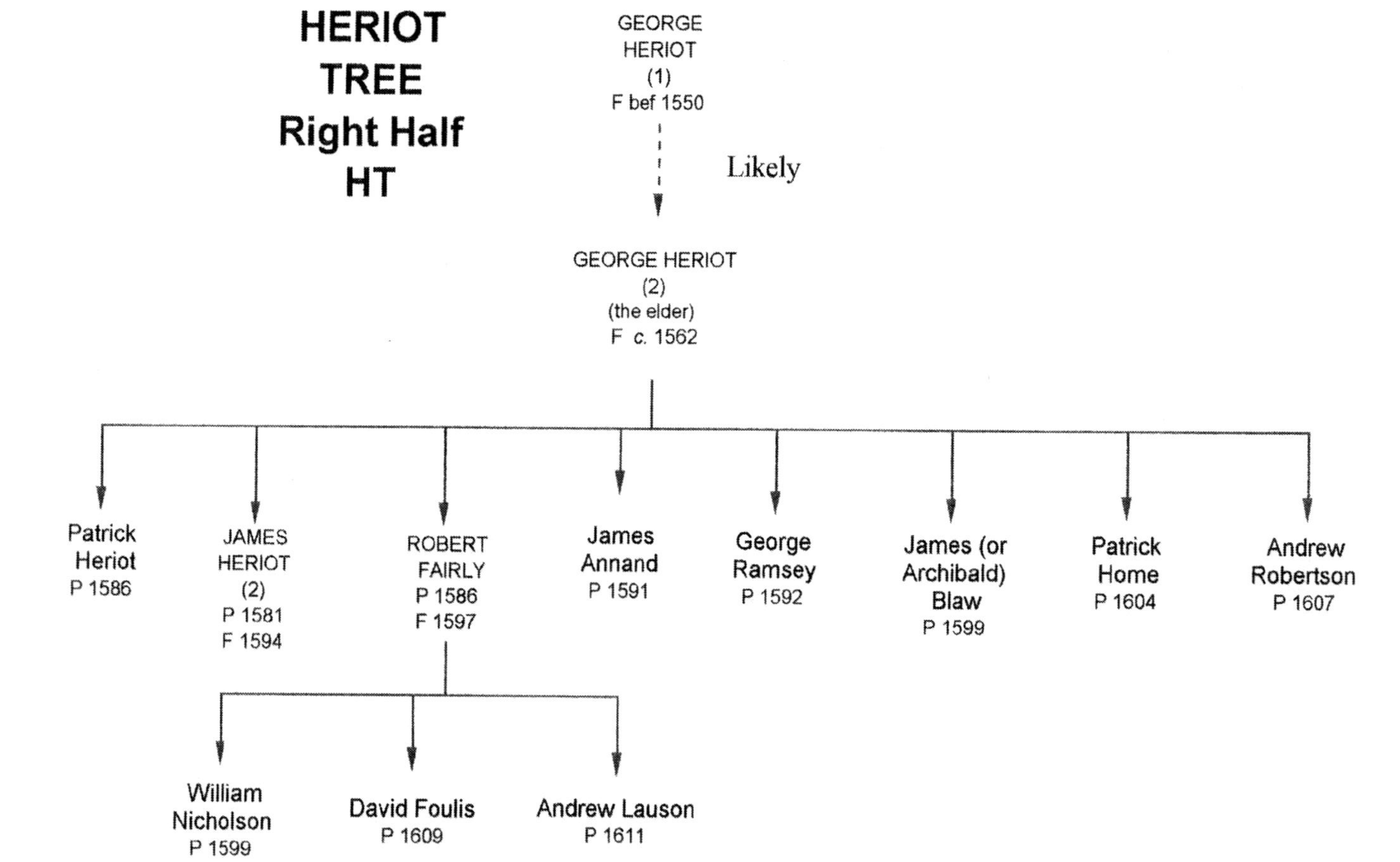
HERIOT
TREE
Right Half
HT
GEORGE
HERIOT
(1)
F bef 1550
Likely
GEORGE HERIOT
(2)
(the elder)
F c. 1562
Patrick
Heriot
P 1586
JAMES
HERIOT
(2)
P 1581
F 1594
ROBERT
FAIRLY
P 1586
F 1597
James
Annand
P 1591
George
Ramsey
P 1592
James (or
Archibald)
Blaw
P 1599
Patrick
Home
P 1604
Andrew
Robertson
P 1607
William
Nicholson
P 1599
David Foulis
P 1609
Andrew Lauson
P 1611
To
Left
Half
1
2
3
4

HEWITT BRANCH Left Half HE

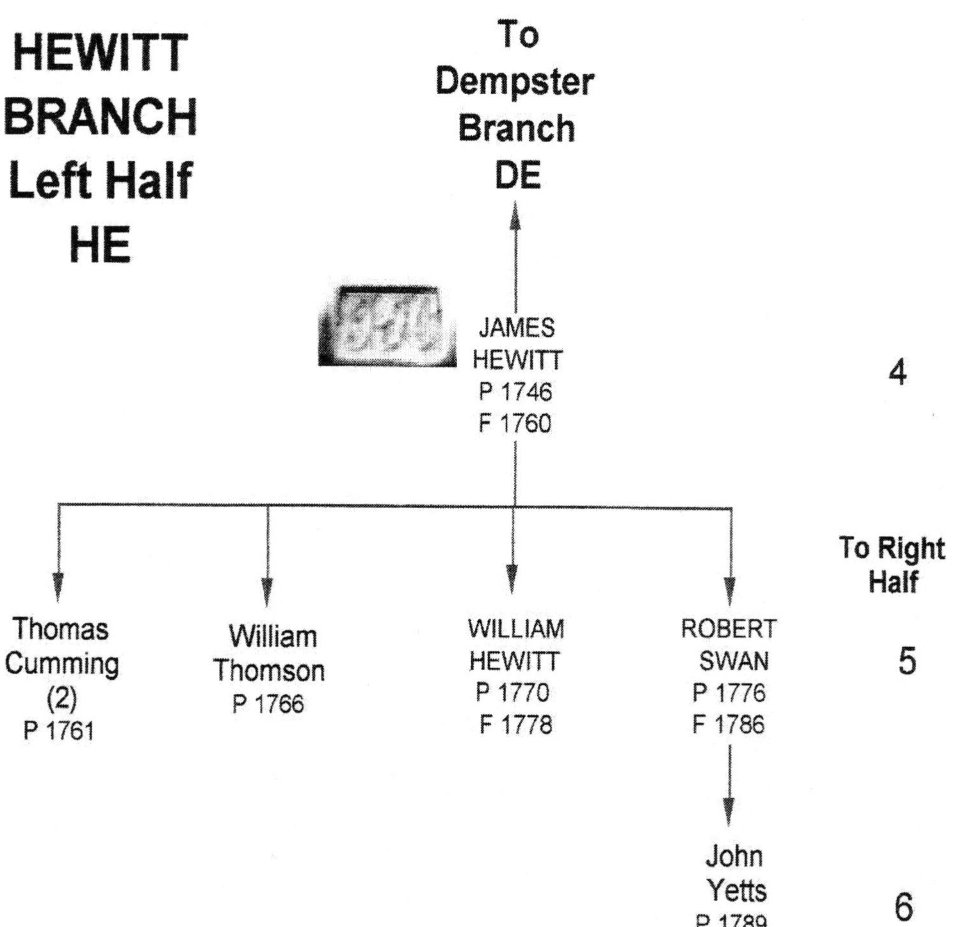

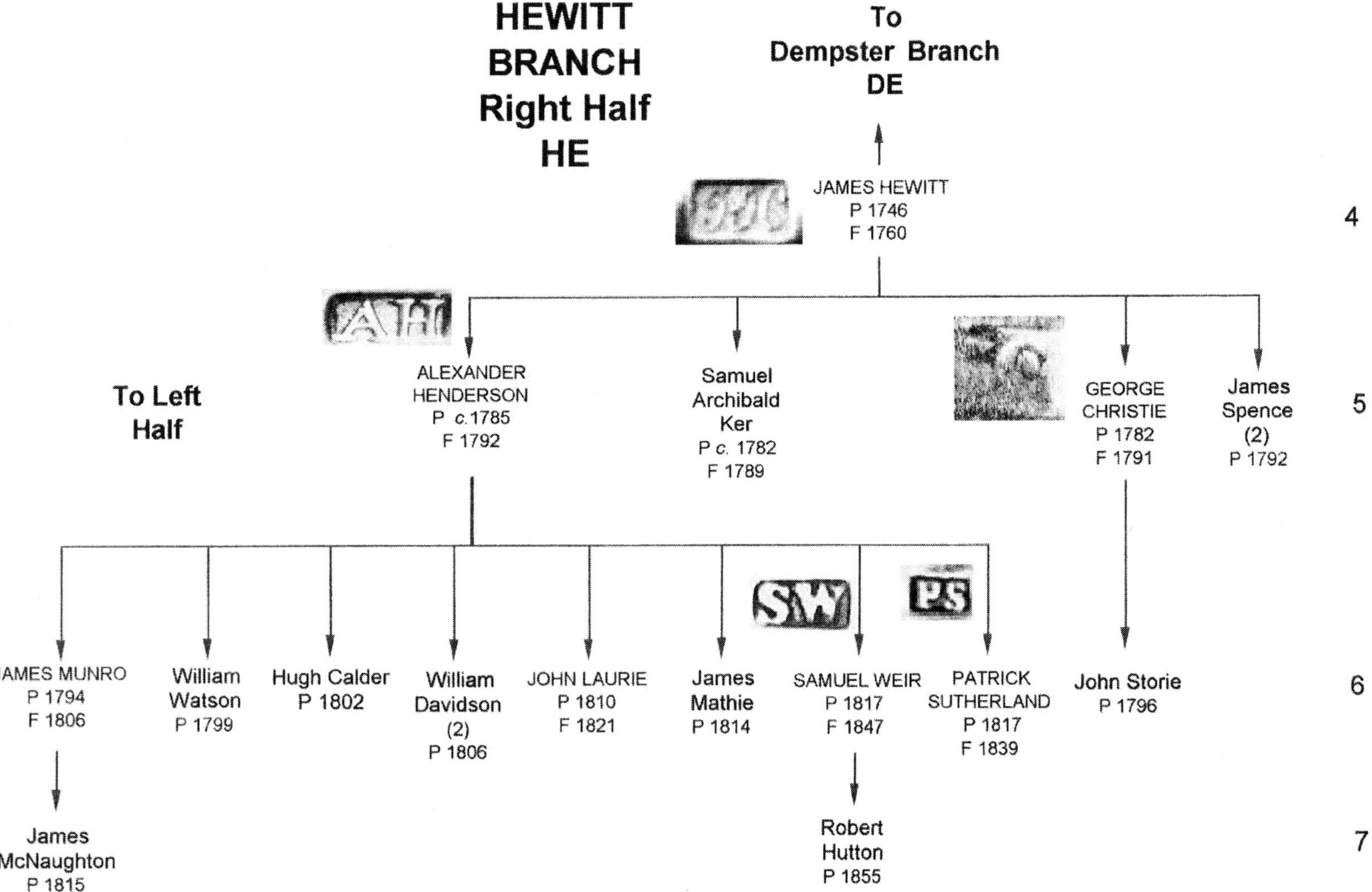
HEWITT BRANCH Right Half HE
To Dempster Branch DE
JAMES HEWITT P 1746 F 1760
4
AH
ALEXANDER HENDERSON P c.1785 F 1792
Samuel Archibald Ker P c. 1782 F 1789
GEORGE CHRISTIE P 1782 F 1791
James Spence (2) P 1792
5
To Left Half
JAMES MUNRO P 1794 F 1806
William Watson P 1799
Hugh Calder P 1802
William Davidson (2) P 1806
JOHN LAURIE P 1810 F 1821
James Mathie P 1814
SW
SAMUEL WEIR P 1817 F 1847
PS
PATRICK SUTHERLAND P 1817 F 1839
John Storie P 1796
6
James McNaughton P 1815
Robert Hutton P 1855
7

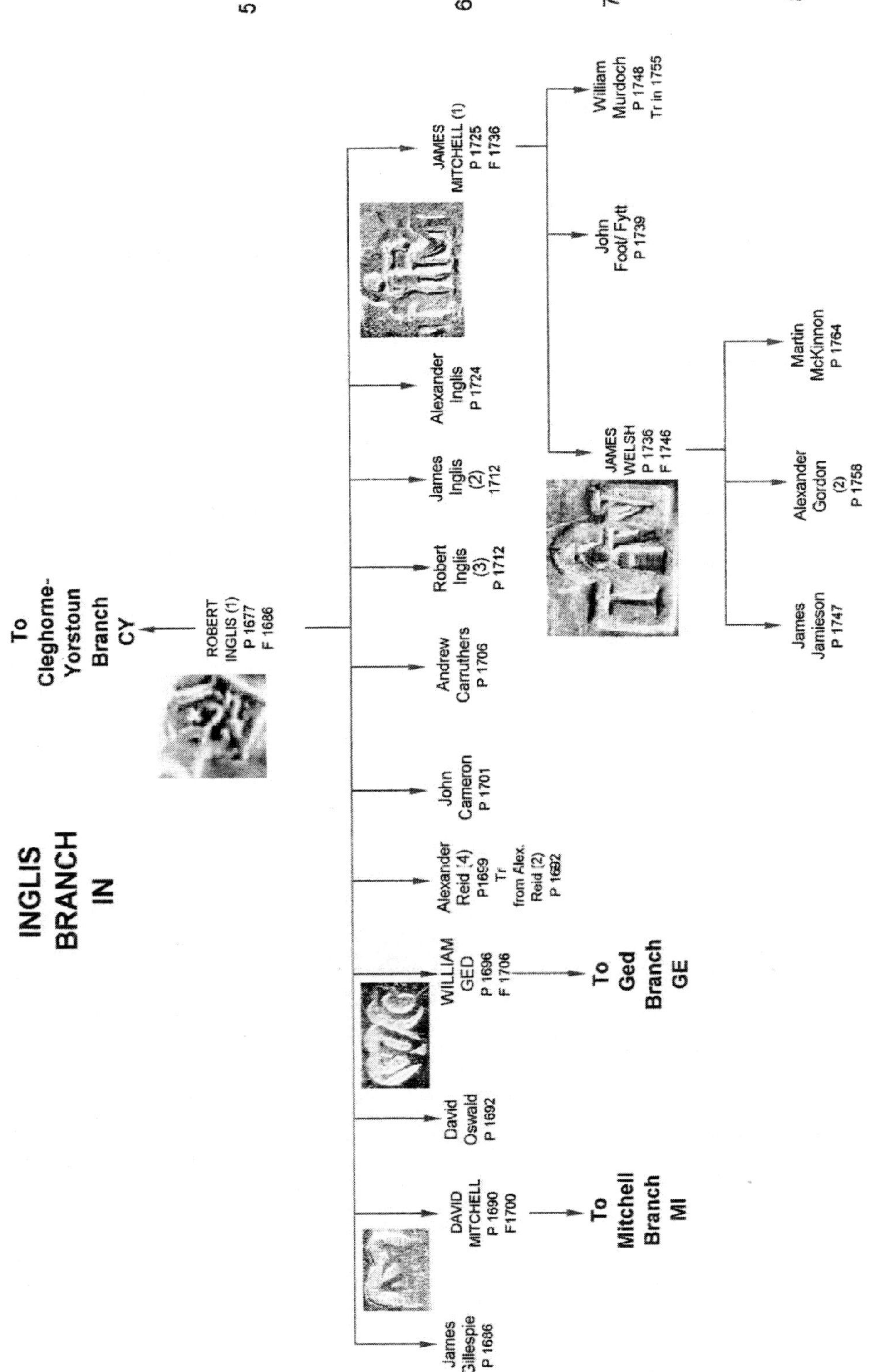
INGLIS BRANCH IN
5
6
7
8
ROBERT INGLIS (1) P 1677 F 1686
To Cleghorne-Yorstoun Branch CY
James Gillespie P 1686
DAVID MITCHELL P 1690 F1700
To Mitchell Branch MI
David Oswald P 1692
WILLIAM GED P 1696 F 1706
To Ged Branch GE
Alexander Reid (4) P1699 Tr from Alex. Reid (2) P 1692
John Cameron P 1701
Andrew Carruthers P 1706
Robert Inglis (3) P 1712
James Inglis (2) 1712
Alexander Inglis P 1724
JAMES MITCHELL (1) P 1725 F 1736
James Jamieson P 1747
Alexander Gordon (2) P 1758
Martin McKinnon P 1764
JAMES WELSH P 1736 F 1746
John Foot/ Fytt P 1739
William Murdoch P 1748 Tr in 1755

JAMES INGLIS BRANCH JI

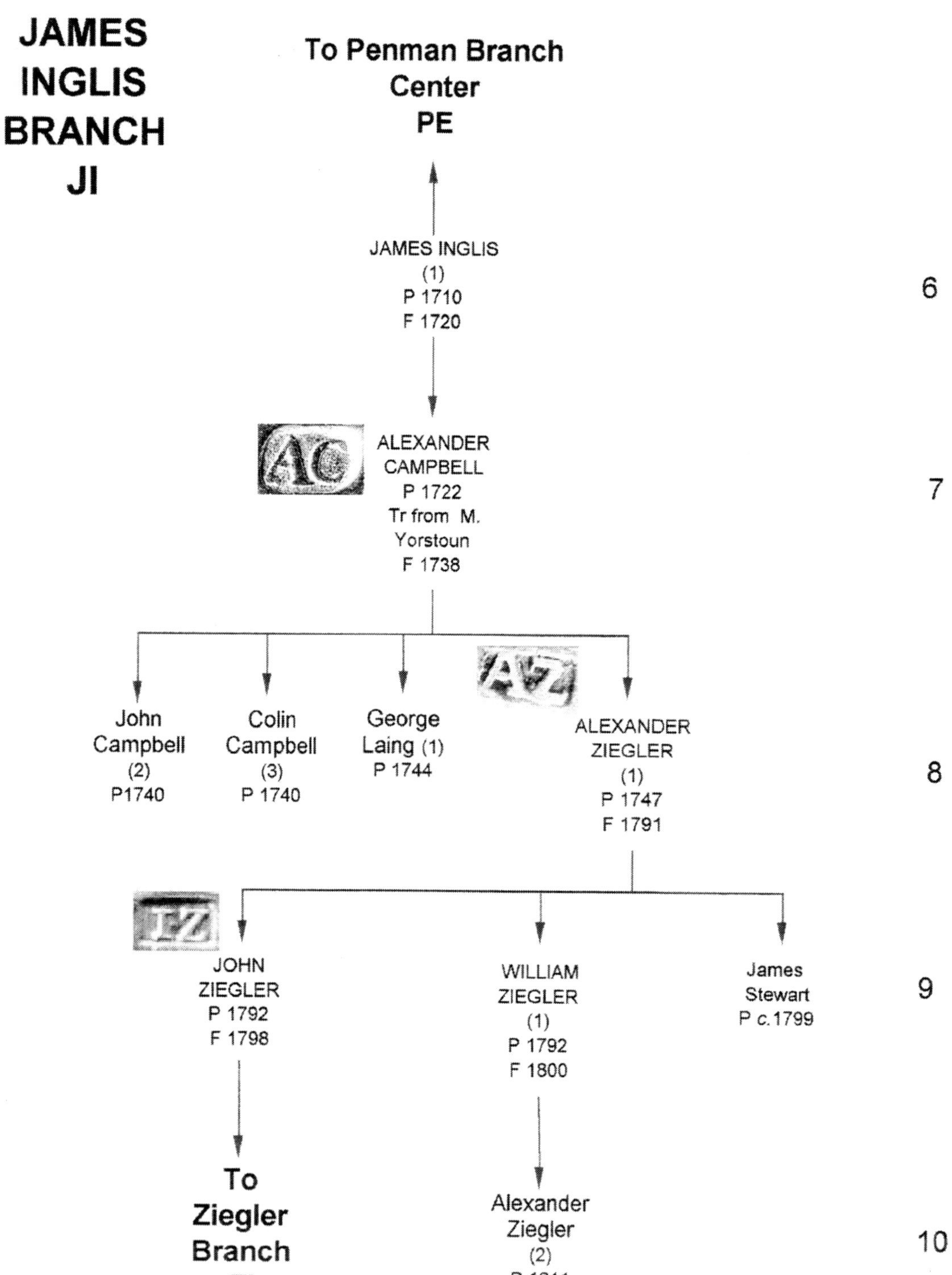

JAMES MCKENZIE (2) BRANCH Left Half JM

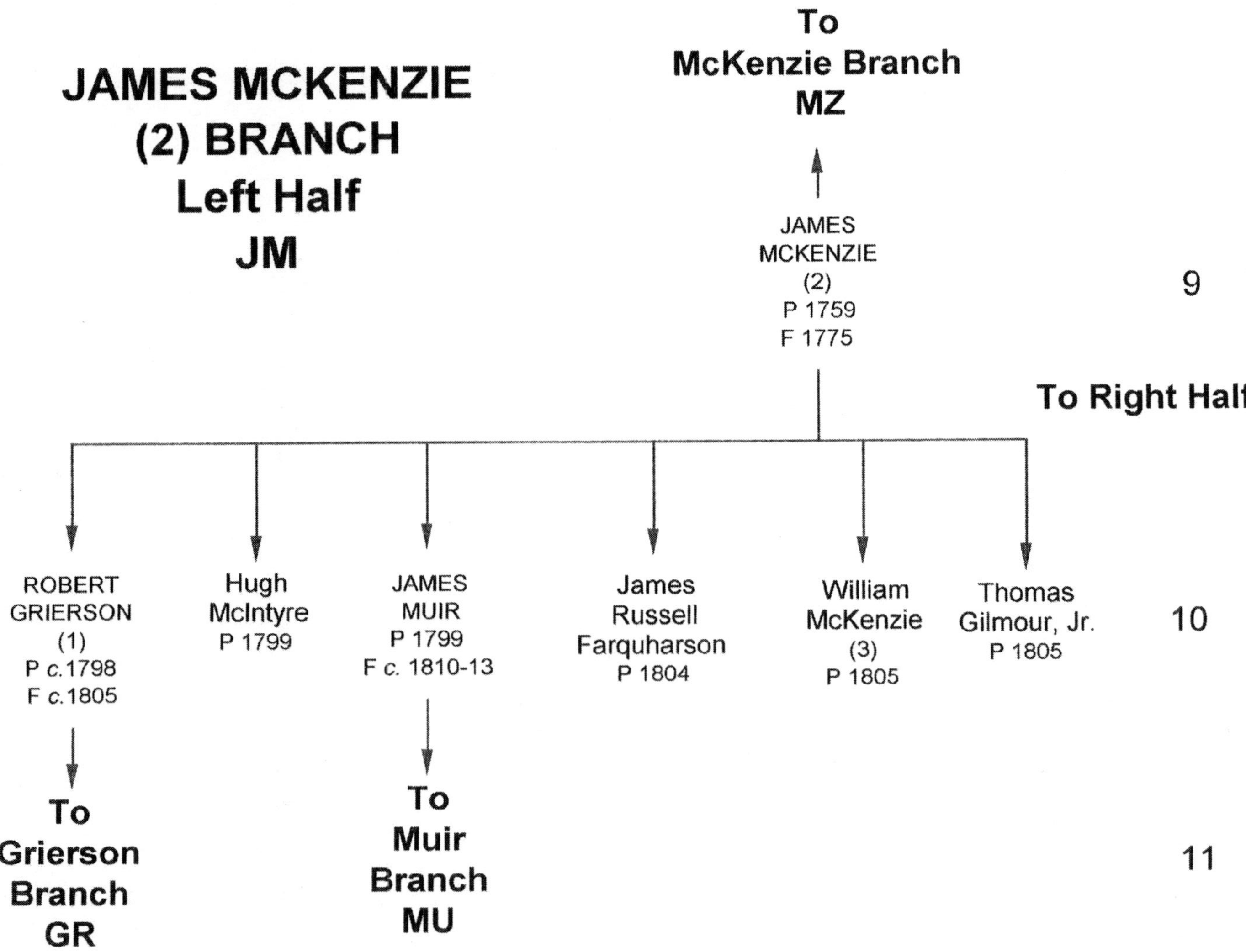

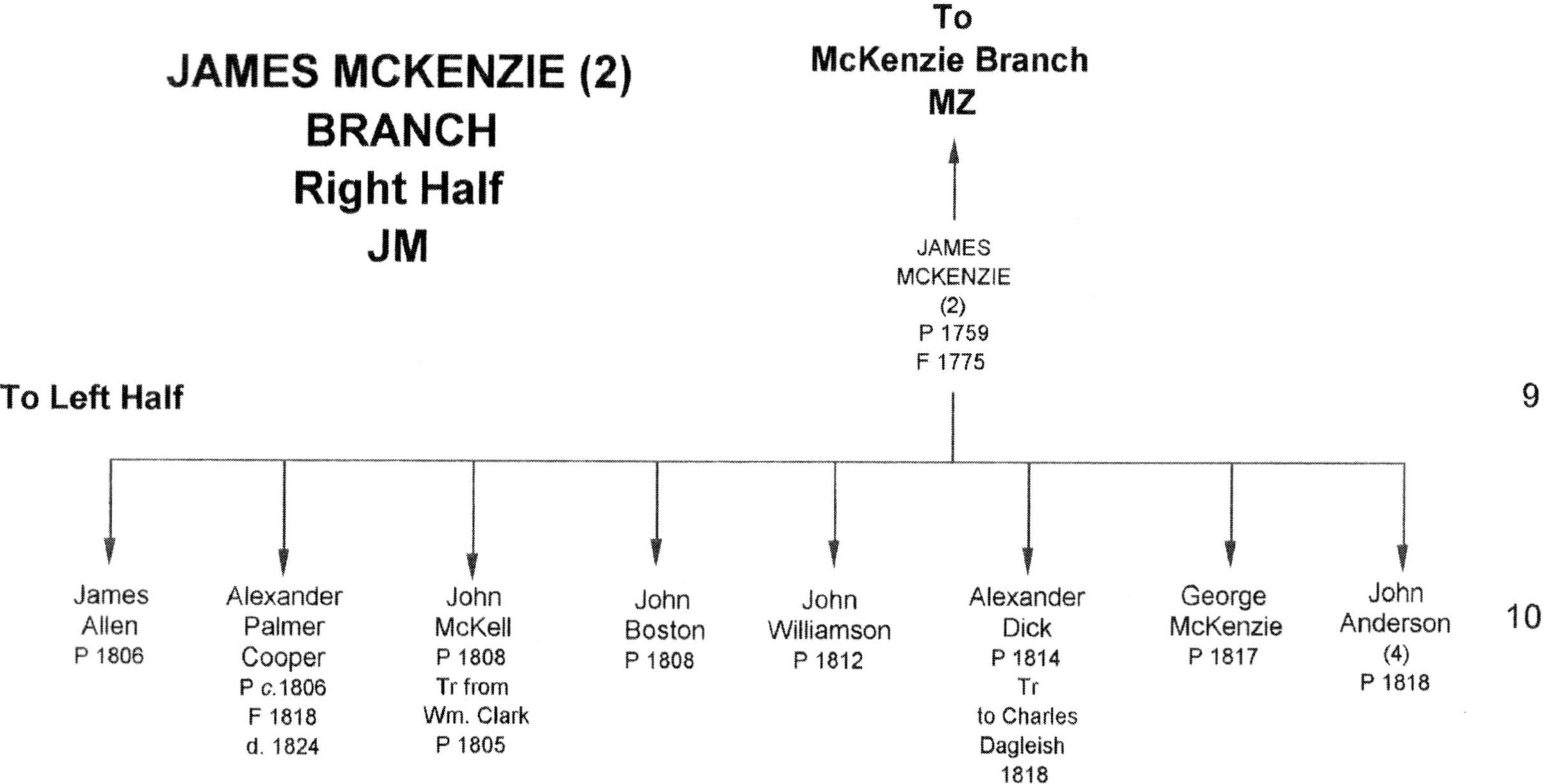
JAMES MCKENZIE (2)
BRANCH
Right Half
JM
To
McKenzie Branch
MZ
JAMES
MCKENZIE
(2)
P 1759
F 1775
To Left Half
9
10
James
Allen
P 1806
Alexander
Palmer
Cooper
P c.1806
F 1818
d. 1824
John
McKell
P 1808
Tr from
Wm. Clark
P 1805
John
Boston
P 1808
John
Williamson
P 1812
Alexander
Dick
P 1814
Tr
to Charles
Dagleish
1818
George
McKenzie
P 1817
John
Anderson
(4)
P 1818

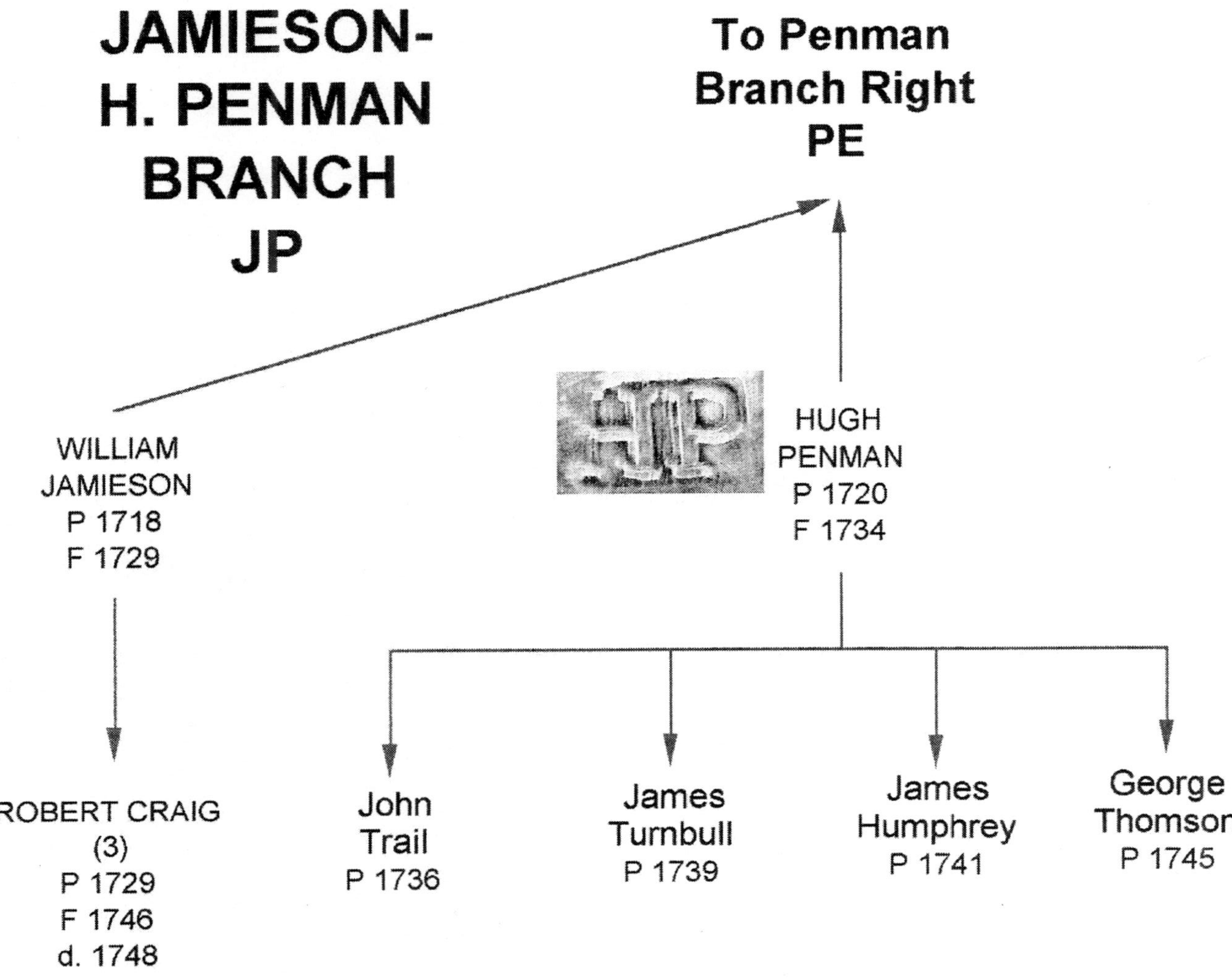
JAMIESON-
H. PENMAN
BRANCH
JP
To Penman
Branch Right
PE
WILLIAM
JAMIESON
P 1718
F 1729
HUGH
PENMAN
P 1720
F 1734
6
ROBERT CRAIG
(3)
P 1729
F 1746
d. 1748
John
Trail
P 1736
James
Turnbull
P 1739
James
Humphrey
P 1741
George
Thomson
P 1745
7

JOHN LAW BRANCH JL

To McAulay-Law Tree ML

4 — JOHN LAW (1) P 1649 F 1662

5 —
- John Colquhoun (1) P 1662 Tr to William Law (1) 1666
- John Stevenson (1) P 1669
- Lawrence Umphra P 1671
- WILLIAM LAW (2) P 1672 F 1686 → **To William Law (2) Branch WL**
- John Meane P 1674
- WALTER SCOTT (1) P 1677 F 1686
  - 6 — James Watson (1) P 1688
  - 6 — Robert Hay P 1689 Tr from David Boige 1689
- Robert Downie P 1679
- ANDREW LAW P 1683 F 1694
  - 6 — Robert Law (2) P 1694
  - 6 — HUGH LAW P 1694 F 1703
  - 6 — James Ker (1) P 1694
  - 6 — Richard Preston P 1695 Tr from Walter Scott 1694/95
- WILLIAM BURTON P 1688 F 1700
- Andrew Johnston P 1692

KER BRANCH Left Half KE

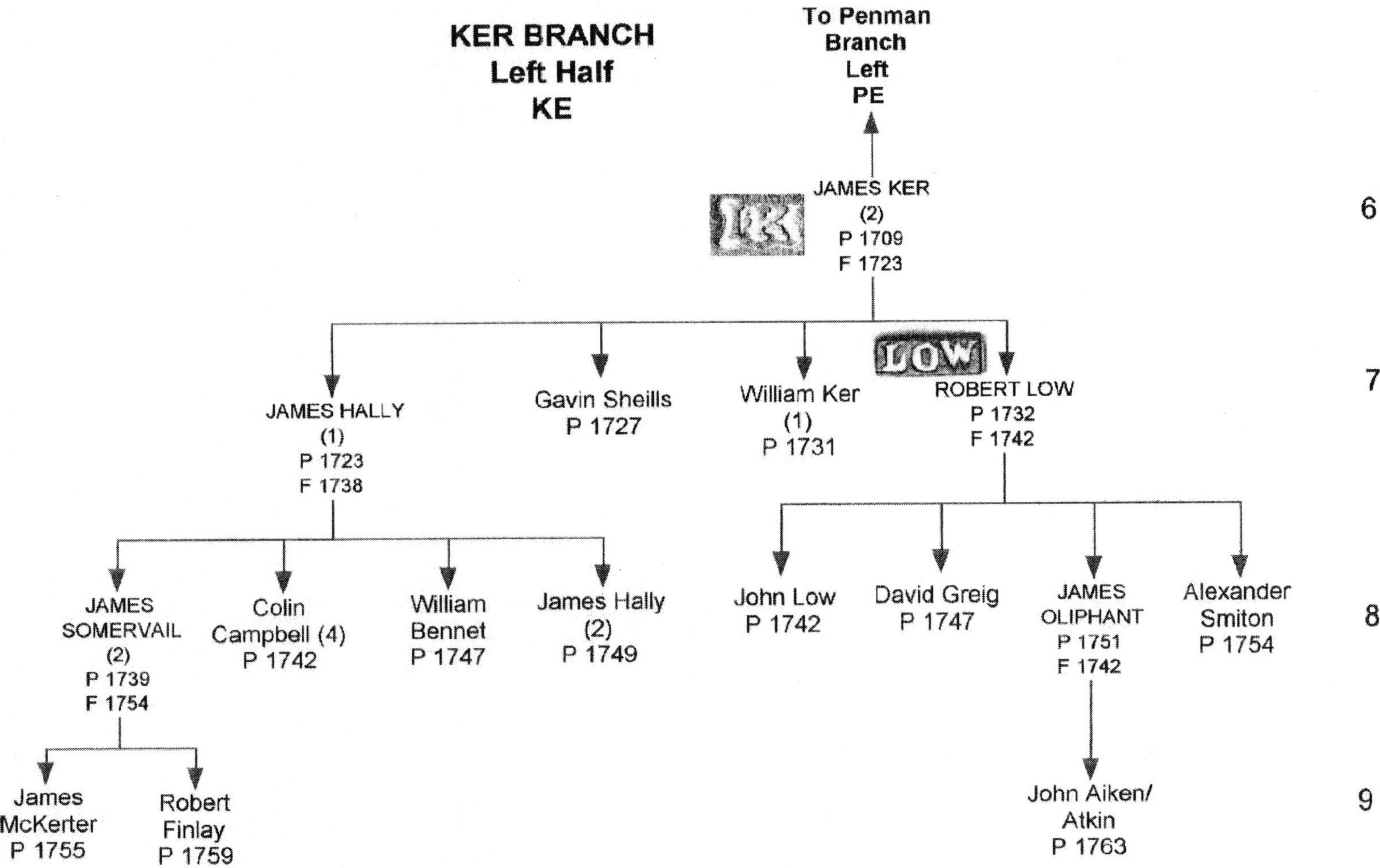

KER BRANCH Right Half KE

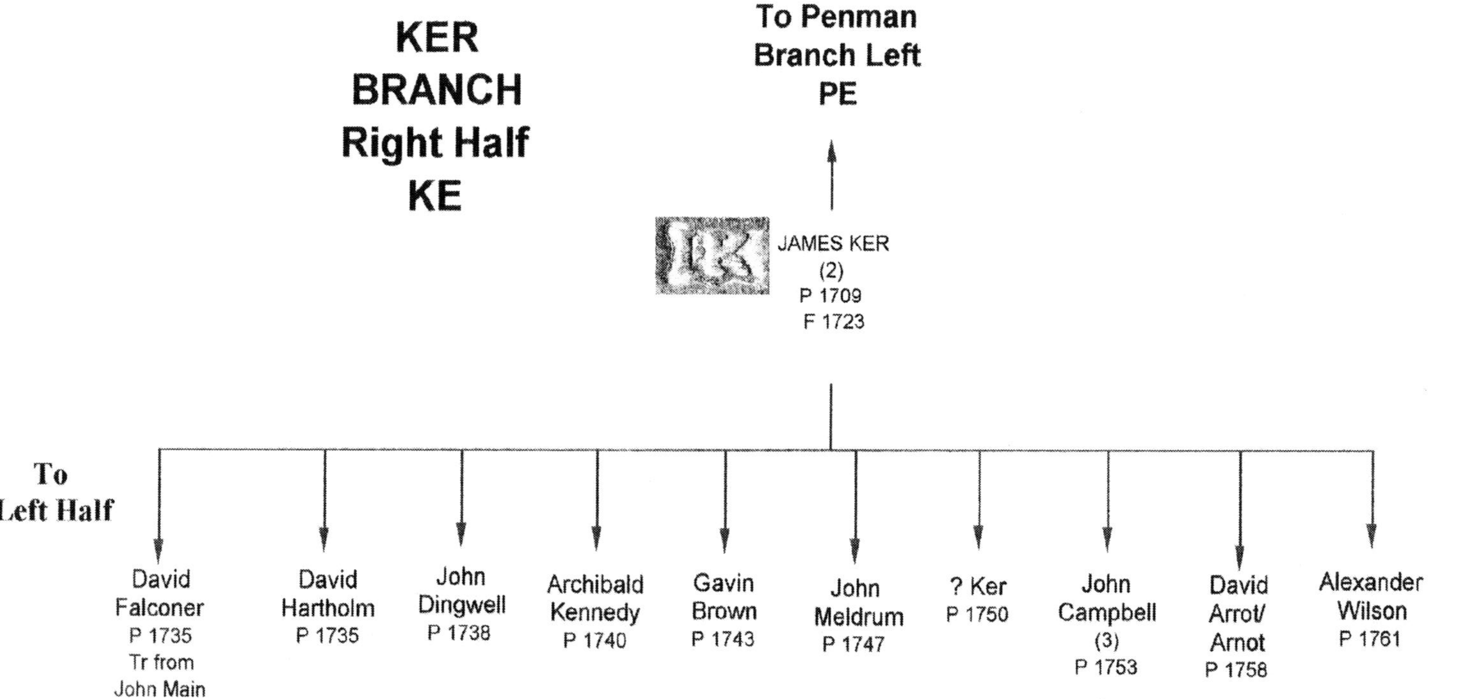

LERRO BRANCH LE

TO Gardner Branch Right Half GA

GEORGE
LERRO
P 1797
Gardner and Co.
F *c.*1810

9

John
Hutchinson
P 1811
Tr to
James
Nasmyth
1816

JOHN CRICHTON
(1)
P 1814
Tr
John Graham
F 1829

10

LINDSAY BRANCH LD

To Cokkie Tree CO

HUGH LINDSAY
P 1577
F 1587

3

Robert Henrie
P 1589

George Lindsay (1)
P 1595

James Livingston
P 1599

John Livingston
P 1605

James Elliott
1618

Gavin Lindsay
P 1626

4

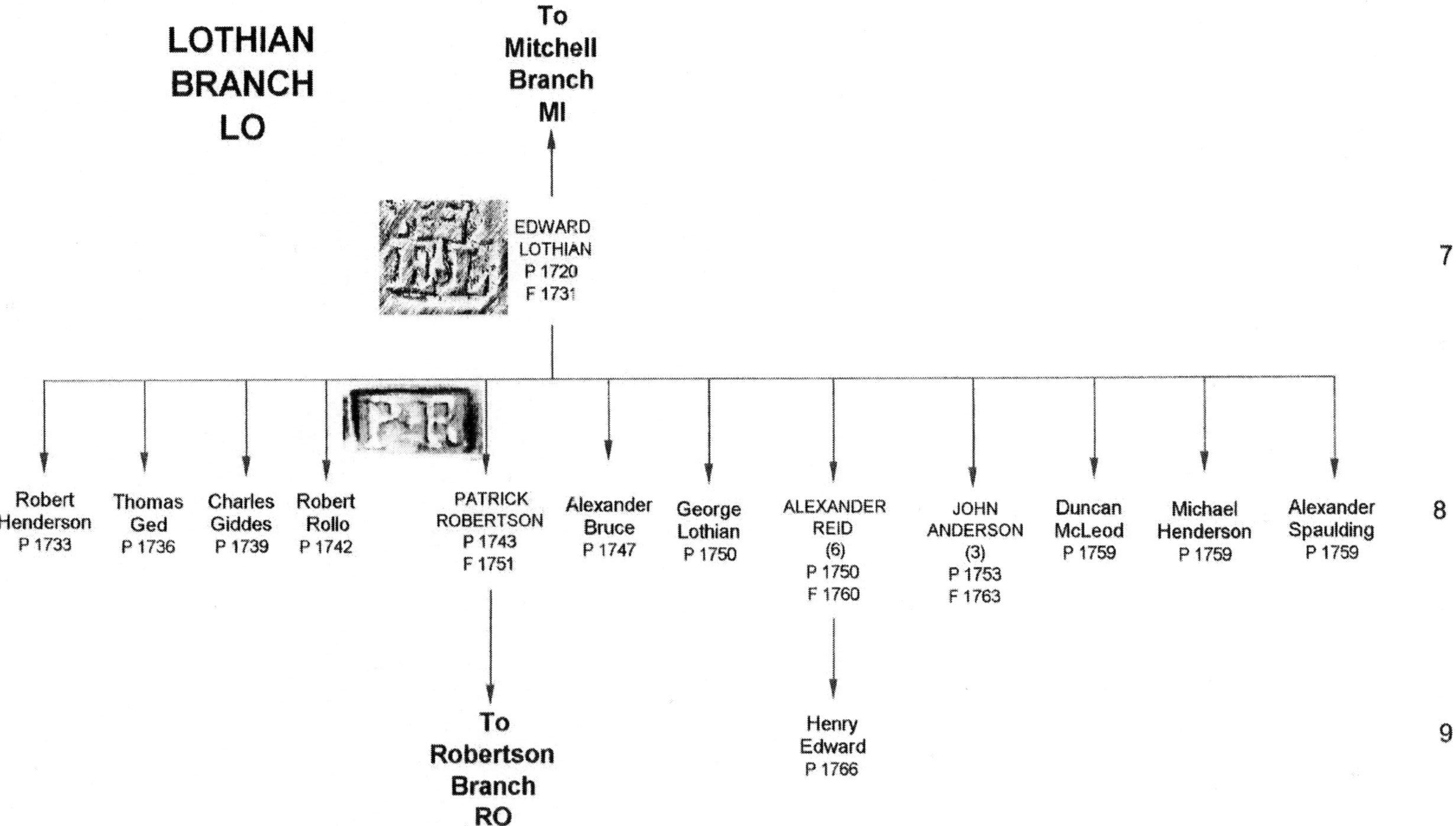
LOTHIAN
BRANCH
LO
To
Mitchell
Branch
MI
EDWARD
LOTHIAN
P 1720
F 1731
7
Robert
Henderson
P 1733
Thomas
Ged
P 1736
Charles
Giddes
P 1739
Robert
Rollo
P 1742
PATRICK
ROBERTSON
P 1743
F 1751
Alexander
Bruce
P 1747
George
Lothian
P 1750
ALEXANDER
REID
(6)
P 1750
F 1760
JOHN
ANDERSON
(3)
P 1753
F 1763
Duncan
McLeod
P 1759
Michael
Henderson
P 1759
Alexander
Spaulding
P 1759
8
To
Robertson
Branch
RO
Henry
Edward
P 1766
9

MAIN BRANCH MA

To Cleghorne-Yorstoun Branch Left Half CY

GEORGE MAIN (1)
P 1676
F 1688 — 5

- John Robertson (2) P 1688
- John Gardner (1) P 1691
- George Paterson P 1693 
- 
  JAMES MITCHELSON (1) P 1696 F 1706 → **To Mitchelson Branch MT**
- Robert Campbell P 1699
- James Main P 1701
- James Walkinshaw P 1702
- Robert Main P 1705
- George Main (2) P 1714
- JOHN MAIN P 1714 F 1729

6

7

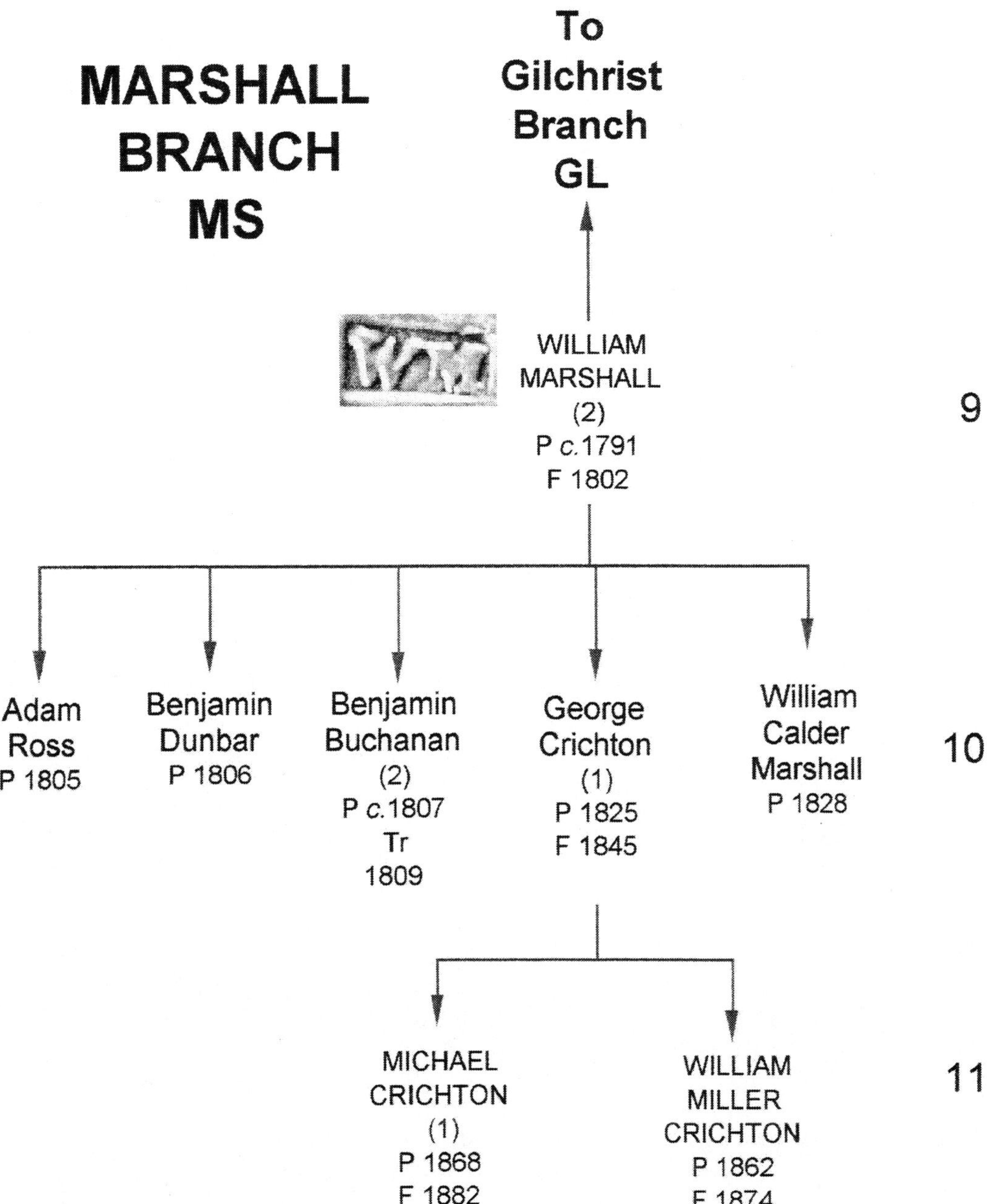
MARSHALL
BRANCH
MS
To
Gilchrist
Branch
GL
WILLIAM
MARSHALL
(2)
P c.1791
F 1802
9
Adam
Ross
P 1805
Benjamin
Dunbar
P 1806
Benjamin
Buchanan
(2)
P c.1807
Tr
1809
George
Crichton
(1)
P 1825
F 1845
William
Calder
Marshall
P 1828
10
MICHAEL
CRICHTON
(1)
P 1868
F 1882
WILLIAM
MILLER
CRICHTON
P 1862
F 1874
11

McAulay-
Law Tree
ML

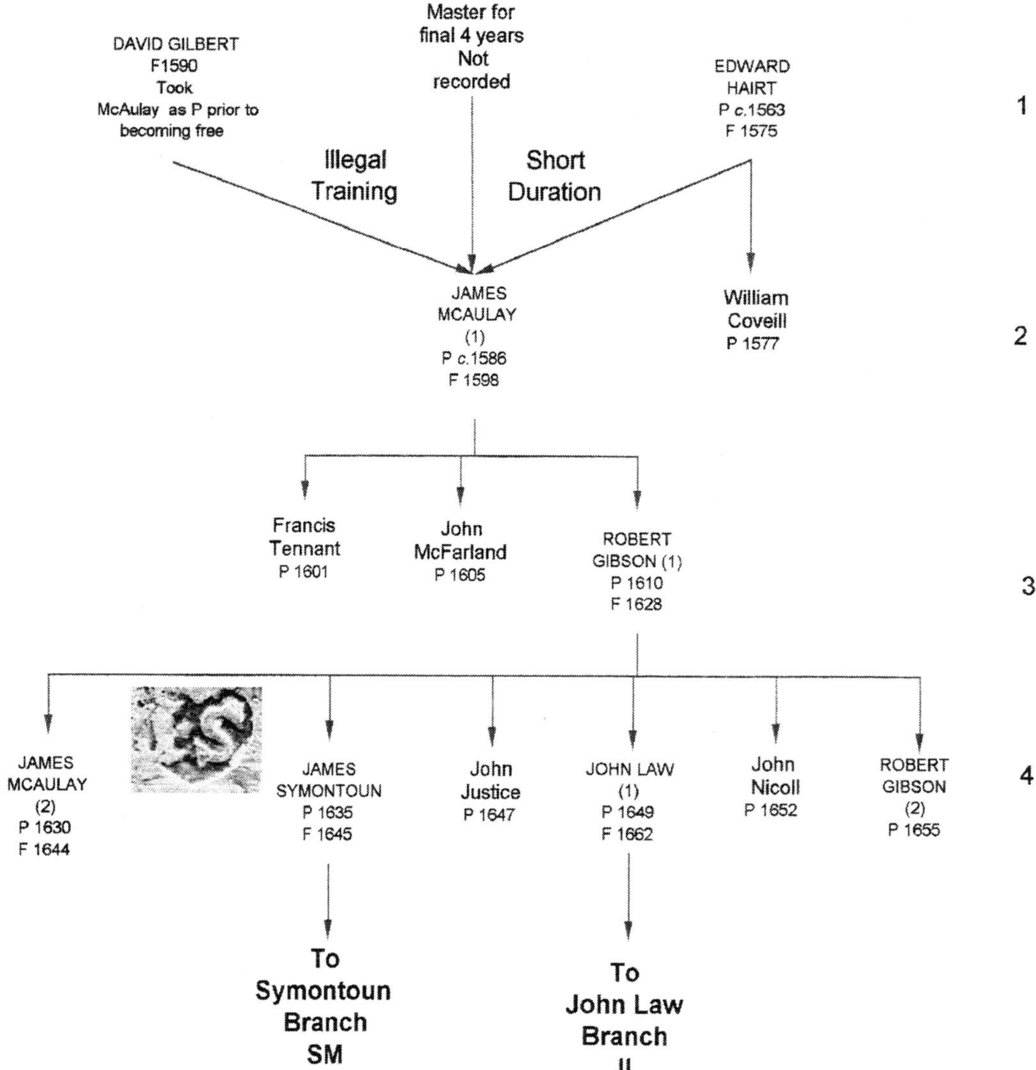

110 – McAulay Law Tree

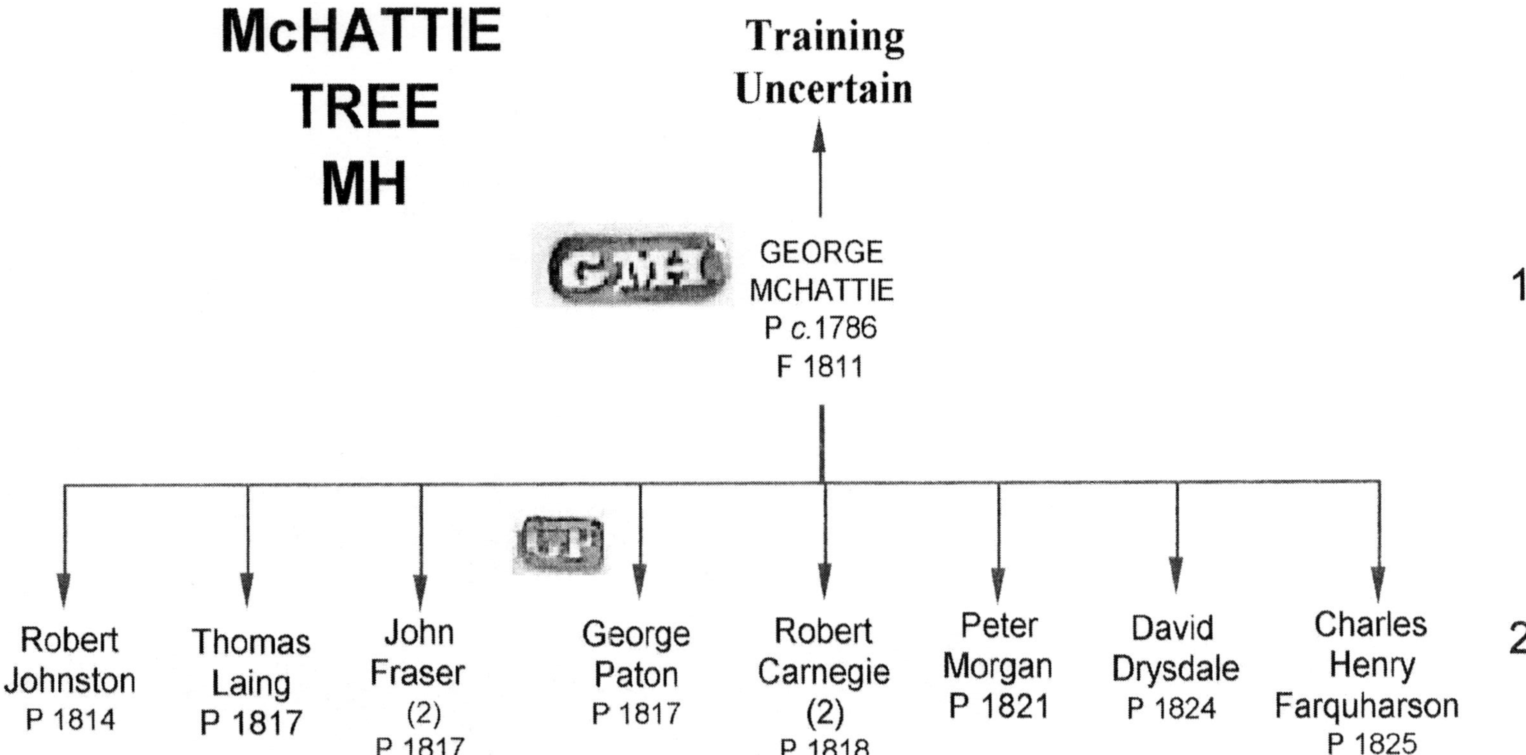
McHATTIE TREE MH
Training Uncertain
GMH
GEORGE MCHATTIE P c.1786 F 1811
1
GP
Robert Johnston P 1814
Thomas Laing P 1817
John Fraser (2) P 1817
George Paton P 1817
Robert Carnegie (2) P 1818
Peter Morgan P 1821
David Drysdale P 1824
Charles Henry Farquharson P 1825
2

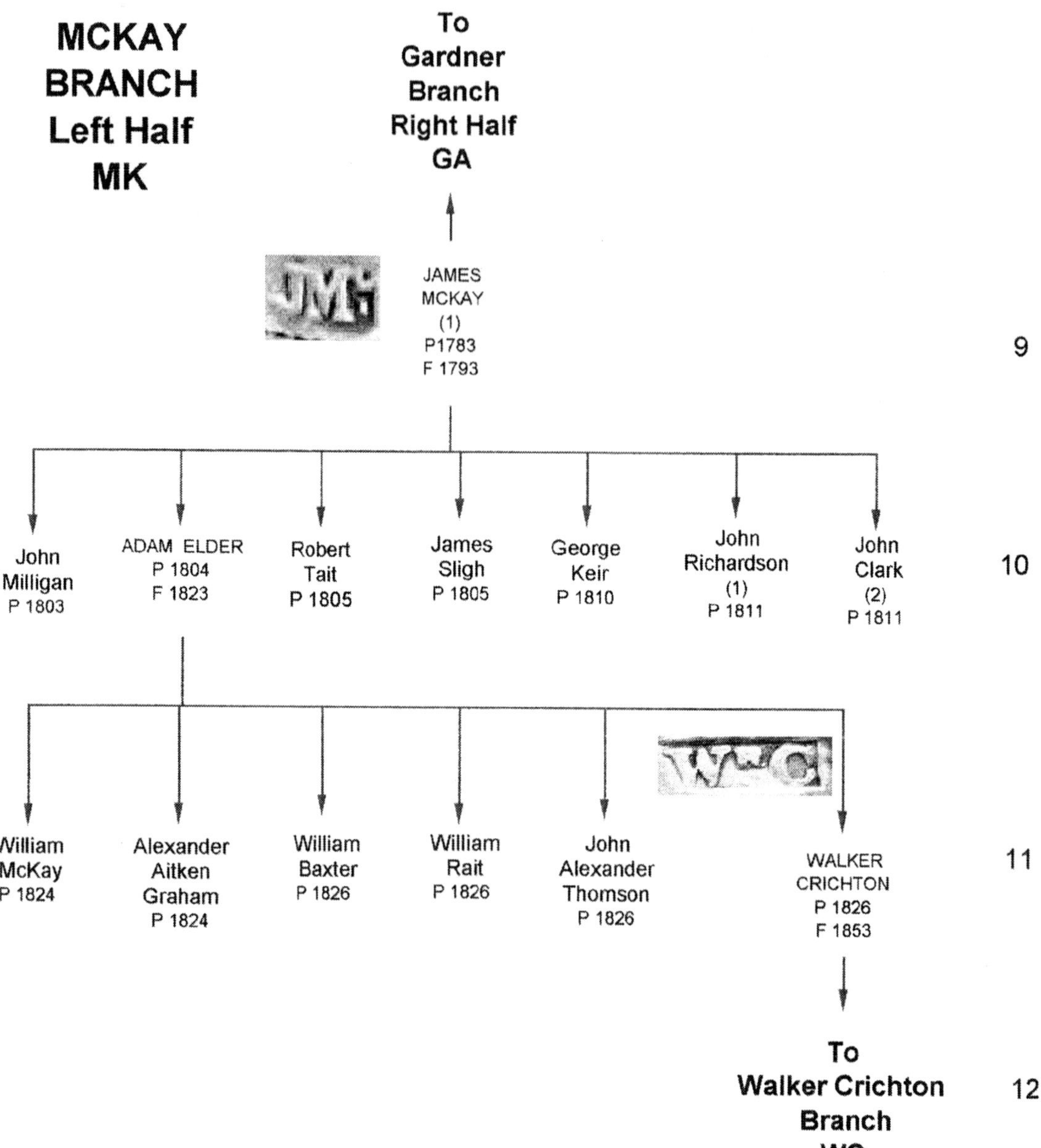
MCKAY BRANCH Left Half MK
To Gardner Branch Right Half GA
JAMES MCKAY (1) P1783 F 1793
9
John Milligan P 1803
ADAM ELDER P 1804 F 1823
Robert Tait P 1805
James Sligh P 1805
George Keir P 1810
John Richardson (1) P 1811
John Clark (2) P 1811
10
William McKay P 1824
Alexander Aitken Graham P 1824
William Baxter P 1826
William Rait P 1826
John Alexander Thomson P 1826
WALKER CRICHTON P 1826 F 1853
11
To Walker Crichton Branch WC
12

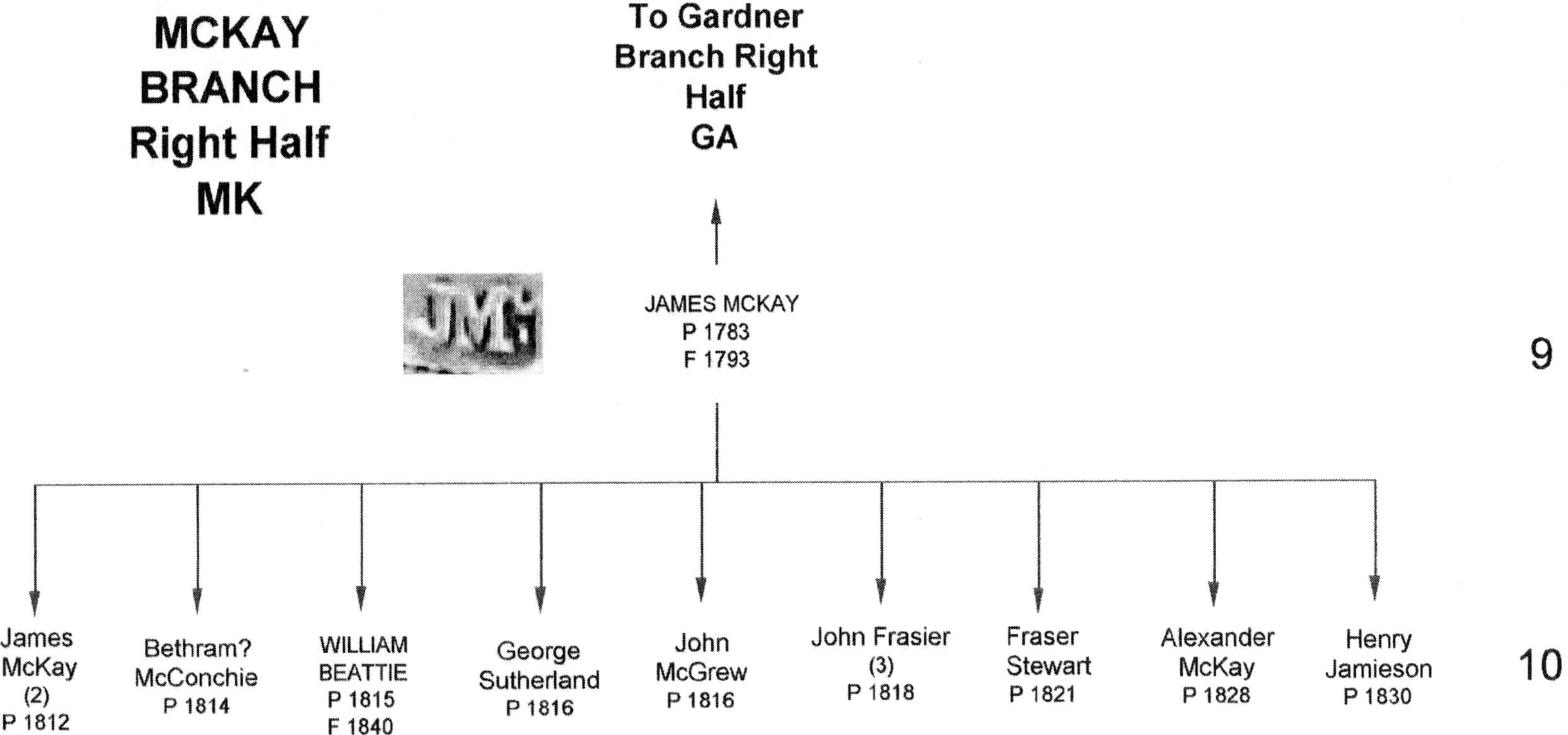
MCKAY
BRANCH
Right Half
MK
To Gardner
Branch Right
Half
GA
JAMES MCKAY
P 1783
F 1793
9
James
McKay
(2)
P 1812
Bethram?
McConchie
P 1814
WILLIAM
BEATTIE
P 1815
F 1840
George
Sutherland
P 1816
John
McGrew
P 1816
John Frasier
(3)
P 1818
Fraser
Stewart
P 1821
Alexander
McKay
P 1828
Henry
Jamieson
P 1830
10

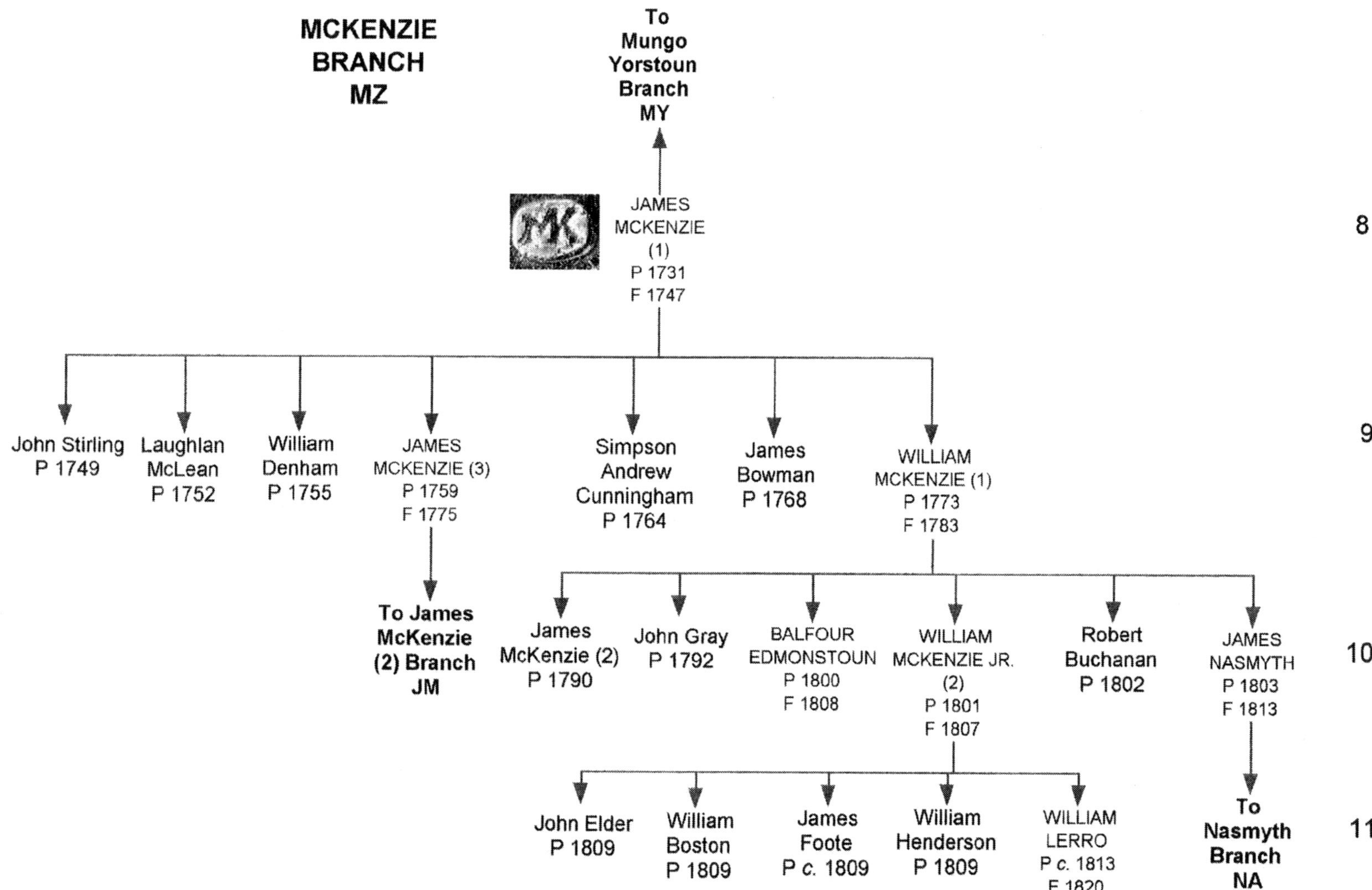
MCKENZIE BRANCH MZ
To Mungo Yorstoun Branch MY
JAMES MCKENZIE (1)
P 1731
F 1747
8
John Stirling P 1749
Laughlan McLean P 1752
William Denham P 1755
JAMES MCKENZIE (3)
P 1759
F 1775
Simpson Andrew Cunningham P 1764
James Bowman P 1768
WILLIAM MCKENZIE (1)
P 1773
F 1783
9
To James McKenzie (2) Branch JM
James McKenzie (2) P 1790
John Gray P 1792
BALFOUR EDMONSTOUN
P 1800
F 1808
WILLIAM MCKENZIE JR. (2)
P 1801
F 1807
Robert Buchanan P 1802
JAMES NASMYTH
P 1803
F 1813
10
John Elder P 1809
William Boston P 1809
James Foote P c. 1809
William Henderson P 1809
WILLIAM LERRO
P c. 1813
F 1820
To Nasmyth Branch NA
11

MELLINUS TREE ME

1
ZACCHARIAS MELLINUS F 1672

2
George Muir P 1672
Luis Nisbit P 1675
George Hepburn P 1679
ALEXANDER KINCAID P 1683 F 1692
ADAM GORDAN P *c.* 1688 F 1696
ROBERT SCOTT P *c.* 1689 F 1697

3
(Alexander Kincaid →)
John Frogg P 1693
Robert Renton P 1696
Archibald Kincaid P 1699
John Philip P 1703
ARCHIBALD URE P 1709 F 1718
JOHN KINCAID P 1709 F 1726
George Ross P 1717
James Napier P 1720
John Kincaid (2) P 1728
(Adam Gordan →) Alexander Neilson P 1698
(Robert Scott →) Thomas Watt (1) P 1698

4
(Archibald Ure →) **To Ure Branch UR**
(John Kincaid →) John Duncan (2) P 1725

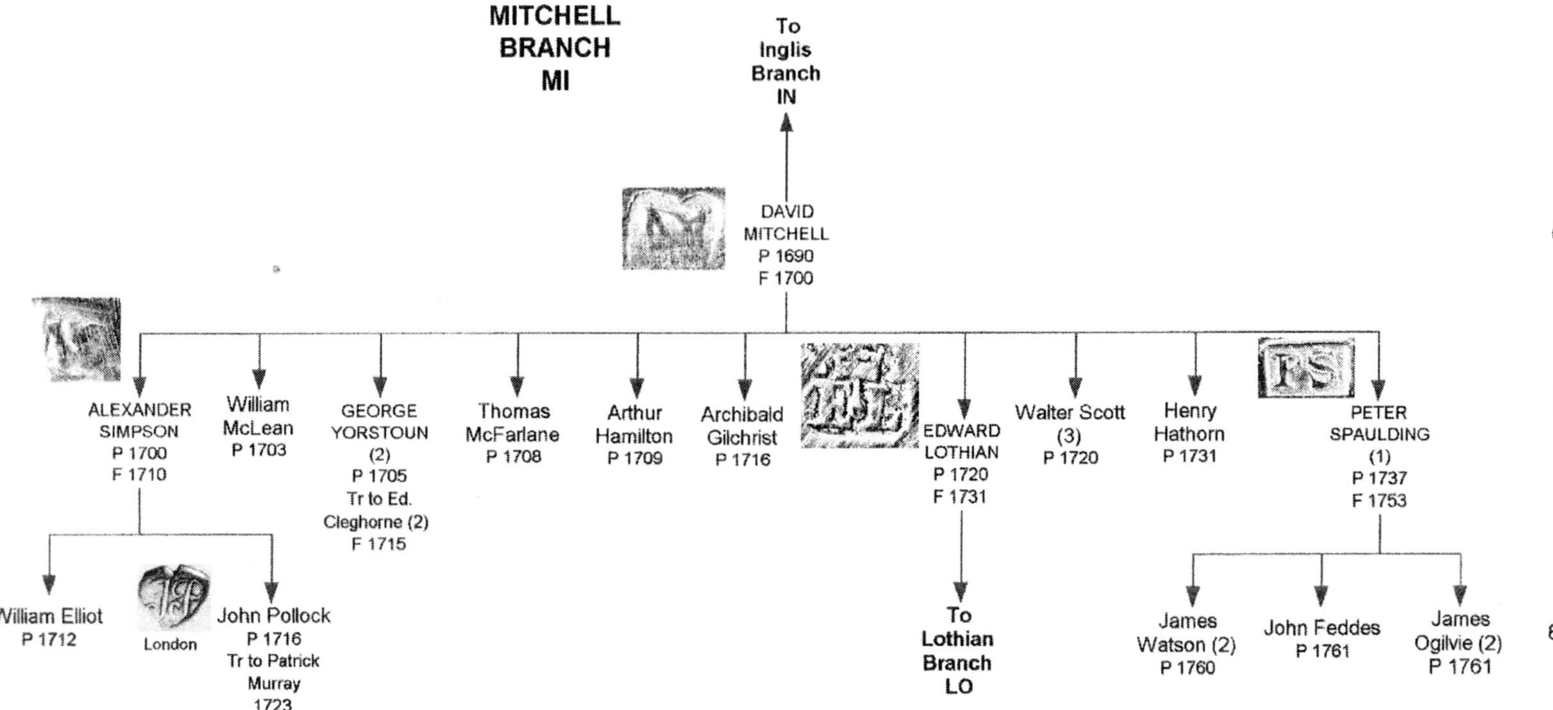
MITCHELL
BRANCH
MI
To
Inglis
Branch
IN
DAVID
MITCHELL
P 1690
F 1700
6
ALEXANDER
SIMPSON
P 1700
F 1710
William
McLean
P 1703
GEORGE
YORSTOUN
(2)
P 1705
Tr to Ed.
Cleghorne (2)
F 1715
Thomas
McFarlane
P 1708
Arthur
Hamilton
P 1709
Archibald
Gilchrist
P 1716
EDWARD
LOTHIAN
P 1720
F 1731
Walter Scott
(3)
P 1720
Henry
Hathorn
P 1731
PETER
SPAULDING
(1)
P 1737
F 1753
7
William Elliot
P 1712
London
John Pollock
P 1716
Tr to Patrick
Murray
1723
To
Lothian
Branch
LO
James
Watson (2)
P 1760
John Feddes
P 1761
James
Ogilvie (2)
P 1761
8

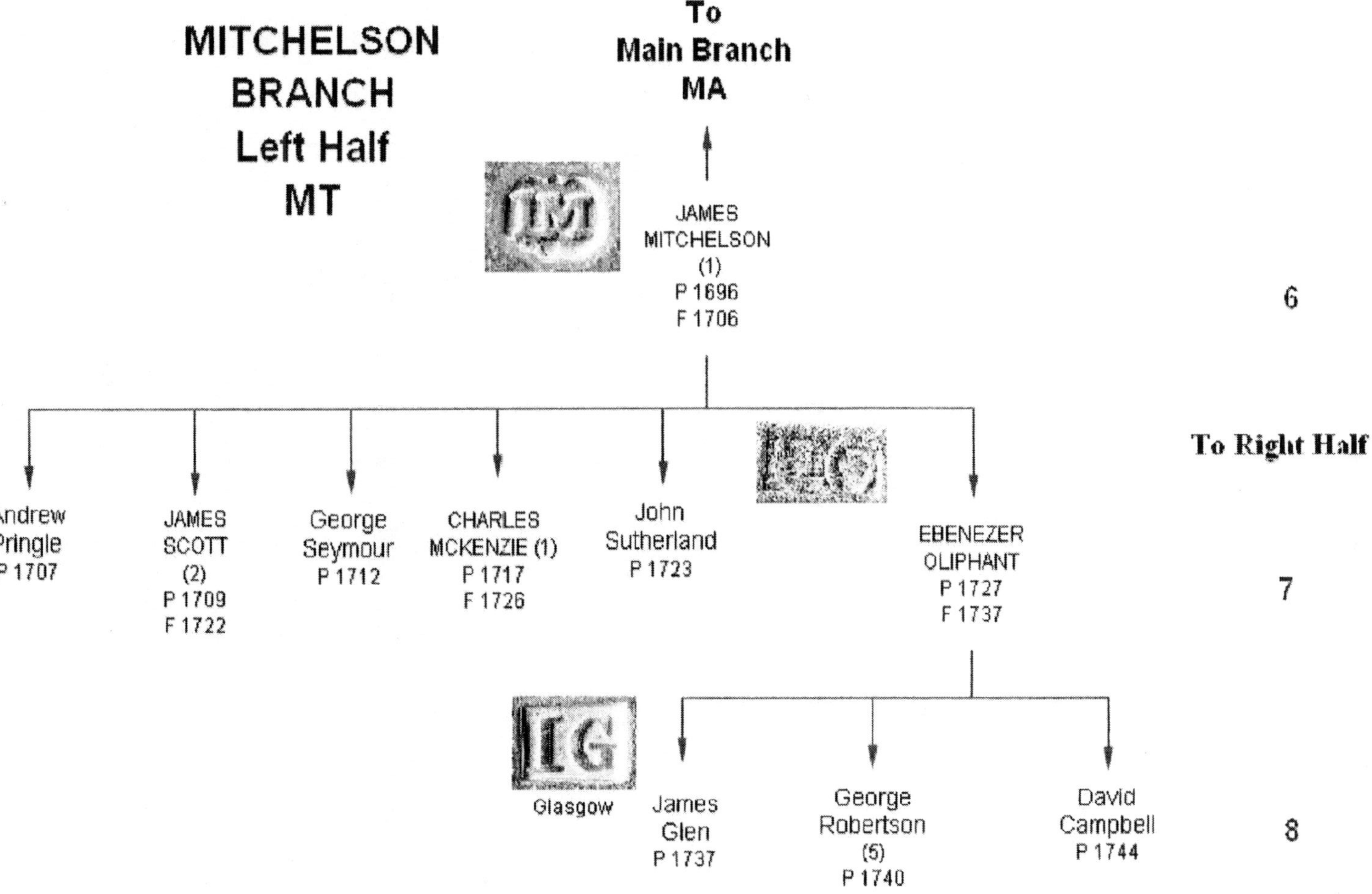
MITCHELSON
BRANCH
Left Half
MT
To
Main Branch
MA
JAMES
MITCHELSON
(1)
P 1696
F 1706
6
To Right Half
Andrew
Pringle
P 1707
JAMES
SCOTT
(2)
P 1709
F 1722
George
Seymour
P 1712
CHARLES
MCKENZIE (1)
P 1717
F 1726
John
Sutherland
P 1723
EBENEZER
OLIPHANT
P 1727
F 1737
7
Glasgow
James
Glen
P 1737
George
Robertson
(5)
P 1740
David
Campbell
P 1744
8

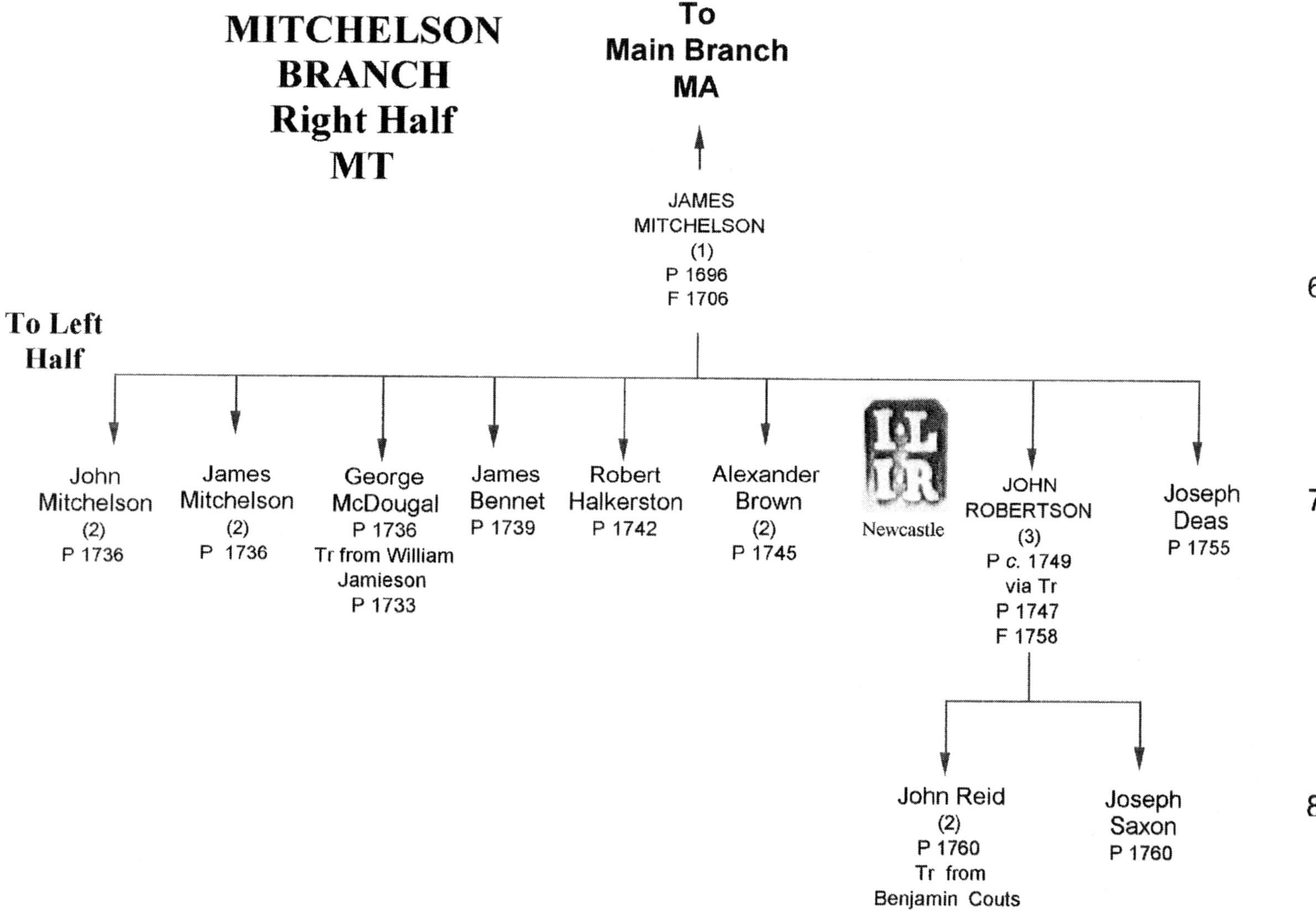
MITCHELSON BRANCH Right Half MT
To Main Branch MA
JAMES MITCHELSON (1) P 1696 F 1706
6
To Left Half
John Mitchelson (2) P 1736
James Mitchelson (2) P 1736
George McDougal P 1736 Tr from William Jamieson P 1733
James Bennet P 1739
Robert Halkerston P 1742
Alexander Brown (2) P 1745
Newcastle
JOHN ROBERTSON (3) P c. 1749 via Tr P 1747 F 1758
Joseph Deas P 1755
7
John Reid (2) P 1760 Tr from Benjamin Couts
Joseph Saxon P 1760
8

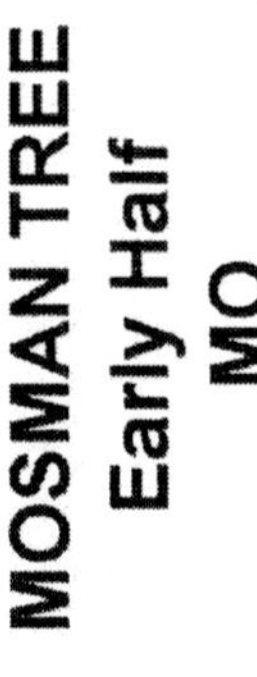
MOSMAN TREE
Early Half
MO

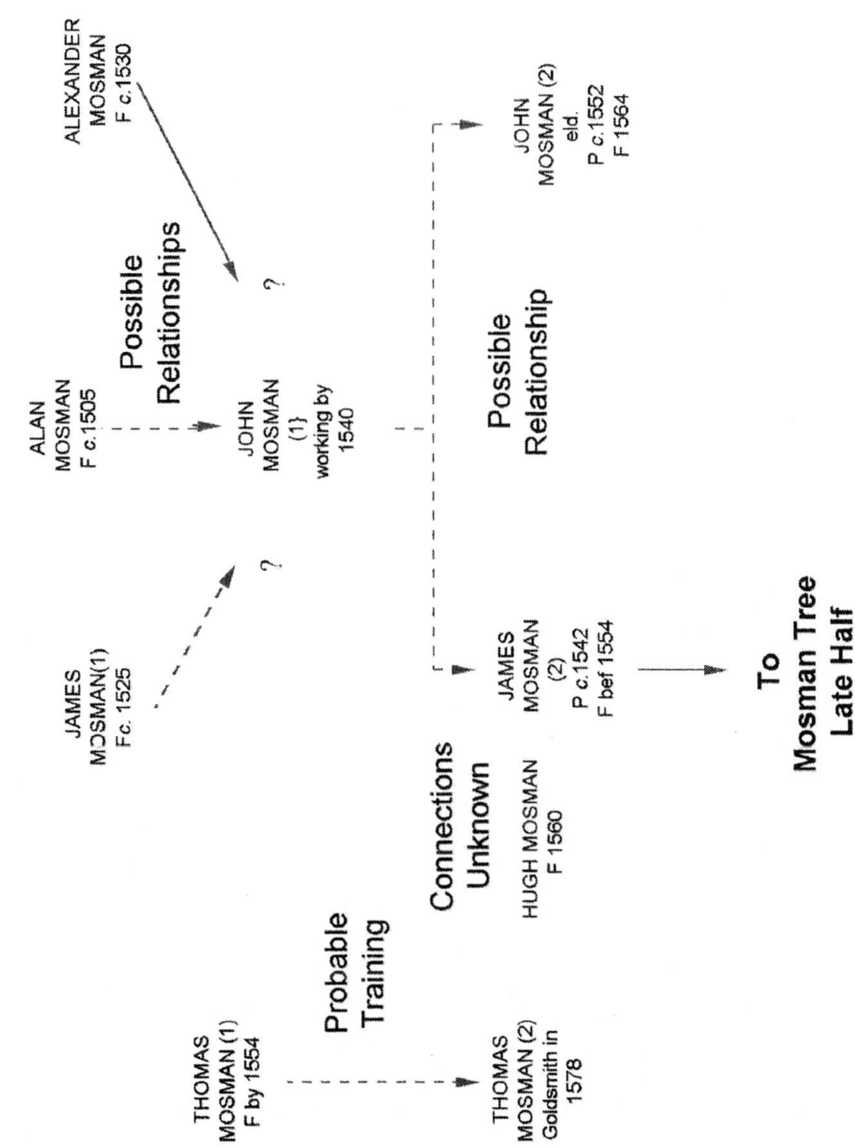
ALAN
MOSMAN
F c.1505
Possible
Relationships
ALEXANDER
MOSMAN
F c.1530
JAMES
MOSMAN(1)
F c. 1525
?
JOHN
MOSMAN
(1)
working by
1540
?
Possible
Relationship
JOHN
MOSMAN (2)
eld.
P c.1552
F 1564
JAMES
MOSMAN
(2)
P c.1542
F bef 1554
To
Mosman Tree
Late Half
Connections
Unknown
HUGH MOSMAN
F 1560
THOMAS
MOSMAN (1)
F by 1554
Probable
Training
THOMAS
MOSMAN (2)
Goldsmith in
1578
0
1
2
3

MOSMAN TREE Late Half MO

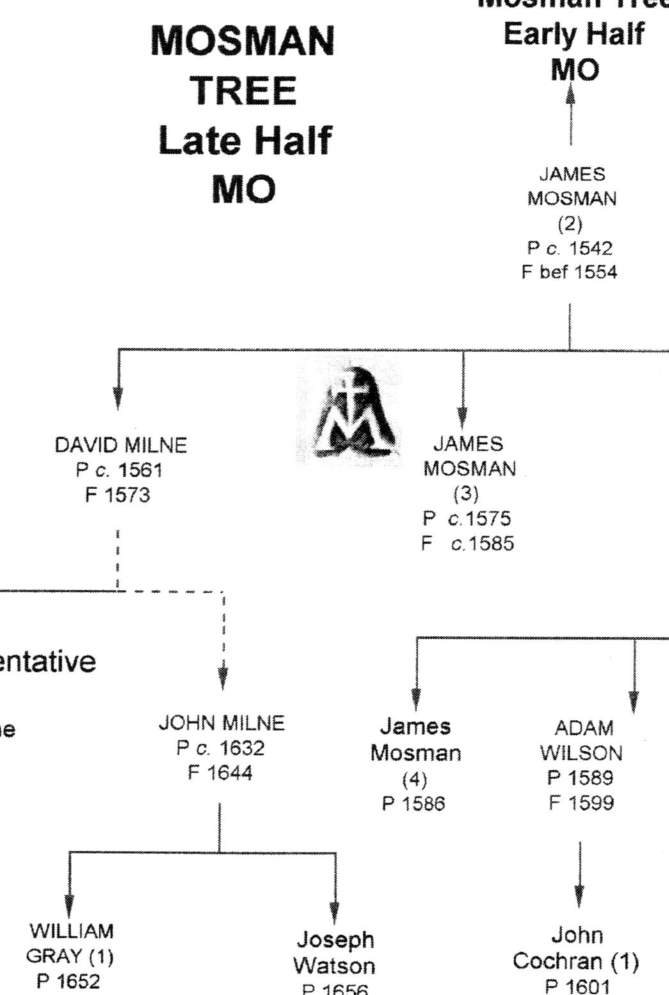

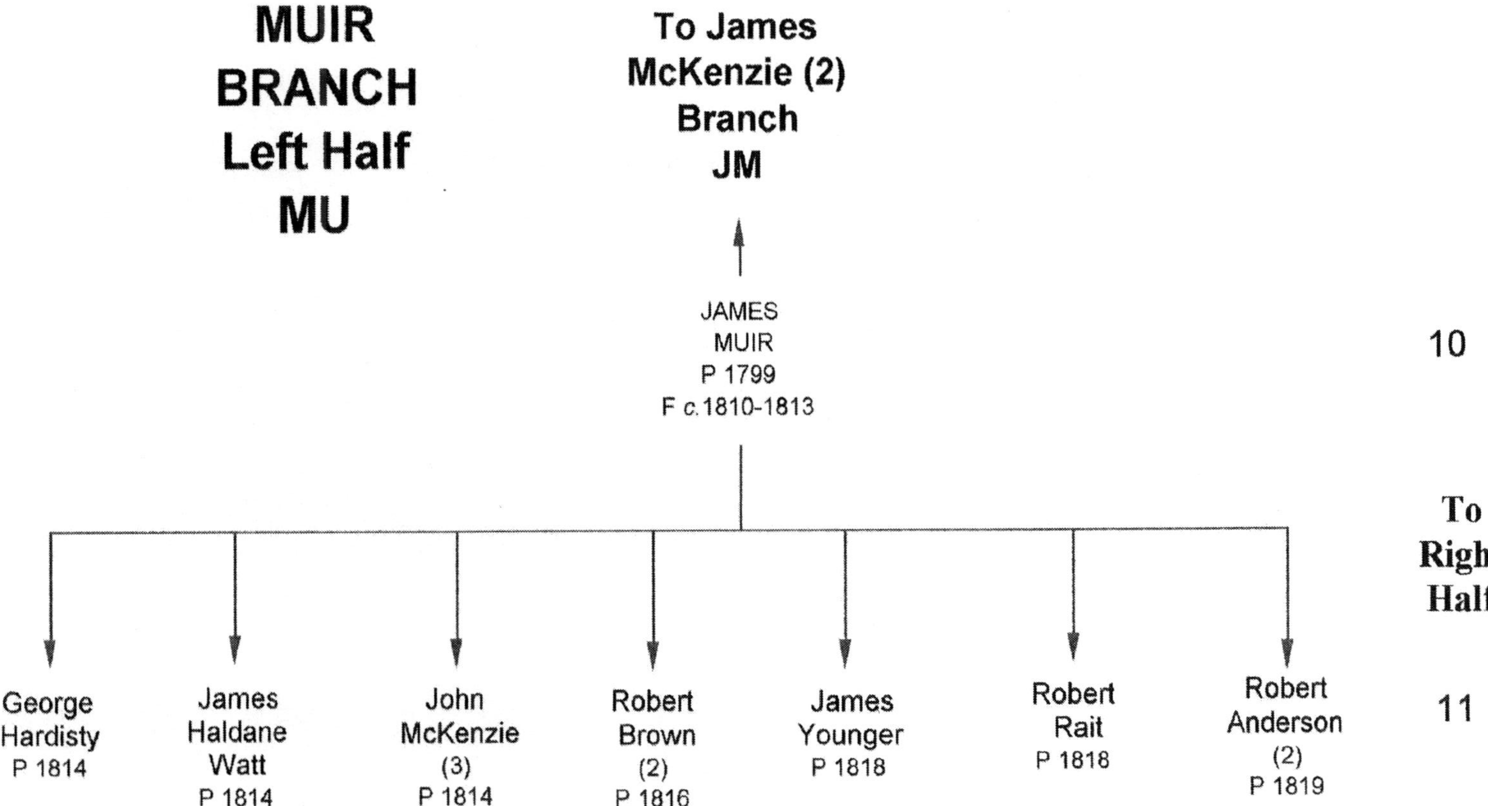
MUIR
BRANCH
Left Half
MU
To James
McKenzie (2)
Branch
JM
JAMES
MUIR
P 1799
F c.1810-1813
10
To
Right
Half
George
Hardisty
P 1814
James
Haldane
Watt
P 1814
John
McKenzie
(3)
P 1814
Robert
Brown
(2)
P 1816
James
Younger
P 1818
Robert
Rait
P 1818
Robert
Anderson
(2)
P 1819
11

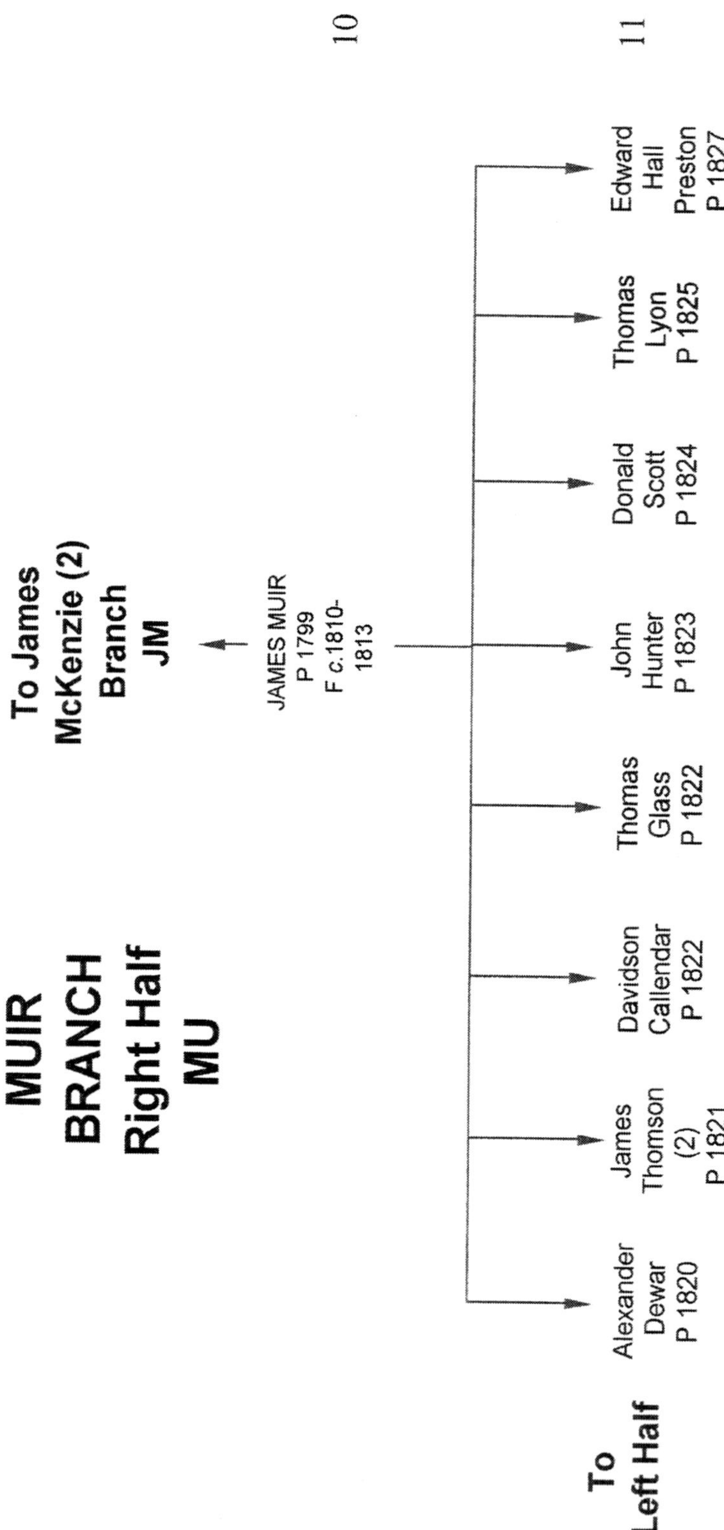
MUIR BRANCH Right Half MU
To James McKenzie (2) Branch JM
To Left Half
JAMES MUIR P 1799 F c.1810-1813
Alexander Dewar P 1820
James Thomson (2) P 1821
Davidson Callendar P 1822
Thomas Glass P 1822
John Hunter P 1823
Donald Scott P 1824
Thomas Lyon P 1825
Edward Hall Preston P 1827
10
11

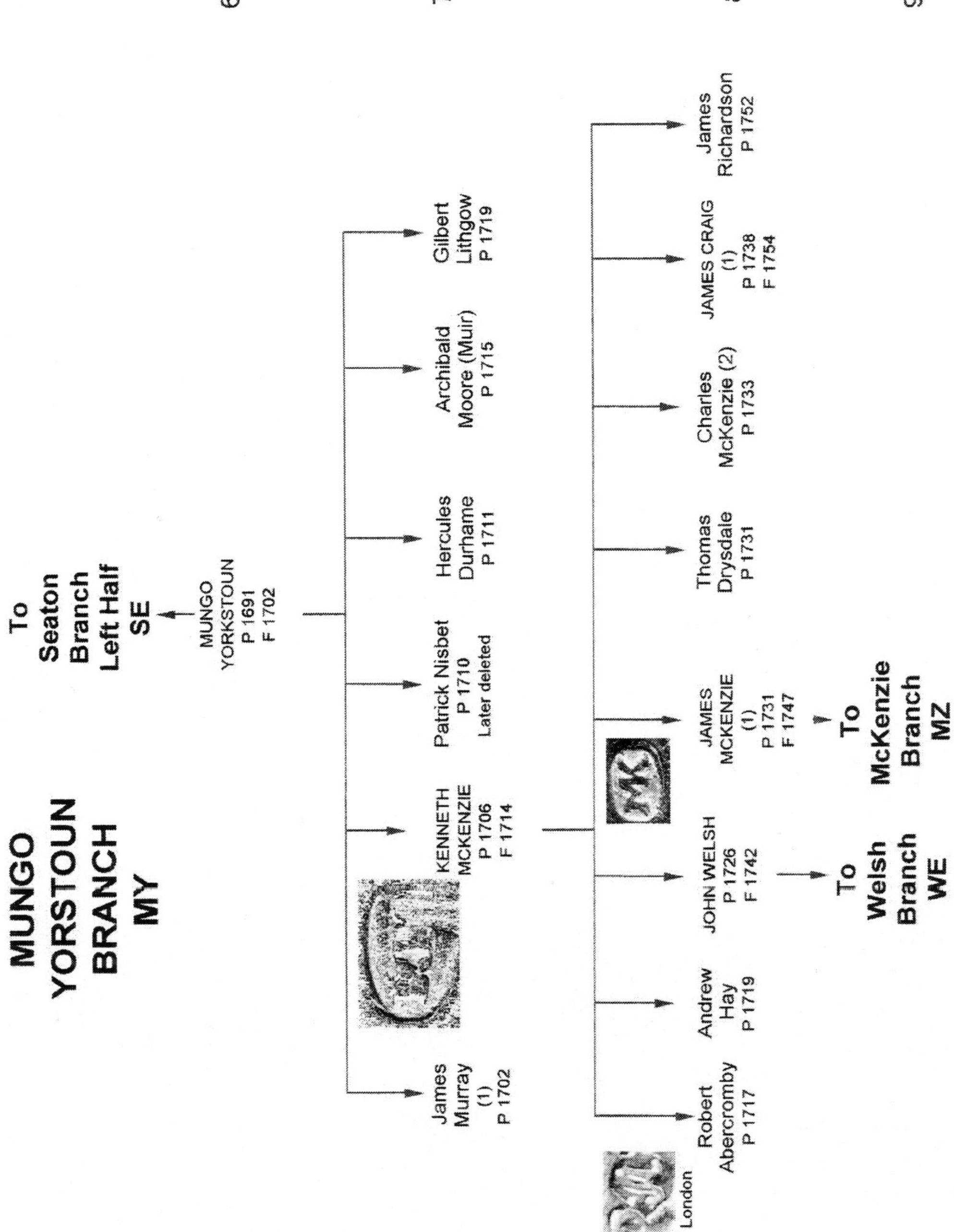

MUNGO
YORSTOUN
BRANCH
MY
To
Seaton
Branch
Left Half
SE
MUNGO
YORKSTOUN
P 1691
F 1702
6
James
Murray
(1)
P 1702
KENNETH
MCKENZIE
P 1706
F 1714
Patrick Nisbet
P 1710
Later deleted
Hercules
Durhame
P 1711
Archibald
Moore (Muir)
P 1715
Gilbert
Lithgow
P 1719
7
London
Robert
Abercromby
P 1717
Andrew
Hay
P 1719
JOHN WELSH
P 1726
F 1742
JAMES
MCKENZIE
(1)
P 1731
F 1747
Thomas
Drysdale
P 1731
Charles
McKenzie (2)
P 1733
JAMES CRAIG
(1)
P 1738
F 1754
James
Richardson
P 1752
8
To
Welsh
Branch
WE
To
McKenzie
Branch
MZ
9

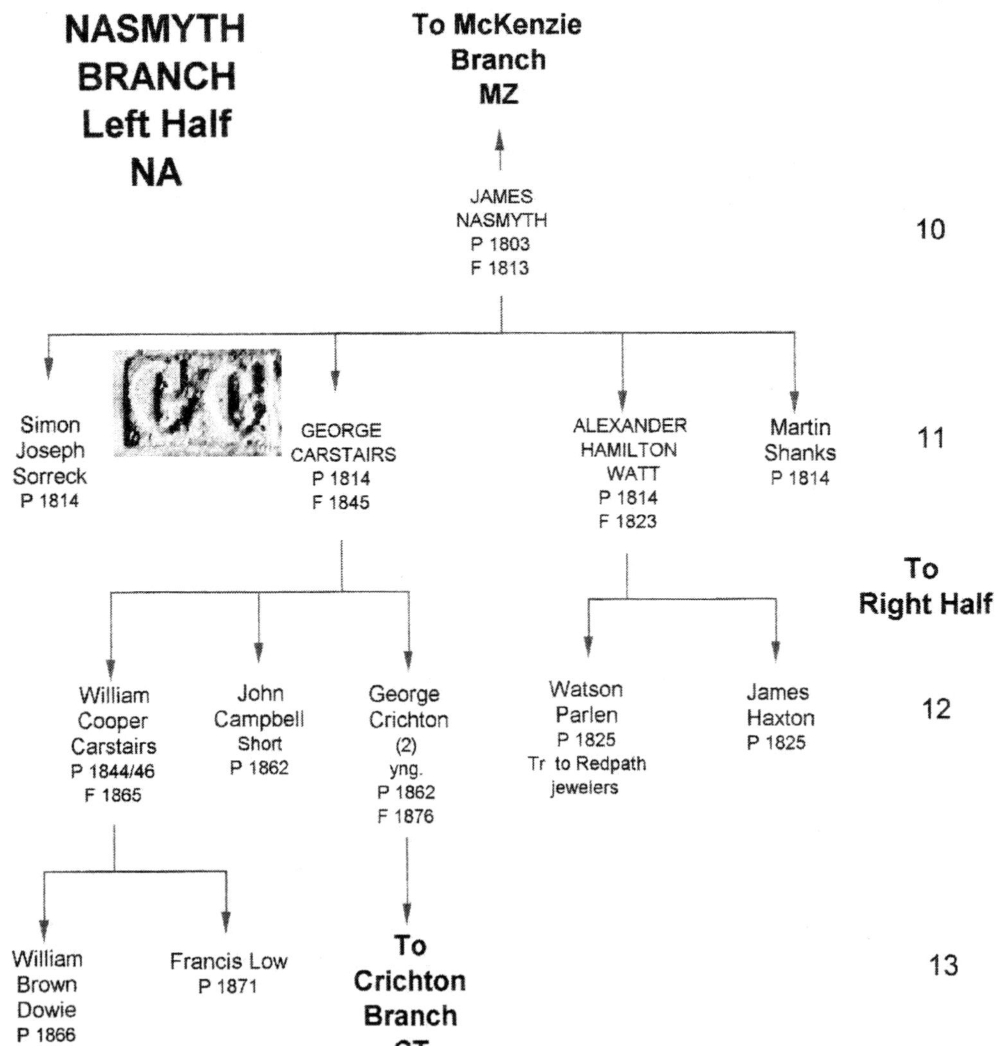
NASMYTH BRANCH Left Half NA
To McKenzie Branch MZ
JAMES NASMYTH P 1803 F 1813
10
Simon Joseph Sorreck P 1814
GEORGE CARSTAIRS P 1814 F 1845
ALEXANDER HAMILTON WATT P 1814 F 1823
Martin Shanks P 1814
11
To Right Half
William Cooper Carstairs P 1844/46 F 1865
John Campbell Short P 1862
George Crichton (2) yng. P 1862 F 1876
Watson Parlen P 1825 Tr to Redpath jewelers
James Haxton P 1825
12
William Brown Dowie P 1866 F 1889
Francis Low P 1871
To Crichton Branch CT
13

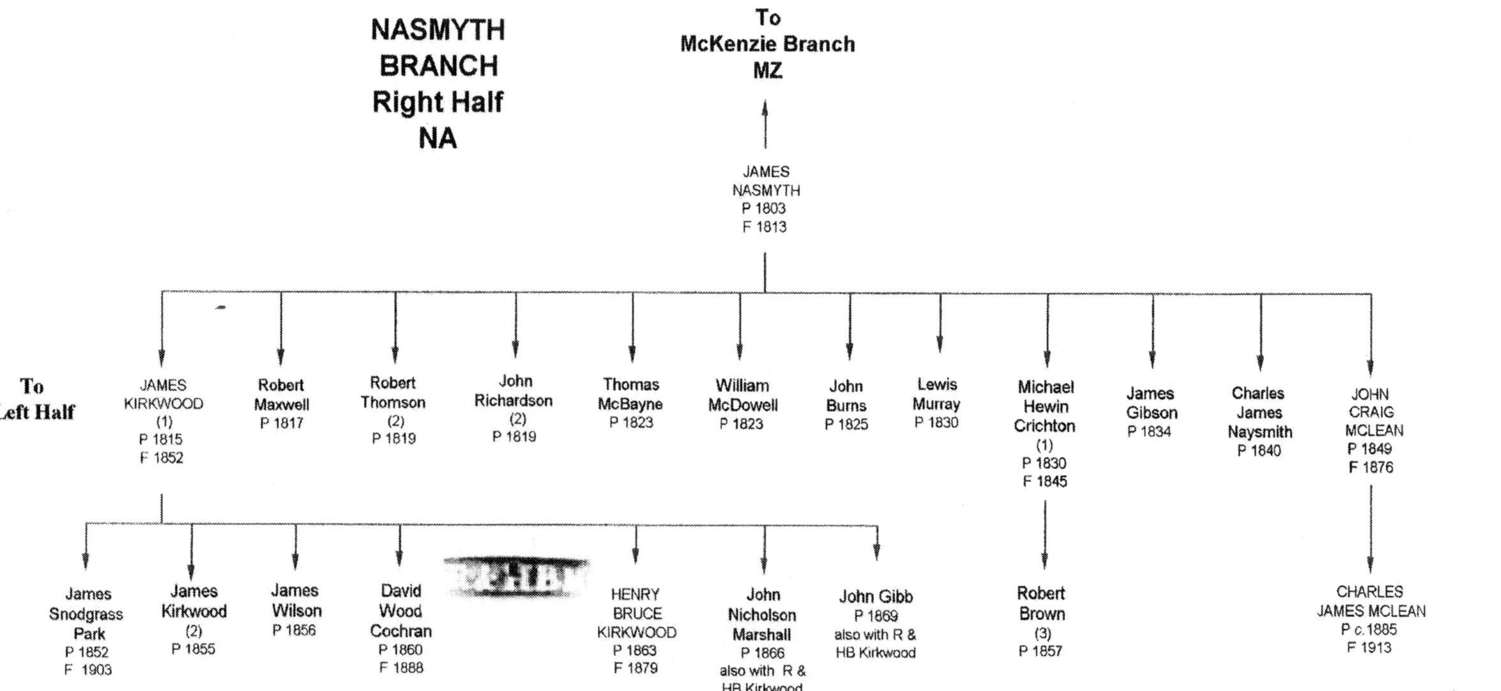
NASMYTH
BRANCH
Right Half
NA
To
McKenzie Branch
MZ
JAMES
NASMYTH
P 1803
F 1813
10
To
Left Half
JAMES
KIRKWOOD
(1)
P 1815
F 1852
Robert
Maxwell
P 1817
Robert
Thomson
(2)
P 1819
John
Richardson
(2)
P 1819
Thomas
McBayne
P 1823
William
McDowell
P 1823
John
Burns
P 1825
Lewis
Murray
P 1830
Michael
Hewin
Crichton
(1)
P 1830
F 1845
James
Gibson
P 1834
Charles
James
Naysmith
P 1840
JOHN
CRAIG
MCLEAN
P 1849
F 1876
11
James
Snodgrass
Park
P 1852
F 1903
James
Kirkwood
(2)
P 1855
James
Wilson
P 1856
David
Wood
Cochran
P 1860
F 1888
HENRY
BRUCE
KIRKWOOD
P 1863
F 1879
John
Nicholson
Marshall
P 1866
also with R &
HB Kirkwood
John Gibb
P 1869
also with R &
HB Kirkwood
Robert
Brown
(3)
P 1857
CHARLES
JAMES MCLEAN
P c.1885
F 1913
12

OLIPHANT BRANCH OL

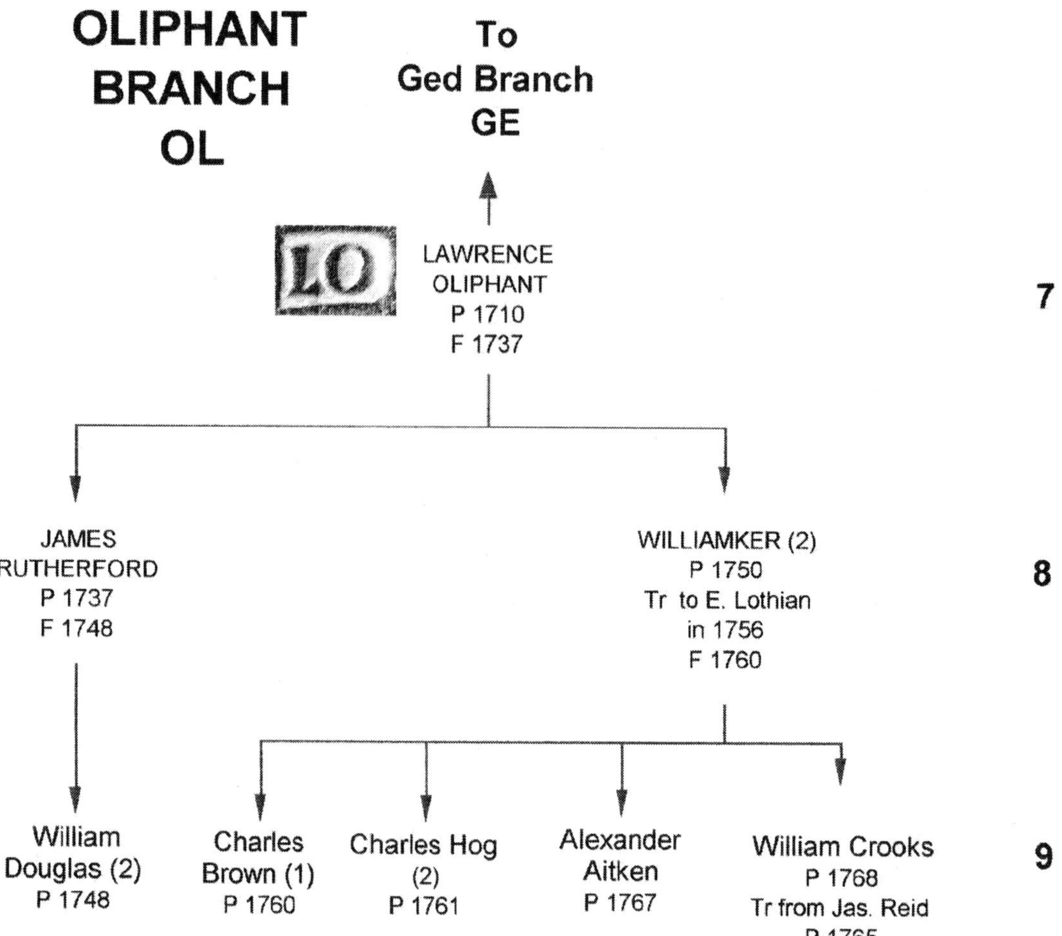

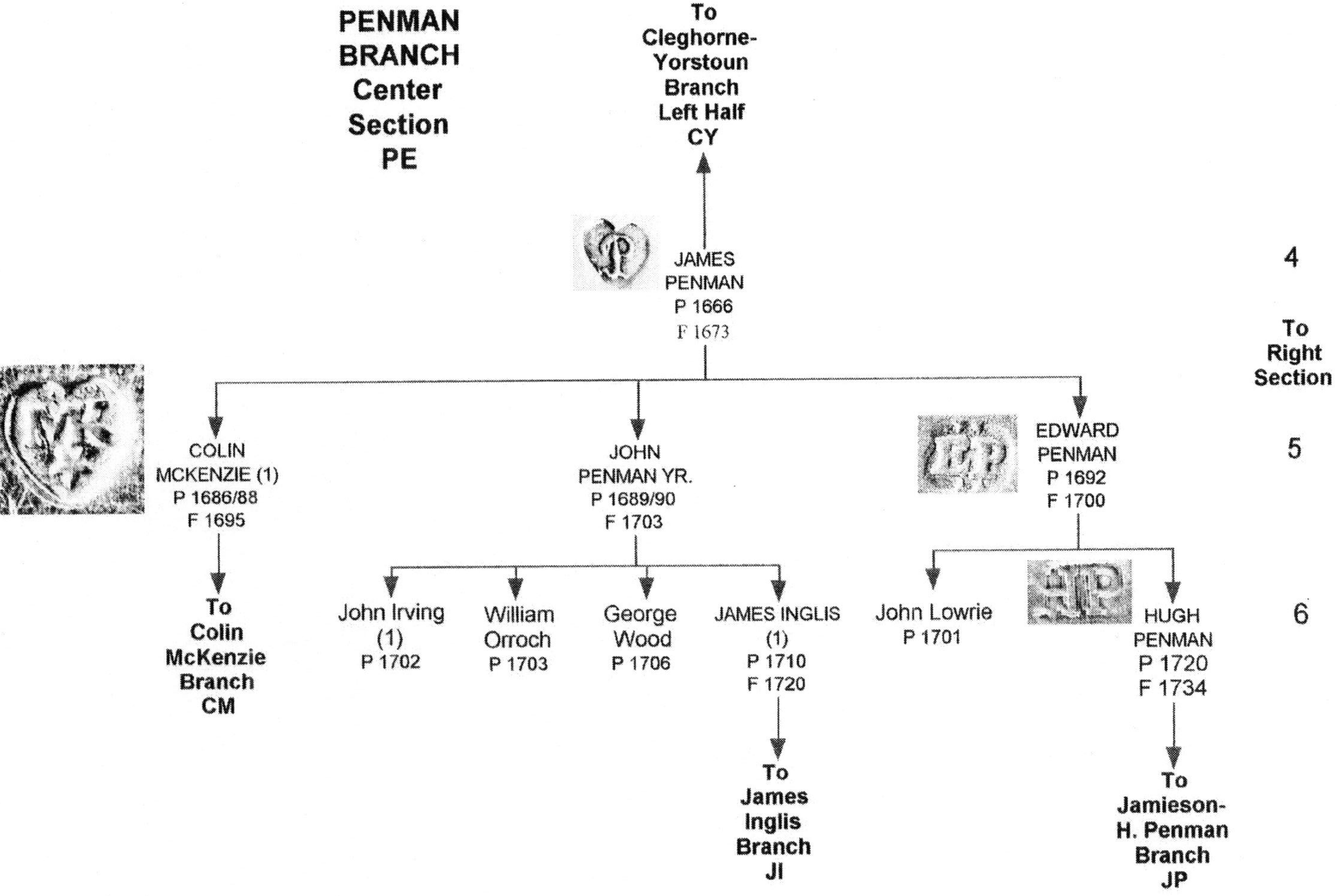
PENMAN
BRANCH
Center
Section
PE
To
Cleghorne-
Yorstoun
Branch
Left Half
CY
JAMES
PENMAN
P 1666
F 1673
4
To
Right
Section
COLIN
MCKENZIE (1)
P 1686/88
F 1695
JOHN
PENMAN YR.
P 1689/90
F 1703
EDWARD
PENMAN
P 1692
F 1700
5
To
Colin
McKenzie
Branch
CM
John Irving
(1)
P 1702
William
Orroch
P 1703
George
Wood
P 1706
JAMES INGLIS
(1)
P 1710
F 1720
John Lowrie
P 1701
HUGH
PENMAN
P 1720
F 1734
6
To
James
Inglis
Branch
JI
To
Jamieson-
H. Penman
Branch
JP

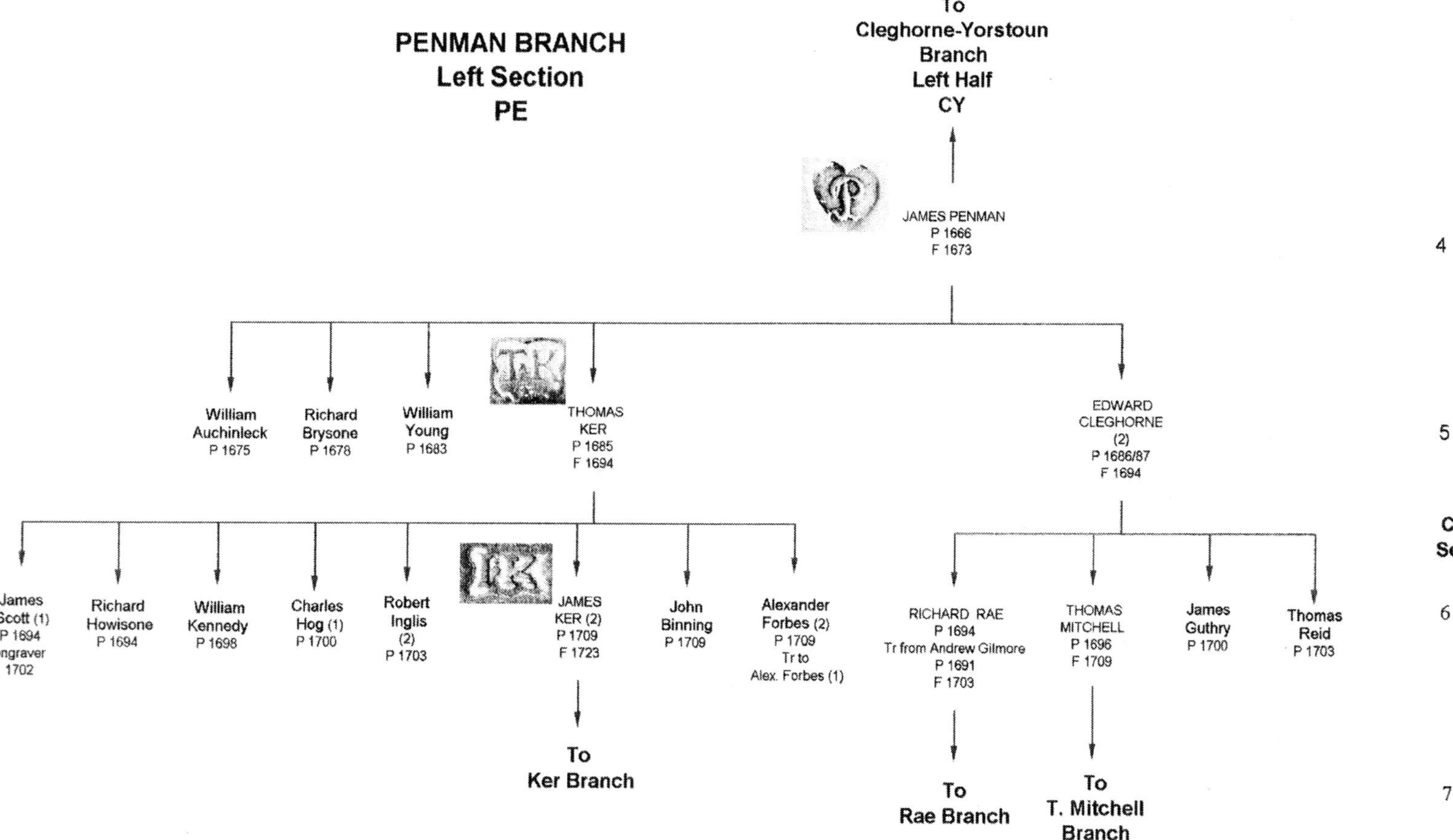
PENMAN BRANCH
Left Section
PE
To
Cleghorne-Yorstoun
Branch
Left Half
CY
JAMES PENMAN
P 1666
F 1673
4
William
Auchinleck
P 1675
Richard
Brysone
P 1678
William
Young
P 1683
THOMAS
KER
P 1685
F 1694
EDWARD
CLEGHORNE
(2)
P 1686/87
F 1694
5
To
Center
Section
James
Scott (1)
P 1694
engraver
1702
Richard
Howisone
P 1694
William
Kennedy
P 1698
Charles
Hog (1)
P 1700
Robert
Inglis
(2)
P 1703
JAMES
KER (2)
P 1709
F 1723
John
Binning
P 1709
Alexander
Forbes (2)
P 1709
Tr to
Alex. Forbes (1)
RICHARD RAE
P 1694
Tr from Andrew Gilmore
P 1691
F 1703
THOMAS
MITCHELL
P 1696
F 1709
James
Guthry
P 1700
Thomas
Reid
P 1703
6
To
Ker Branch
To
Rae Branch
To
T. Mitchell
Branch
7

PENMAN BRANCH
Right Section
PE

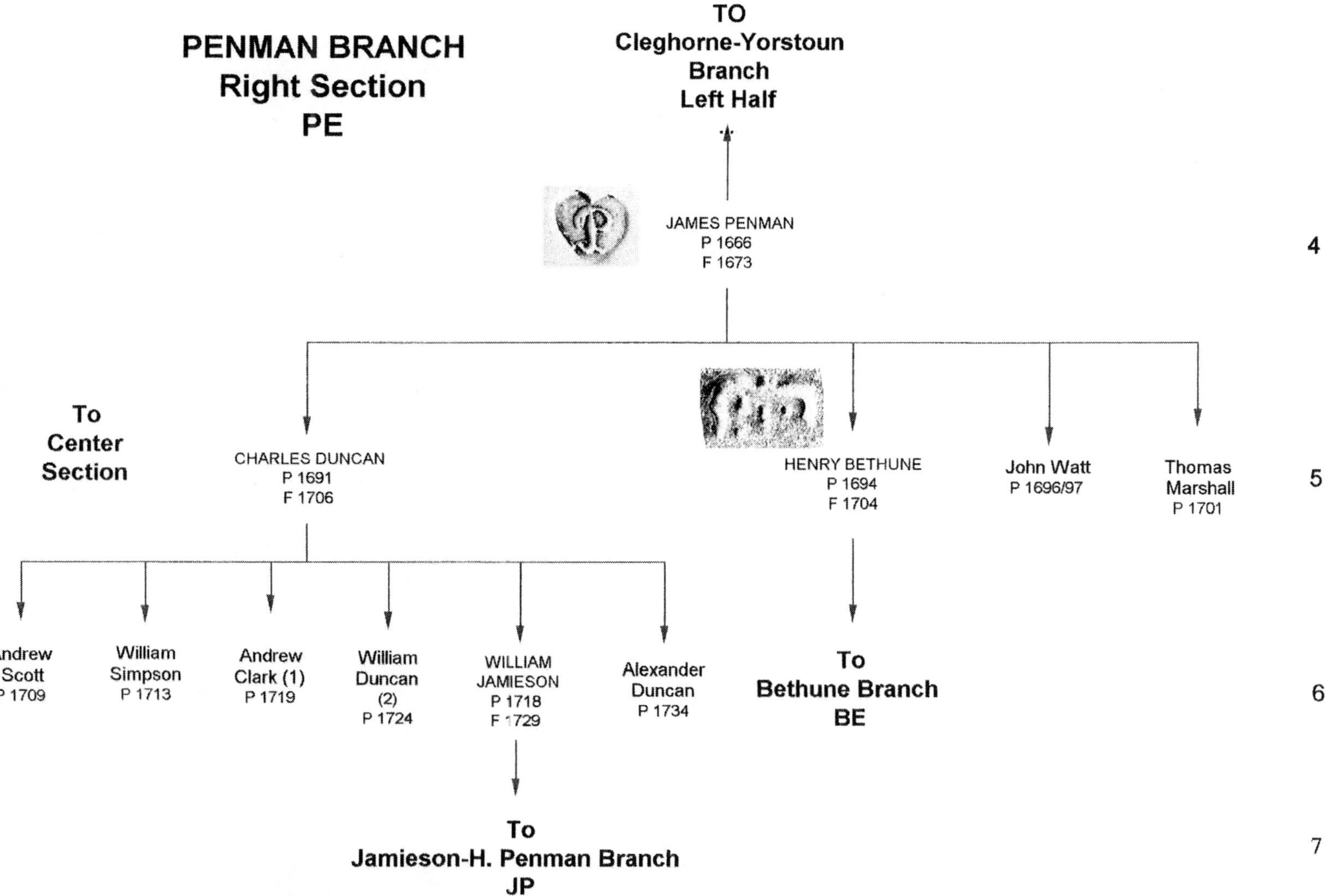

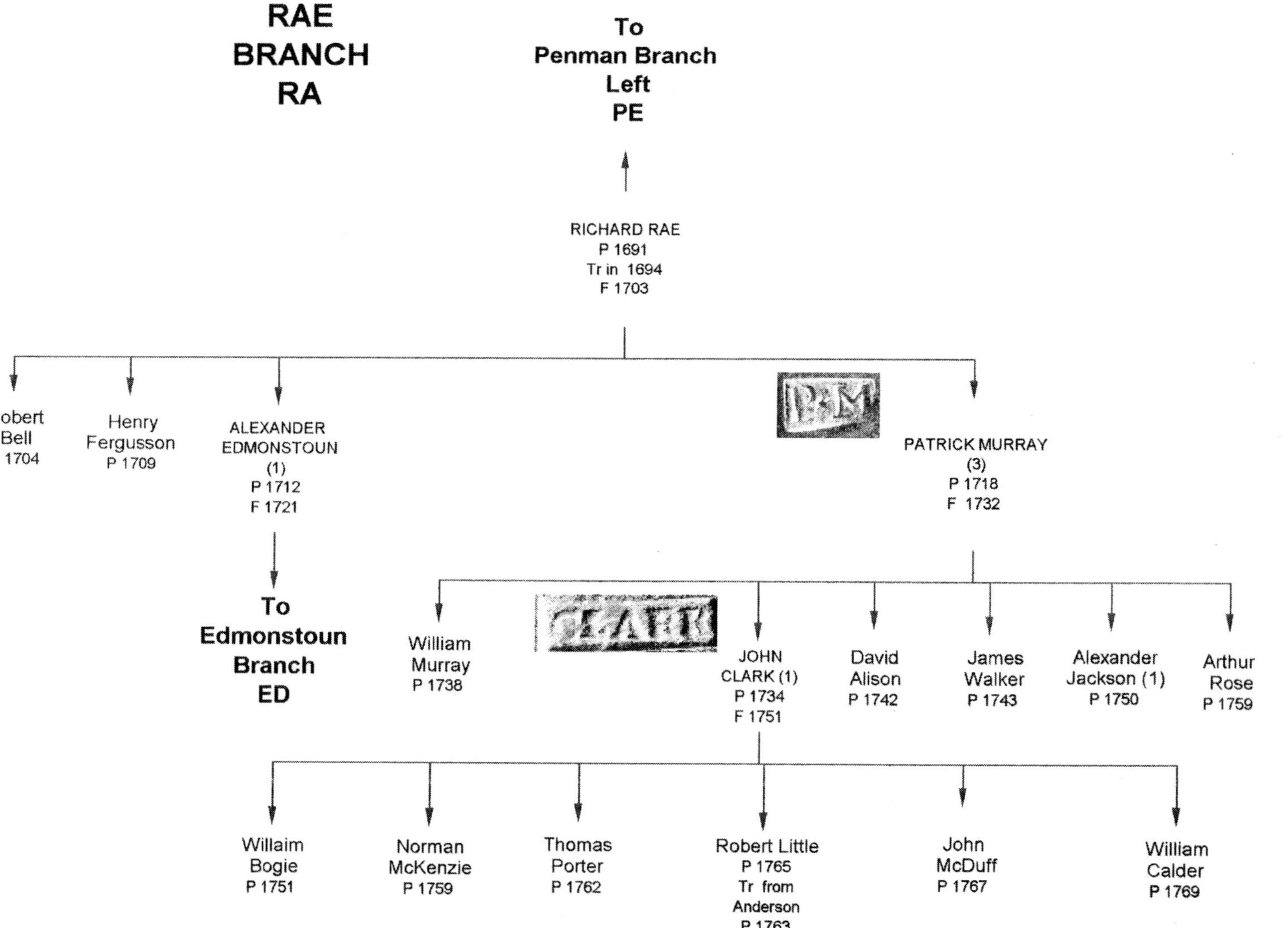

RAE
BRANCH
RA
To
Penman Branch
Left
PE
RICHARD RAE
P 1691
Tr in 1694
F 1703
6
Robert
Bell
P 1704
Henry
Fergusson
P 1709
ALEXANDER
EDMONSTOUN
(1)
P 1712
F 1721
P·M
PATRICK MURRAY
(3)
P 1718
F 1732
7
To
Edmonstoun
Branch
ED
William
Murray
P 1738
CLARK
JOHN
CLARK (1)
P 1734
F 1751
David
Alison
P 1742
James
Walker
P 1743
Alexander
Jackson (1)
P 1750
Arthur
Rose
P 1759
8
Willaim
Bogie
P 1751
Norman
McKenzie
P 1759
Thomas
Porter
P 1762
Robert Little
P 1765
Tr from
Anderson
P 1763
John
McDuff
P 1767
William
Calder
P 1769
9

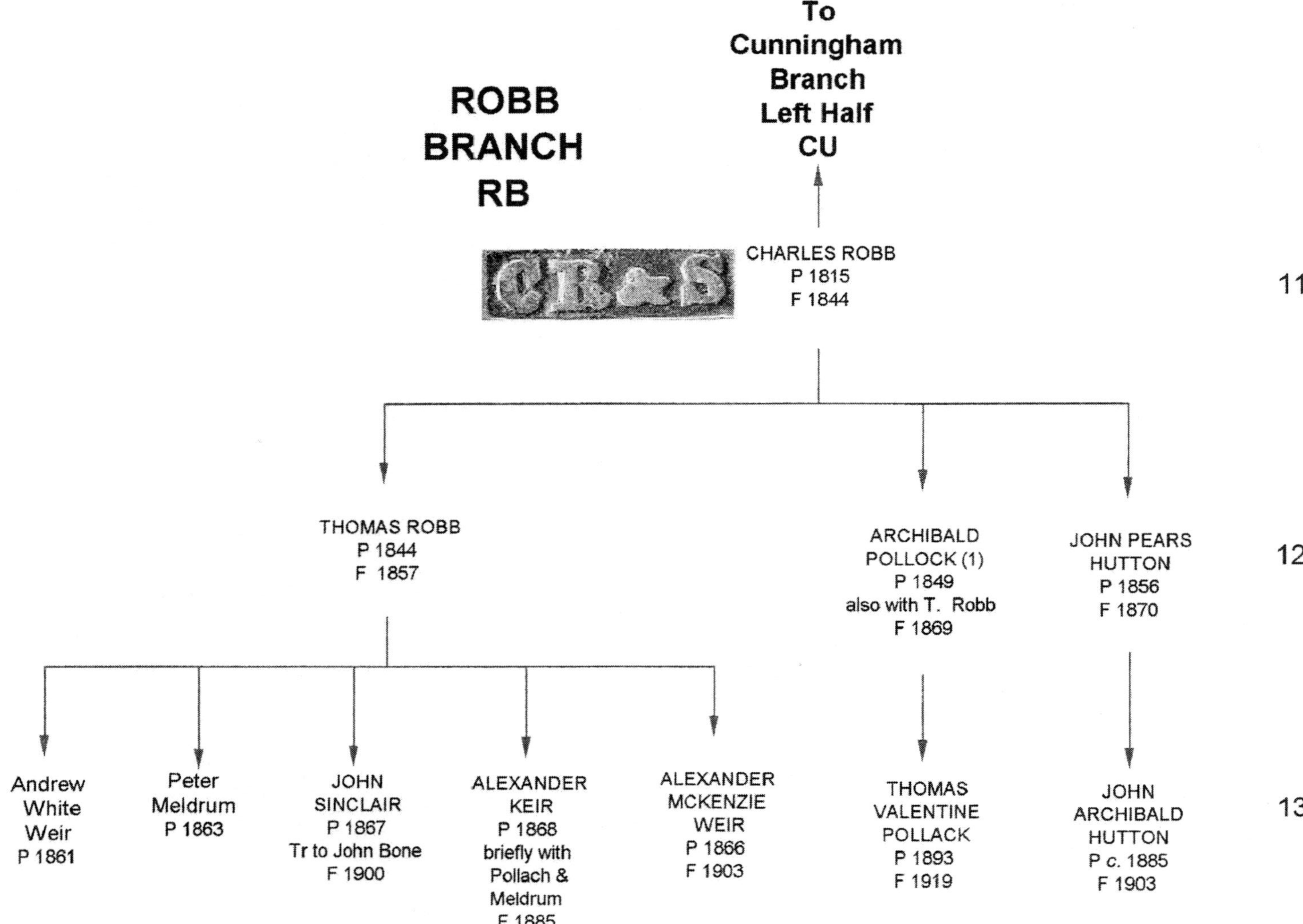
ROBB
BRANCH
RB
CR&S
To
Cunningham
Branch
Left Half
CU
CHARLES ROBB
P 1815
F 1844
11
THOMAS ROBB
P 1844
F 1857
ARCHIBALD
POLLOCK (1)
P 1849
also with T. Robb
F 1869
JOHN PEARS
HUTTON
P 1856
F 1870
12
Andrew
White
Weir
P 1861
Peter
Meldrum
P 1863
JOHN
SINCLAIR
P 1867
Tr to John Bone
F 1900
ALEXANDER
KEIR
P 1868
briefly with
Pollach &
Meldrum
F 1885
ALEXANDER
MCKENZIE
WEIR
P 1866
F 1903
THOMAS
VALENTINE
POLLACK
P 1893
F 1919
JOHN
ARCHIBALD
HUTTON
P c. 1885
F 1903
13

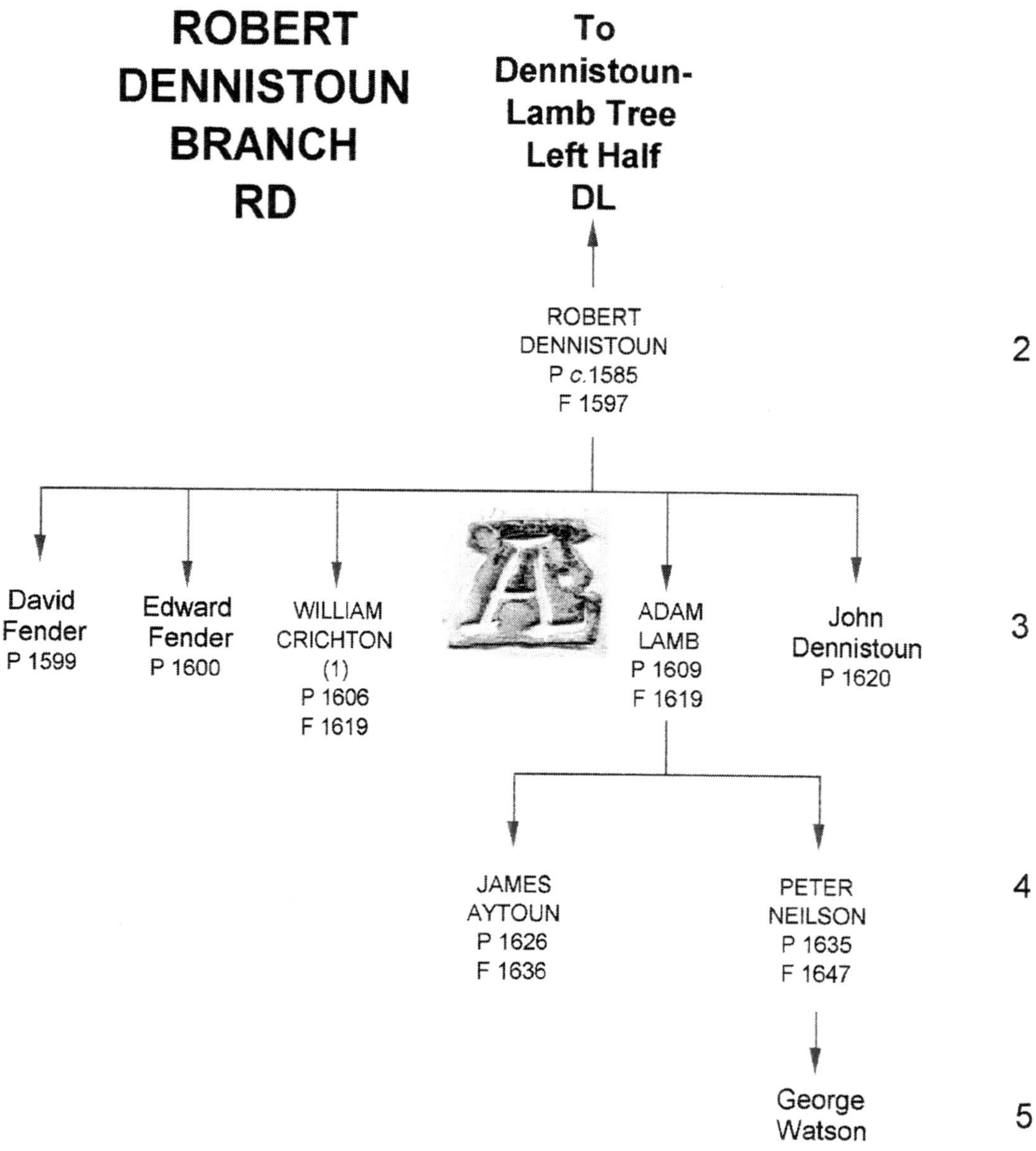
ROBERT DENNISTOUN BRANCH RD
To Dennistoun-Lamb Tree Left Half DL
ROBERT DENNISTOUN P c.1585 F 1597
2
David Fender P 1599
Edward Fender P 1600
WILLIAM CRICHTON (1) P 1606 F 1619
ADAM LAMB P 1609 F 1619
John Dennistoun P 1620
3
JAMES AYTOUN P 1626 F 1636
PETER NEILSON P 1635 F 1647
4
George Watson P 1653
5

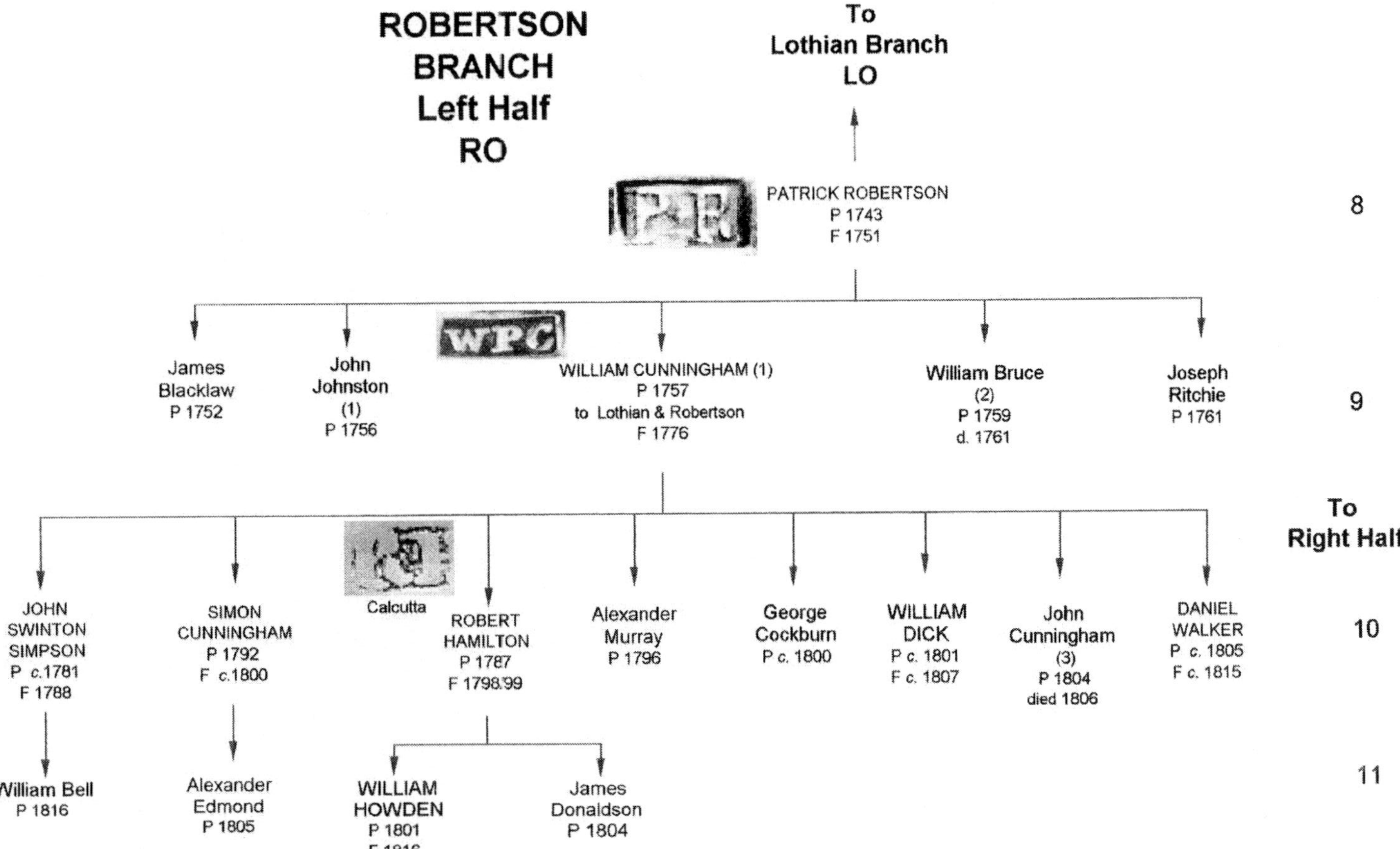
ROBERTSON BRANCH Left Half RO
To Lothian Branch LO
PATRICK ROBERTSON P 1743 F 1751
8
WPC
James Blacklaw P 1752
John Johnston (1) P 1756
WILLIAM CUNNINGHAM (1) P 1757 to Lothian & Robertson F 1776
William Bruce (2) P 1759 d. 1761
Joseph Ritchie P 1761
9
To Right Half
Calcutta
JOHN SWINTON SIMPSON P c.1781 F 1788
SIMON CUNNINGHAM P 1792 F c.1800
ROBERT HAMILTON P 1787 F 1798/99
Alexander Murray P 1796
George Cockburn P c. 1800
WILLIAM DICK P c. 1801 F c. 1807
John Cunningham (3) P 1804 died 1806
DANIEL WALKER P c. 1805 F c. 1815
10
William Bell P 1816
Alexander Edmond P 1805
WILLIAM HOWDEN P 1801 F 1816
James Donaldson P 1804
11

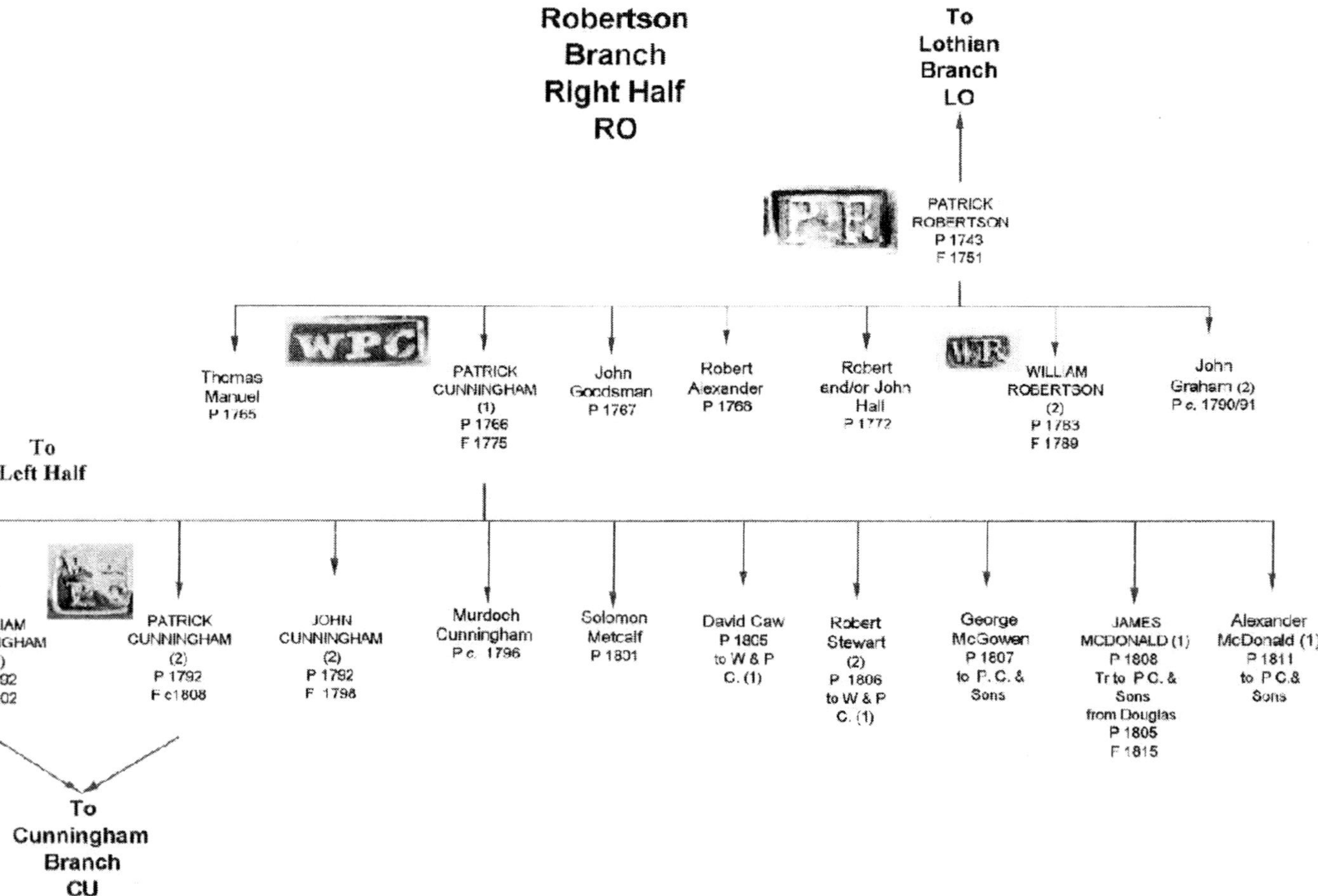
Robertson
Branch
Right Half
RO
To
Lothian
Branch
LO
PATRICK
ROBERTSON
P 1743
F 1751
8
Thomas
Manuel
P 1765
WPC
PATRICK
CUNNINGHAM
(1)
P 1766
F 1775
John
Goodsman
P 1767
Robert
Alexander
P 1768
Robert
and/or John
Hall
P 1772
WR
WILLIAM
ROBERTSON
(2)
P 1783
F 1789
John
Graham (2)
P c. 1790/91
9
To
Left Half
WILLIAM
CUNNINGHAM
(2)
P 1792
F 1802
PATRICK
CUNNINGHAM
(2)
P 1792
F c1808
JOHN
CUNNINGHAM
(2)
P 1792
F 1798
Murdoch
Cunningham
P c. 1796
Solomon
Metcalf
P 1801
David Caw
P 1805
to W & P
C. (1)
Robert
Stewart
(2)
P 1806
to W & P
C. (1)
George
McGowen
P 1807
to P. C. &
Sons
JAMES
MCDONALD (1)
P 1808
Tr to P.C. &
Sons
from Douglas
P 1805
F 1815
Alexander
McDonald (1)
P 1811
to P C.&
Sons
10
To
Cunningham
Branch
CU
11

RYND TREE RY

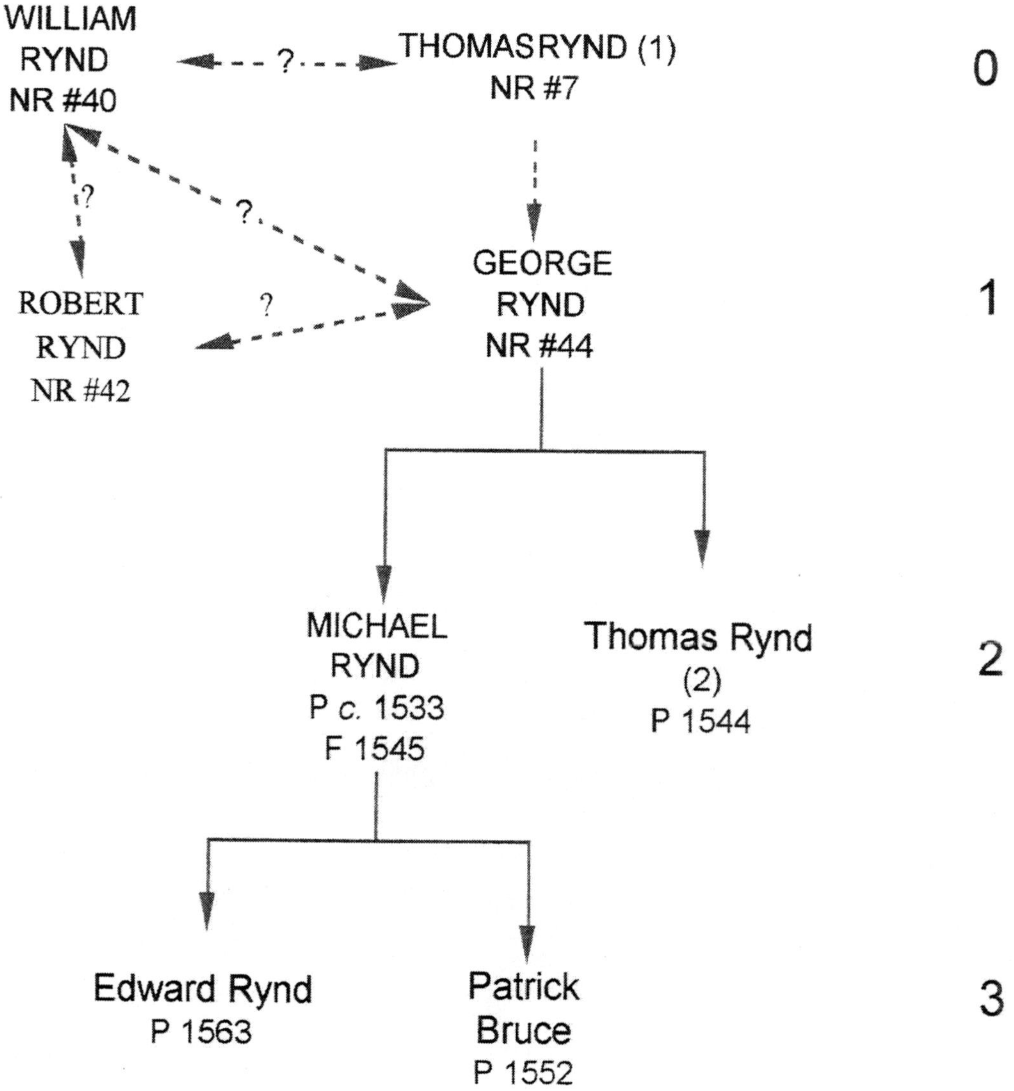
WILLIAM RYND NR #40
?
THOMAS RYND (1) NR #7
0
?
?
ROBERT RYND NR #42
?
GEORGE RYND NR #44
1
MICHAEL RYND P *c.* 1533 F 1545
Thomas Rynd (2) P 1544
2
Edward Rynd P 1563
Patrick Bruce P 1552
3

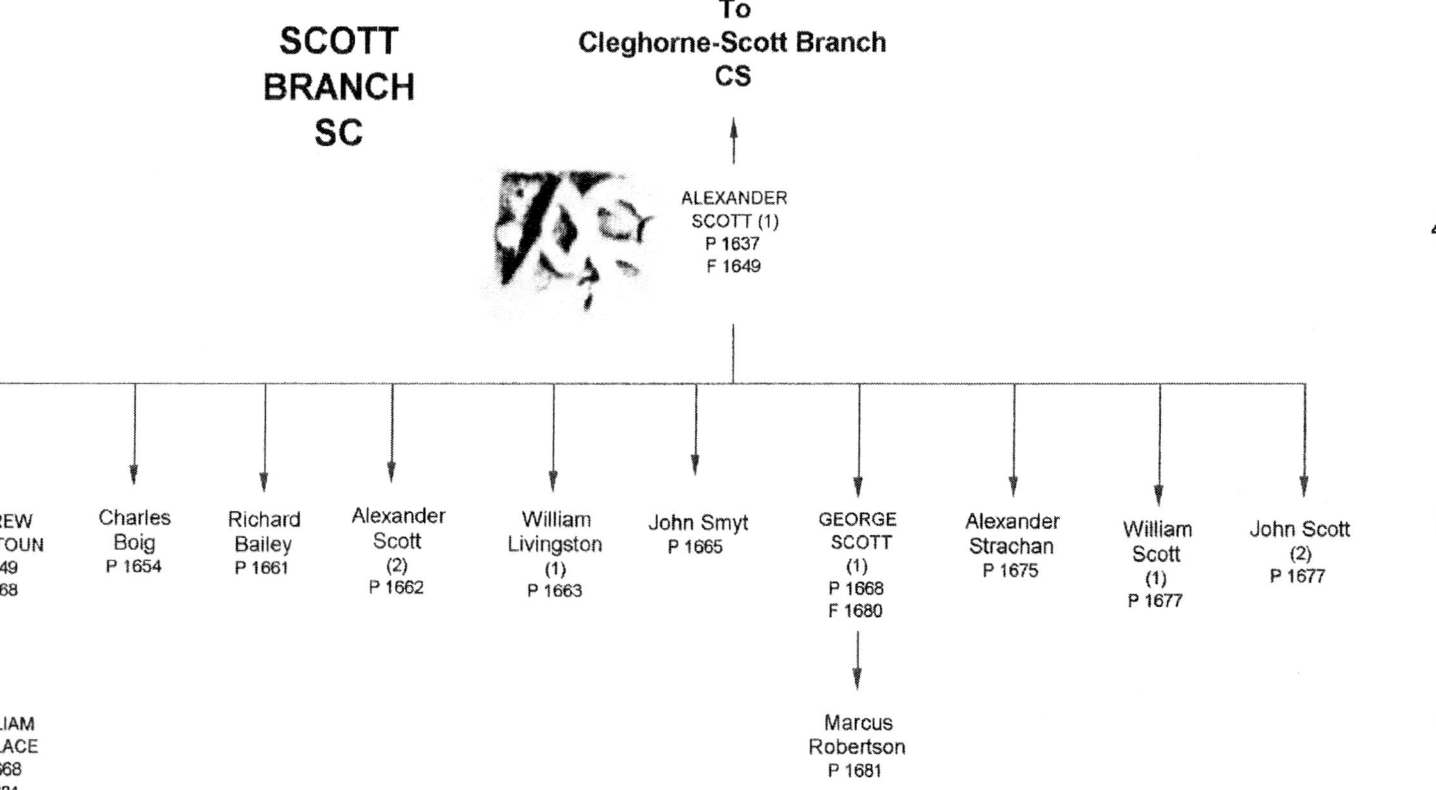
SCOTT
BRANCH
SC
To
Cleghorne-Scott Branch
CS
ALEXANDER
SCOTT (1)
P 1637
F 1649
4
ANDREW
MERSTOUN
P 1649
F 1668
Charles
Boig
P 1654
Richard
Bailey
P 1661
Alexander
Scott
(2)
P 1662
William
Livingston
(1)
P 1663
John Smyt
P 1665
GEORGE
SCOTT
(1)
P 1668
F 1680
Alexander
Strachan
P 1675
William
Scott
(1)
P 1677
John Scott
(2)
P 1677
5
WILLIAM
WALLACE
P 1668
F 1681
Marcus
Robertson
P 1681
6

SEATON BRANCH Left Half SE

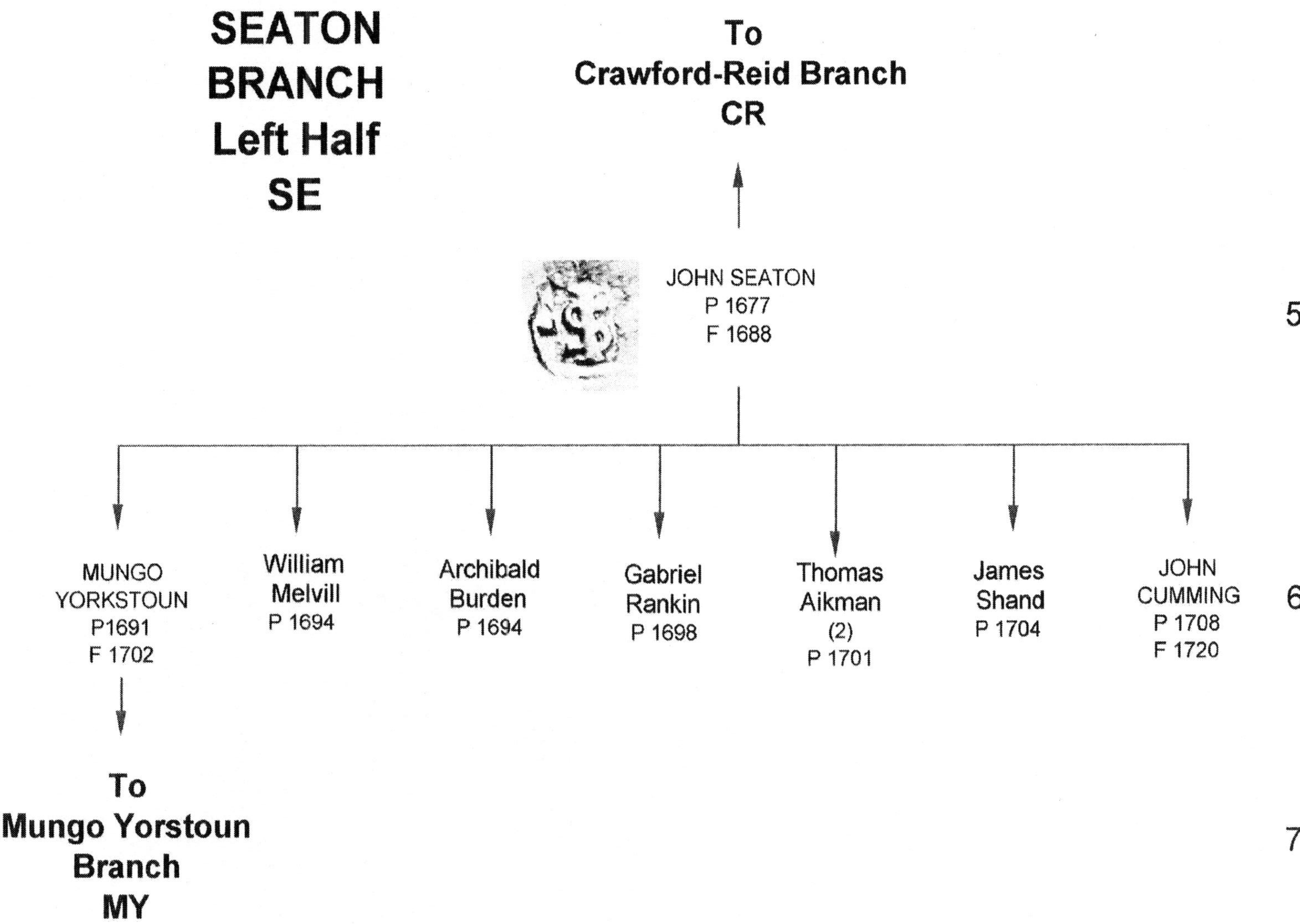

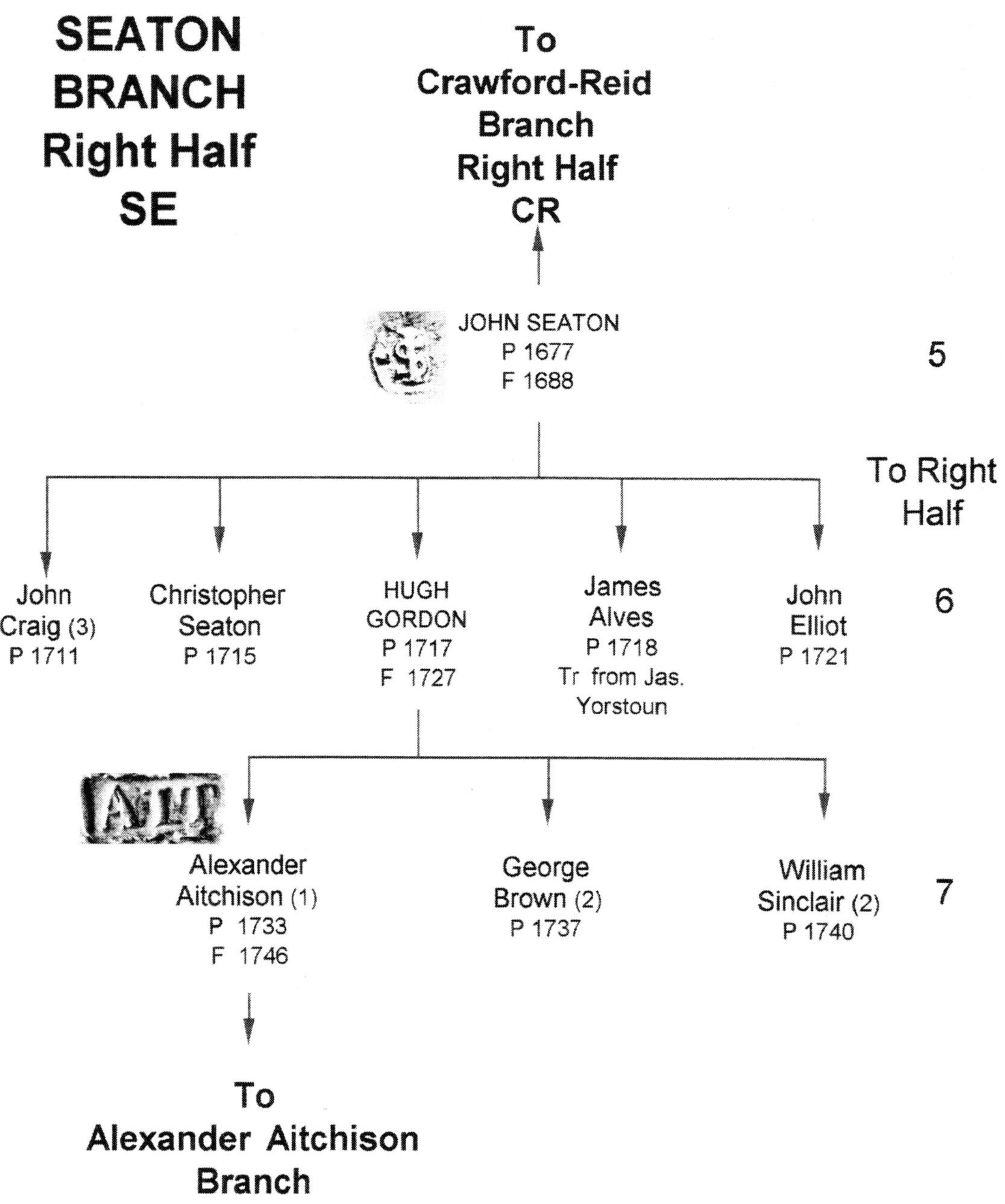

SEATON BRANCH Right Half SE
To Crawford-Reid Branch Right Half CR
JOHN SEATON P 1677 F 1688
5
To Right Half
John Craig (3) P 1711
Christopher Seaton P 1715
HUGH GORDON P 1717 F 1727
James Alves P 1718 Tr from Jas. Yorstoun
John Elliot P 1721
6
Alexander Aitchison (1) P 1733 F 1746
George Brown (2) P 1737
William Sinclair (2) P 1740
7
To Alexander Aitchison Branch AI

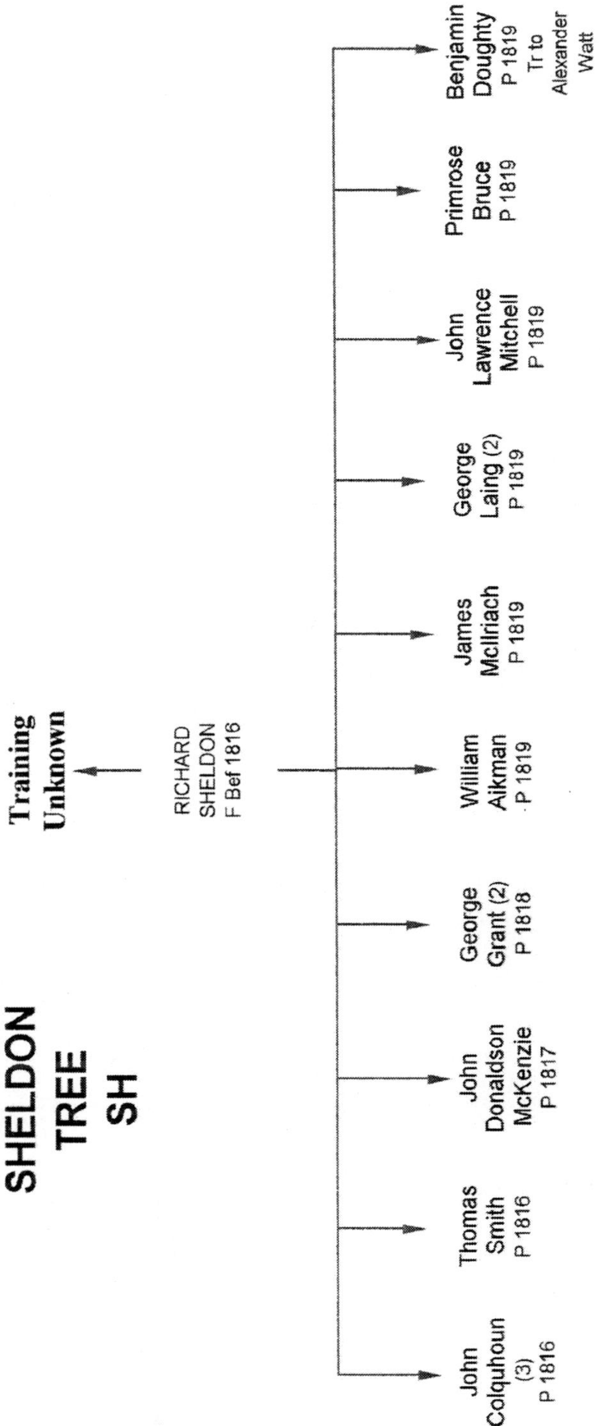

SHELDON TREE SH
Training Unknown
RICHARD SHELDON F Bef 1816
John Colquhoun (3) P 1816
Thomas Smith P 1816
John Donaldson McKenzie P 1817
George Grant (2) P 1818
William Aikman P 1819
James McIlriach P 1819
George Laing (2) P 1819
John Lawrence Mitchell P 1819
Primrose Bruce P 1819
Benjamin Doughty P 1819 Tr to Alexander Watt
1
2

STALKER
TREE
ST

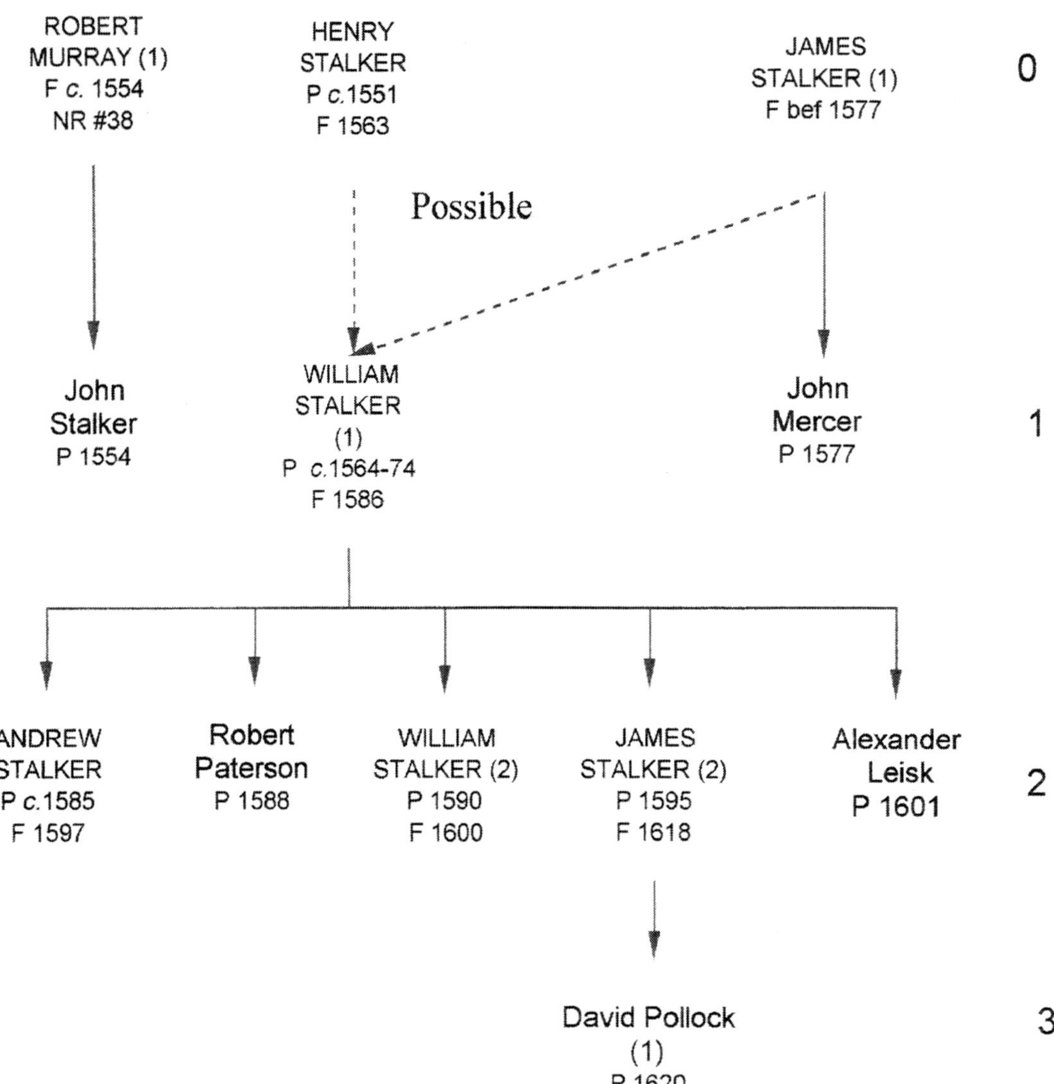

SYME TREE SY

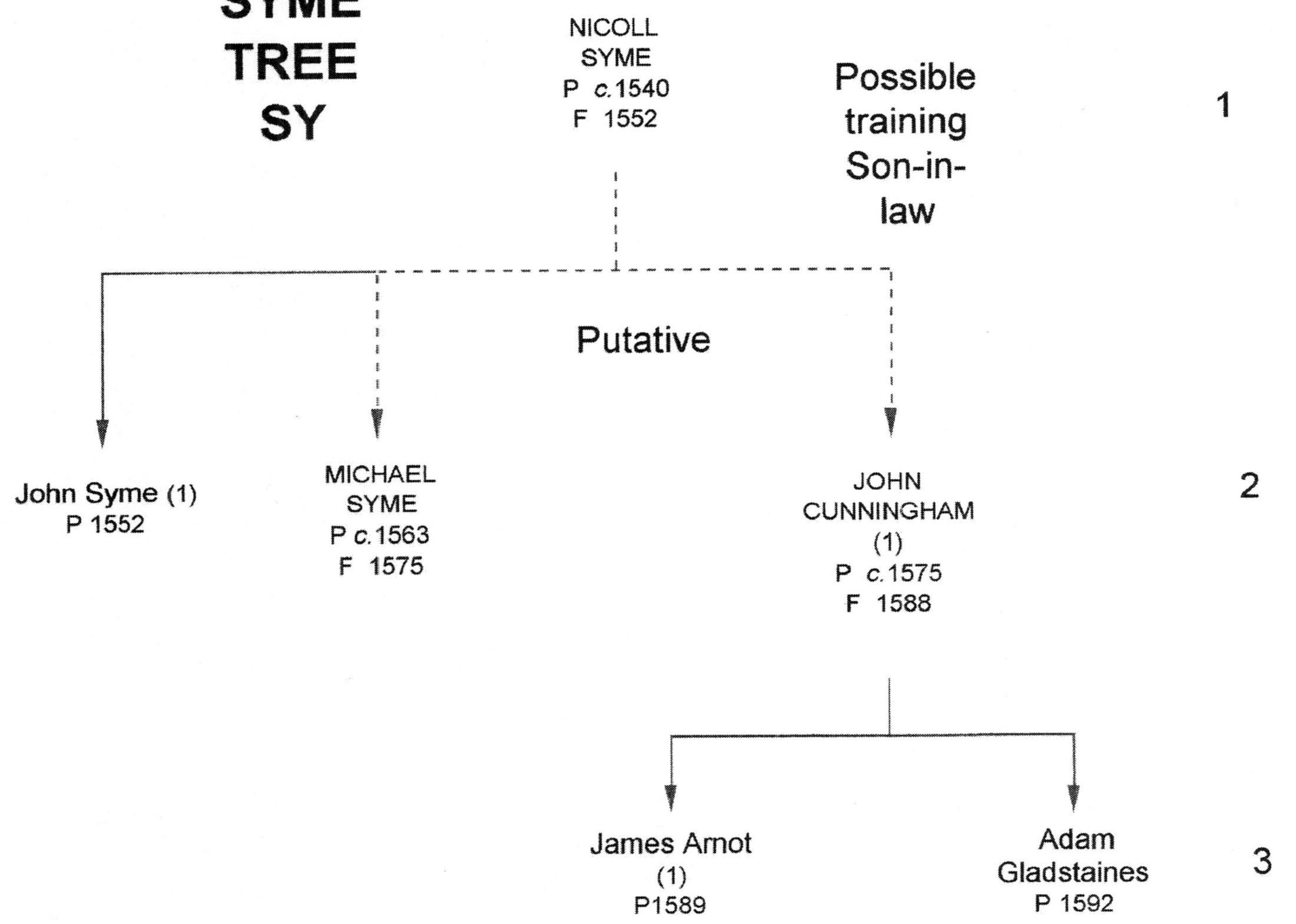

NICOLL SYME
P *c.*1540
F 1552

Possible training Son-in-law

1

Putative

John Syme (1)
P 1552

MICHAEL SYME
P *c.*1563
F 1575

JOHN CUNNINGHAM (1)
P *c.*1575
F 1588

2

James Arnot (1)
P1589

Adam Gladstaines
P 1592

3

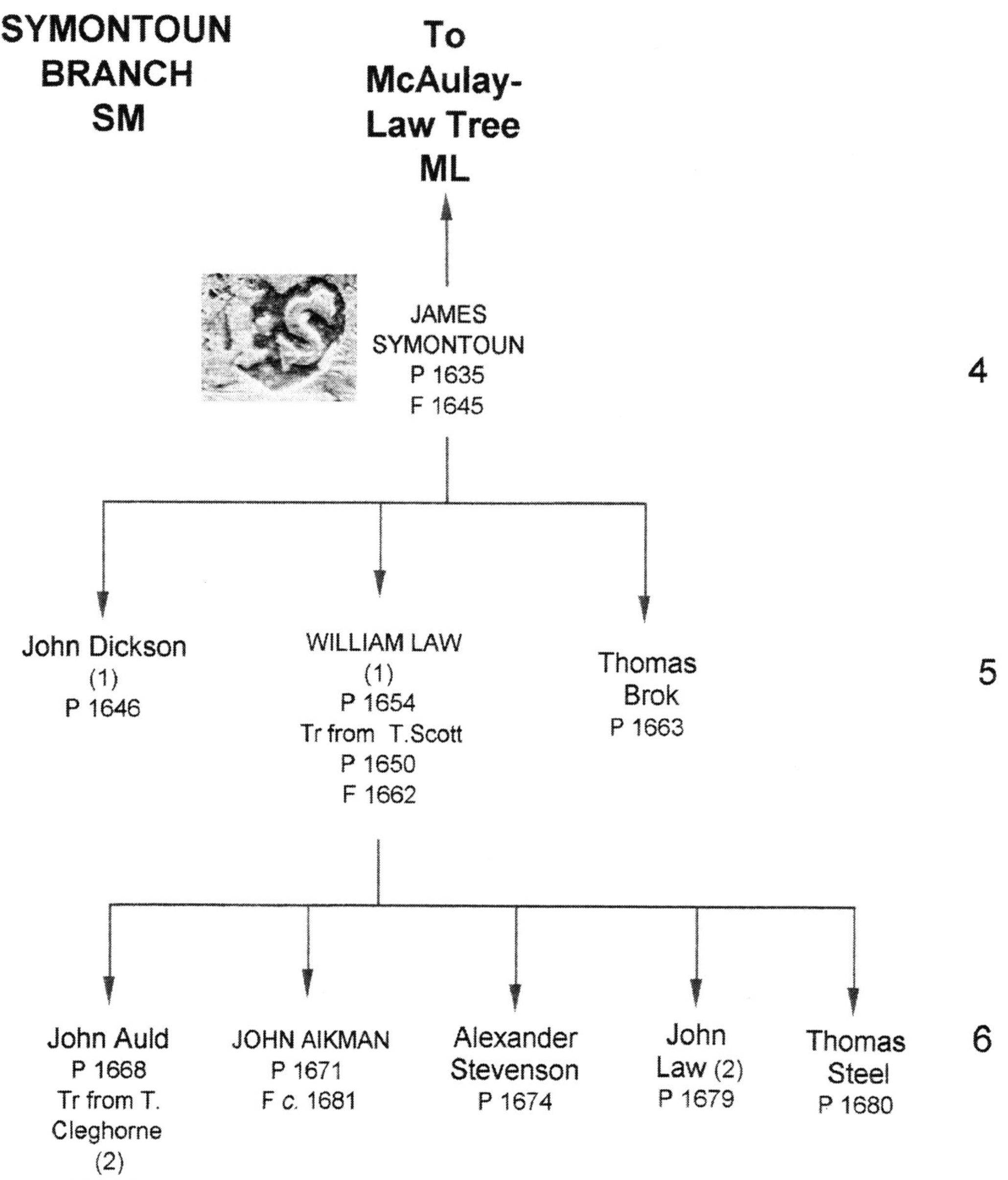
SYMONTOUN BRANCH SM
To McAulay-Law Tree ML
JAMES SYMONTOUN
P 1635
F 1645
4
John Dickson
(1)
P 1646
WILLIAM LAW
(1)
P 1654
Tr from T.Scott
P 1650
F 1662
Thomas Brok
P 1663
5
John Auld
P 1668
Tr from T. Cleghorne
(2)
P 1666
JOHN AIKMAN
P 1671
F c. 1681
Alexander Stevenson
P 1674
John Law (2)
P 1679
Thomas Steel
P 1680
6

TAIT BRANCH
TA

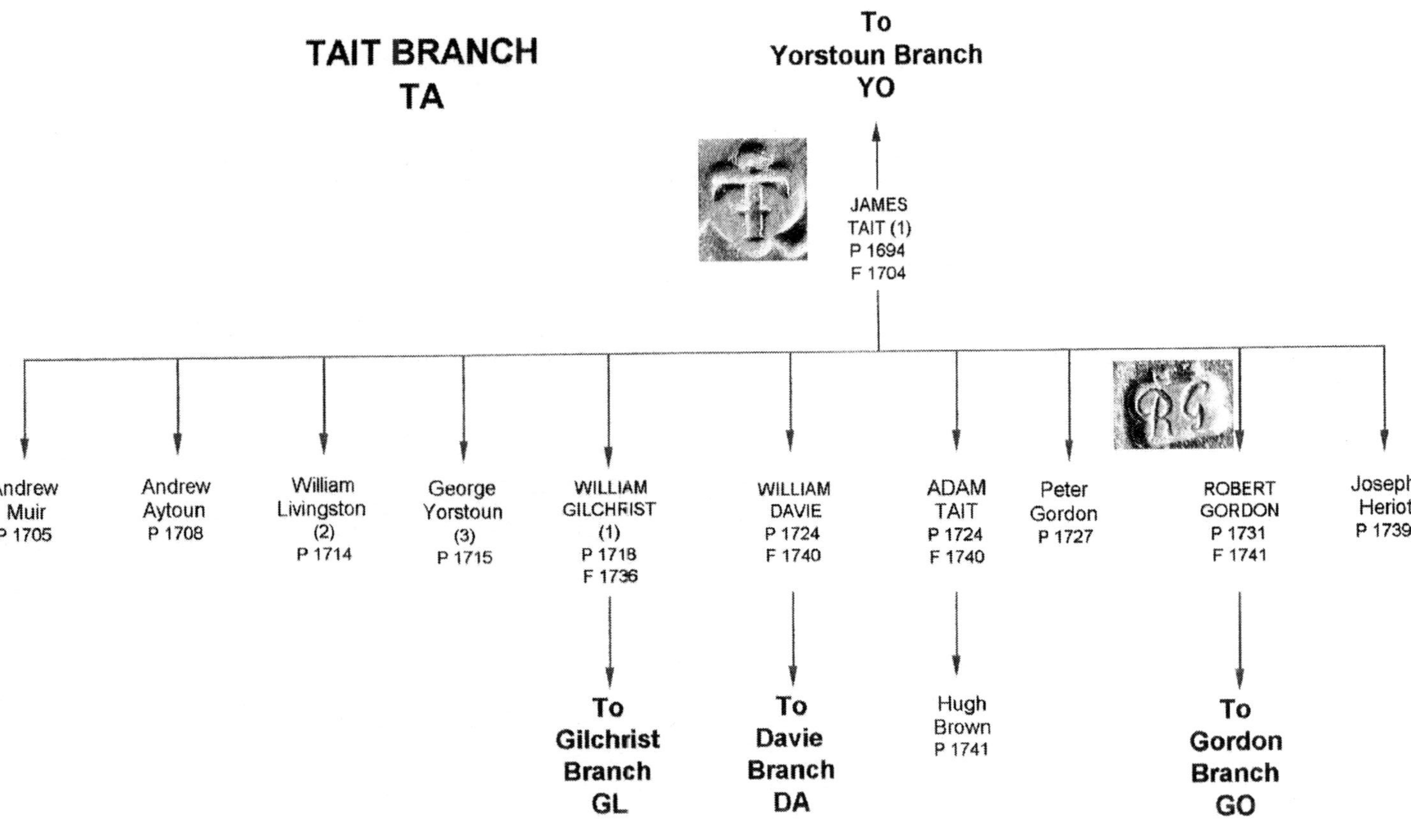

Thomas Mitchell Branch TM

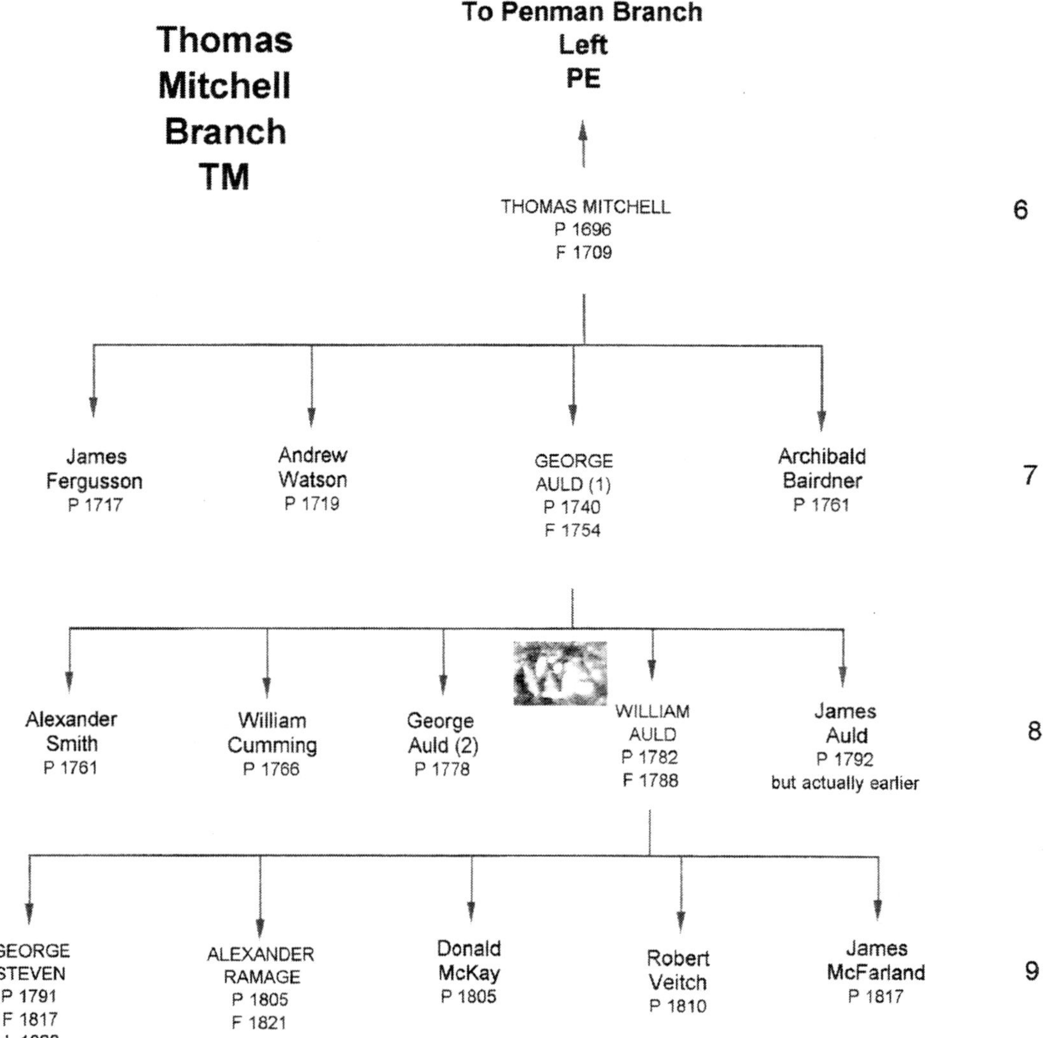

THREIPLAND-REID BRANCH TR

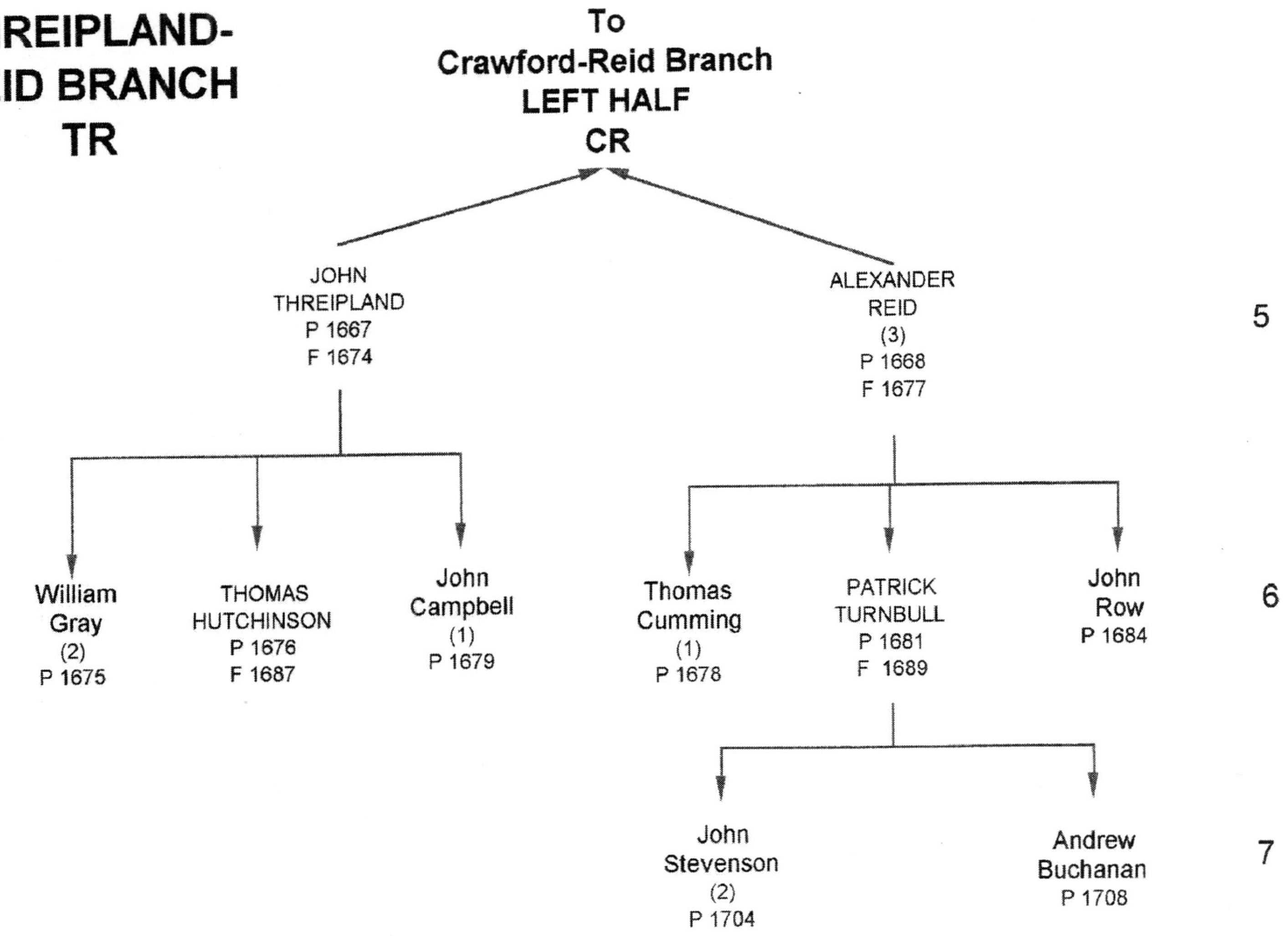

To
Crawford-Reid Branch
LEFT HALF
CR

JOHN THREIPLAND
P 1667
F 1674

ALEXANDER REID
(3)
P 1668
F 1677

5

William Gray
(2)
P 1675

THOMAS HUTCHINSON
P 1676
F 1687

John Campbell
(1)
P 1679

Thomas Cumming
(1)
P 1678

PATRICK TURNBULL
P 1681
F 1689

John Row
P 1684

6

John Stevenson
(2)
P 1704

Andrew Buchanan
P 1708

7

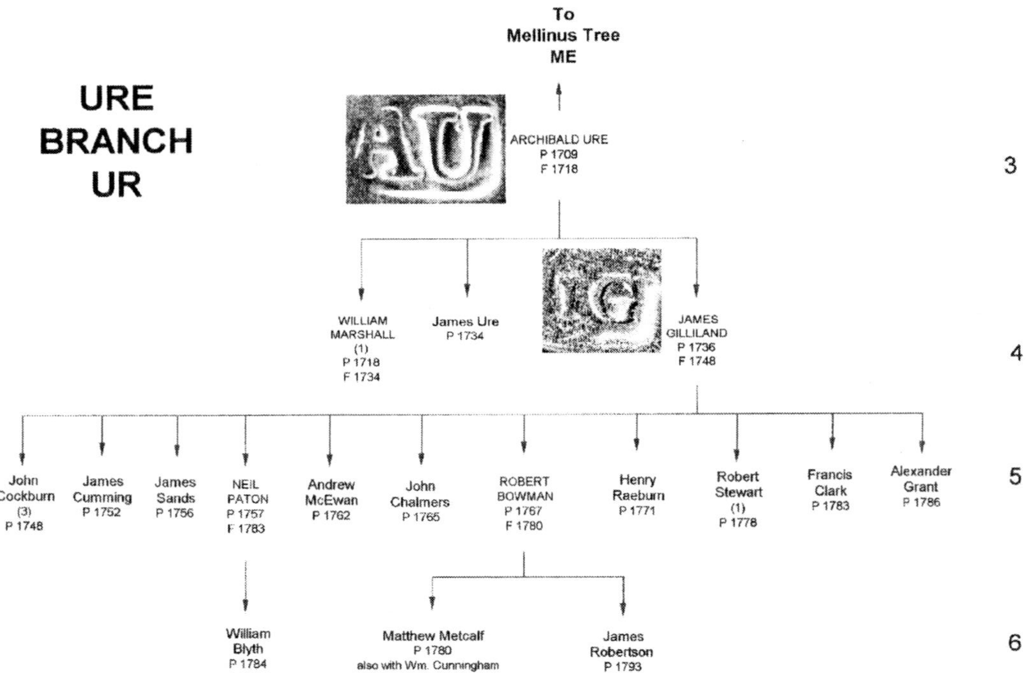
URE
BRANCH
UR
To
Mellinus Tree
ME
ARCHIBALD URE
P 1709
F 1718
3
WILLIAM
MARSHALL
(1)
P 1718
F 1734
James Ure
P 1734
JAMES
GILLILAND
P 1736
F 1748
4
John
Cockburn
(3)
P 1748
James
Cumming
P 1752
James
Sands
P 1756
NEIL
PATON
P 1757
F 1783
Andrew
McEwan
P 1762
John
Chalmers
P 1765
ROBERT
BOWMAN
P 1767
F 1780
Henry
Raeburn
P 1771
Robert
Stewart
(1)
P 1778
Francis
Clark
P 1783
Alexander
Grant
P 1786
5
William
Blyth
P 1784
Matthew Metcalf
P 1780
also with Wm. Cunningham
James
Robertson
P 1793
6

WALKER CRICHTON BRANCH WC

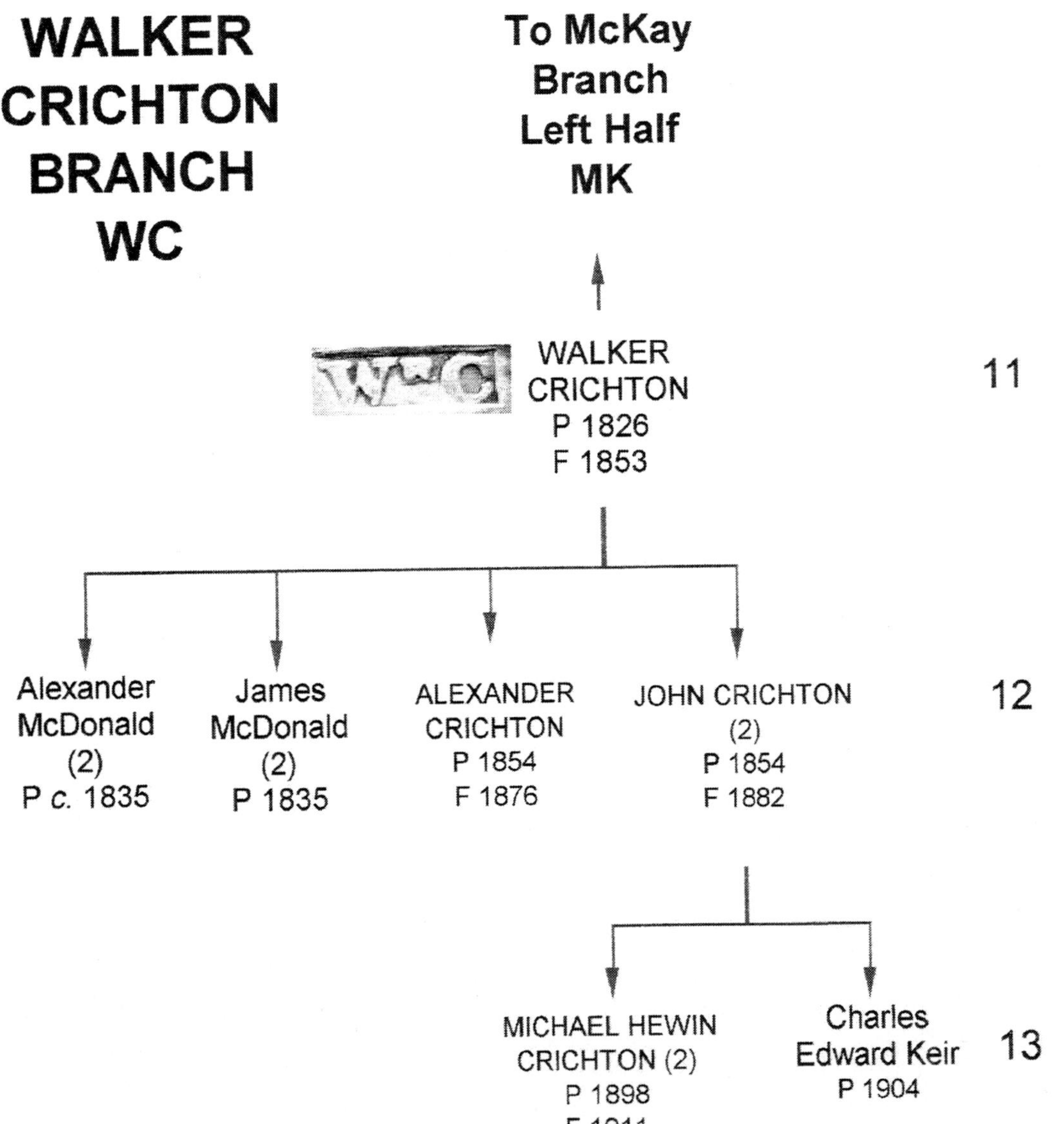

8

9

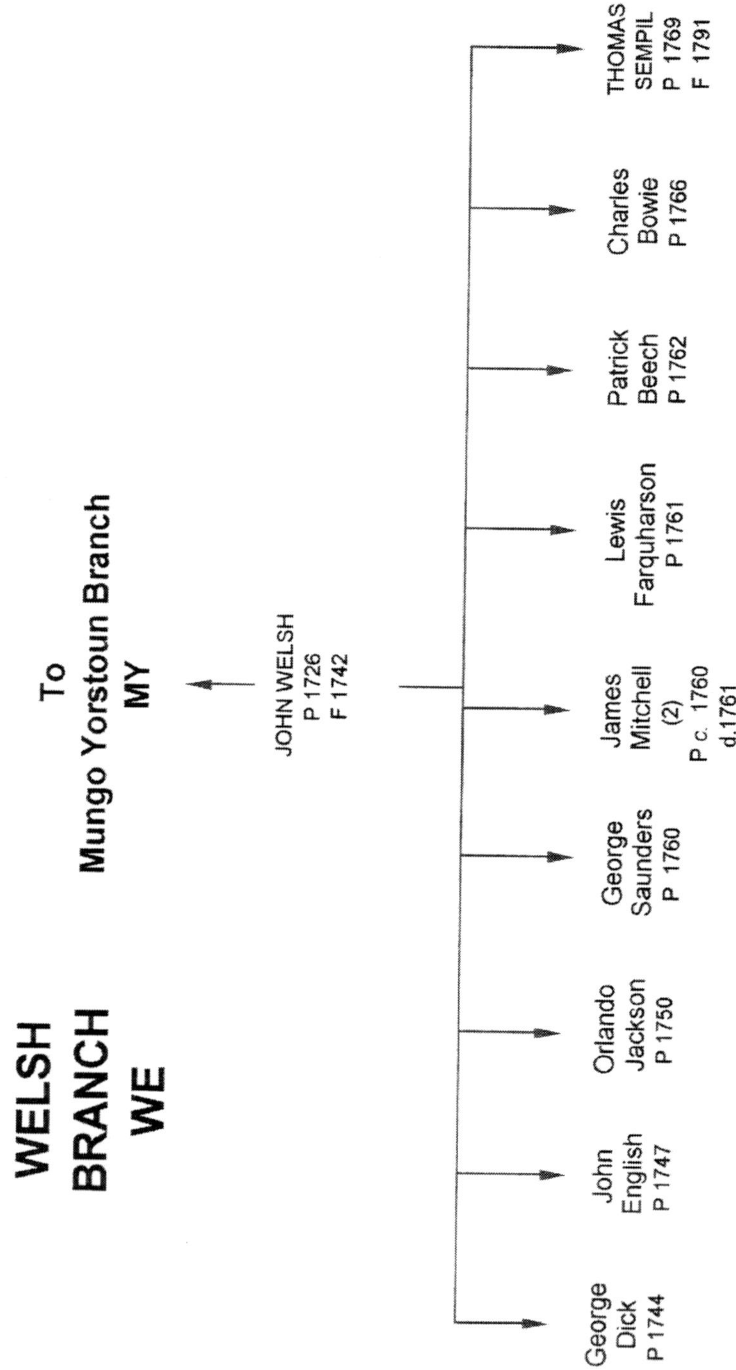

WELSH
BRANCH
WE
To
Mungo Yorstoun Branch
MY
JOHN WELSH
P 1726
F 1742
George
Dick
P 1744
John
English
P 1747
Orlando
Jackson
P 1750
George
Saunders
P 1760
James
Mitchell
(2)
P c. 1760
d.1761
Lewis
Farquharson
P 1761
Patrick
Beech
P 1762
Charles
Bowie
P 1766
THOMAS
SEMPIL
P 1769
F 1791

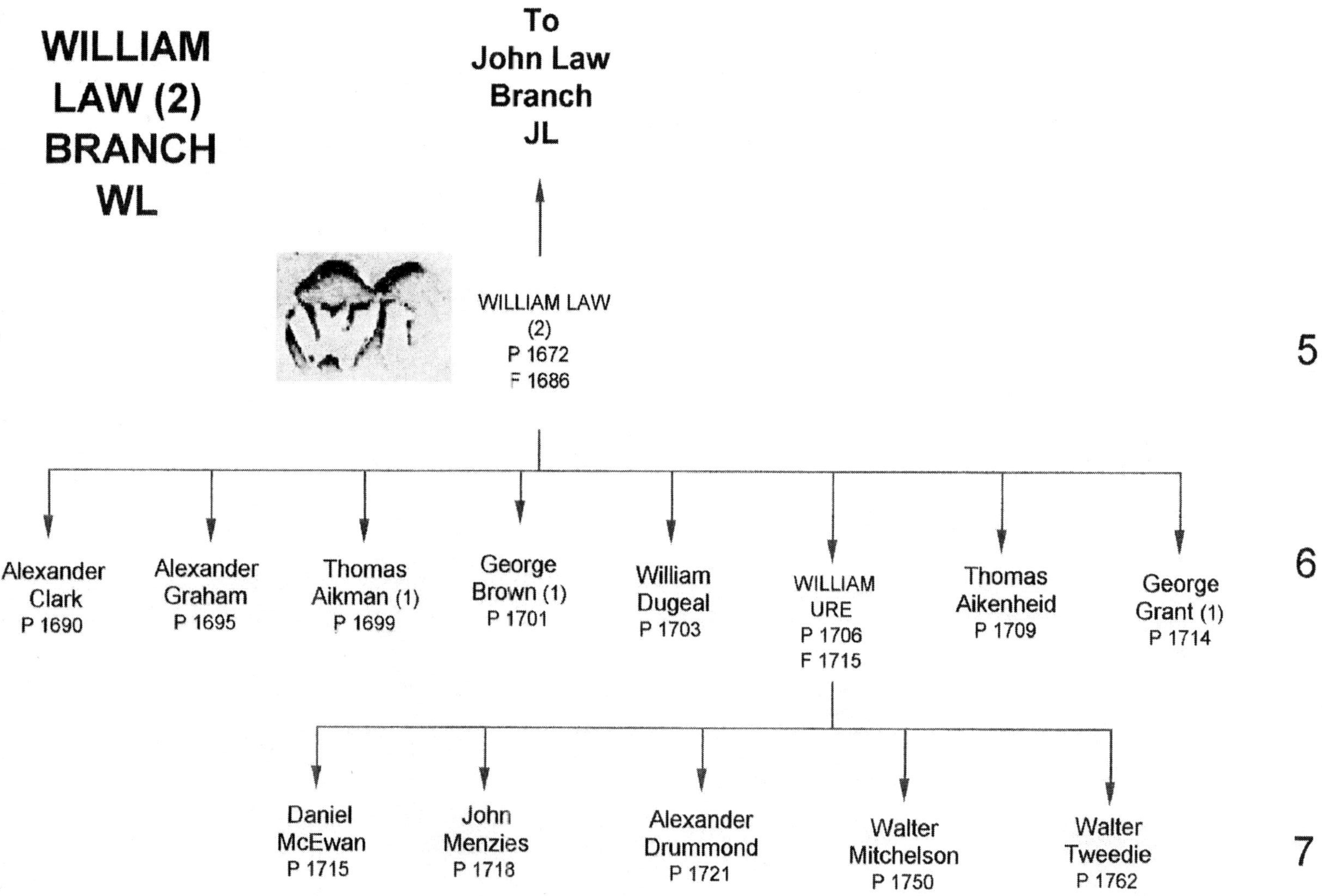
WILLIAM LAW (2) BRANCH WL
To John Law Branch JL
WILLIAM LAW (2) P 1672 F 1686
5
Alexander Clark P 1690
Alexander Graham P 1695
Thomas Aikman (1) P 1699
George Brown (1) P 1701
William Dugeal P 1703
WILLIAM URE P 1706 F 1715
Thomas Aikenheid P 1709
George Grant (1) P 1714
6
Daniel McEwan P 1715
John Menzies P 1718
Alexander Drummond P 1721
Walter Mitchelson P 1750
Walter Tweedie P 1762
7

WILLIAM TAYLOR BRANCH WT

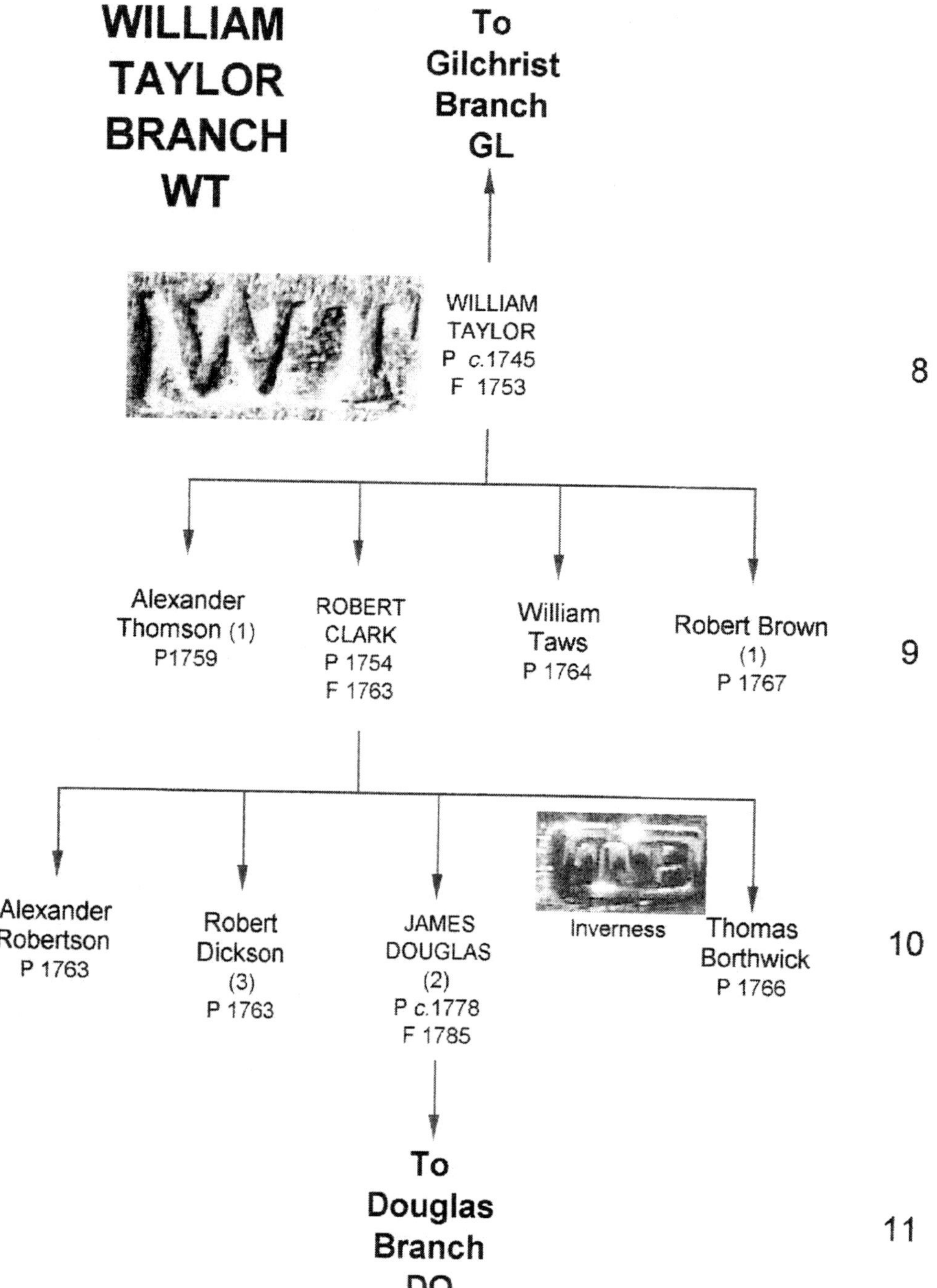

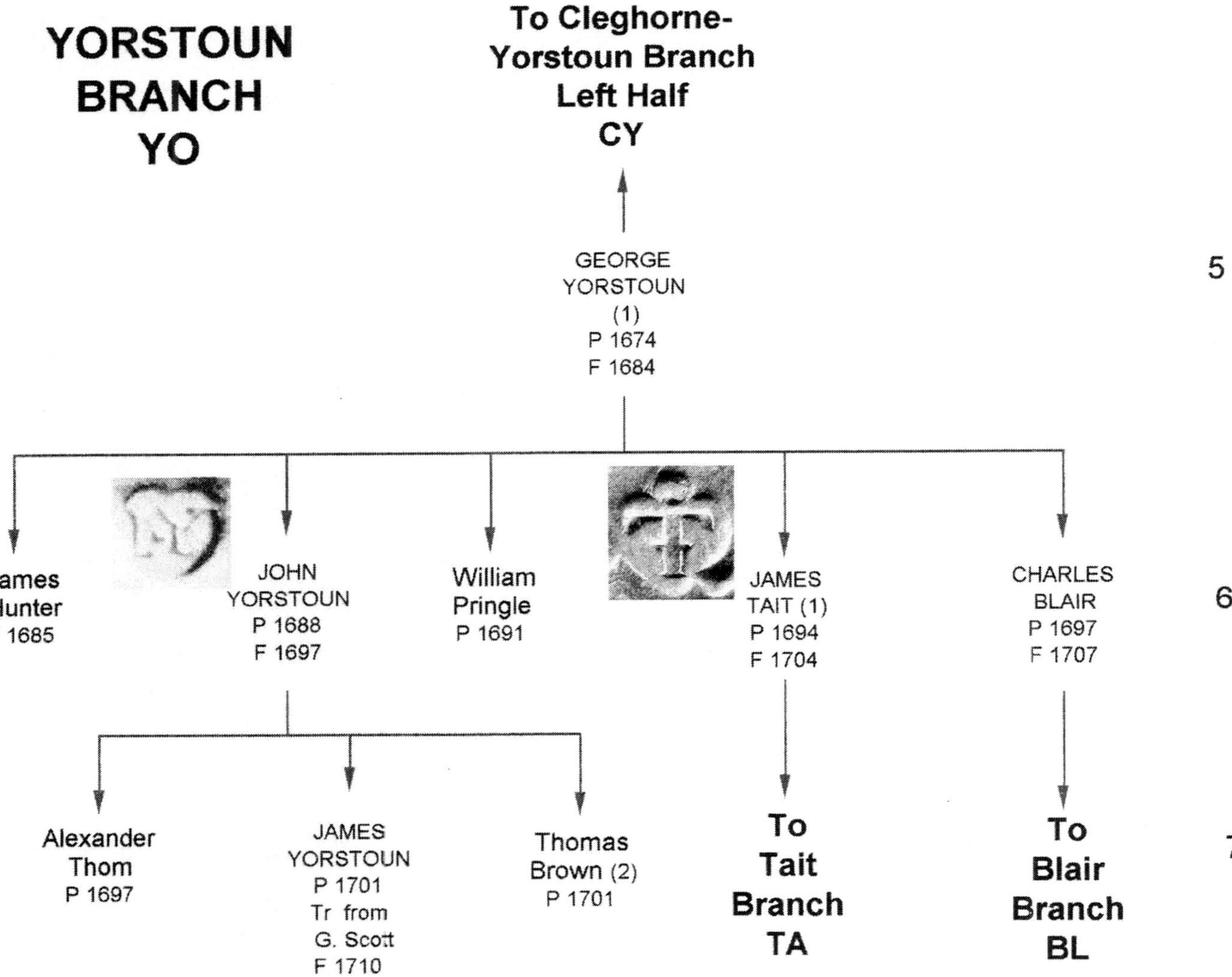

YORSTOUN
BRANCH
YO
To Cleghorne-
Yorstoun Branch
Left Half
CY
GEORGE
YORSTOUN
(1)
P 1674
F 1684
5
James
Hunter
P 1685
JOHN
YORSTOUN
P 1688
F 1697
William
Pringle
P 1691
JAMES
TAIT (1)
P 1694
F 1704
CHARLES
BLAIR
P 1697
F 1707
6
Alexander
Thom
P 1697
JAMES
YORSTOUN
P 1701
Tr from
G. Scott
F 1710
Thomas
Brown (2)
P 1701
To
Tait
Branch
TA
To
Blair
Branch
BL
7

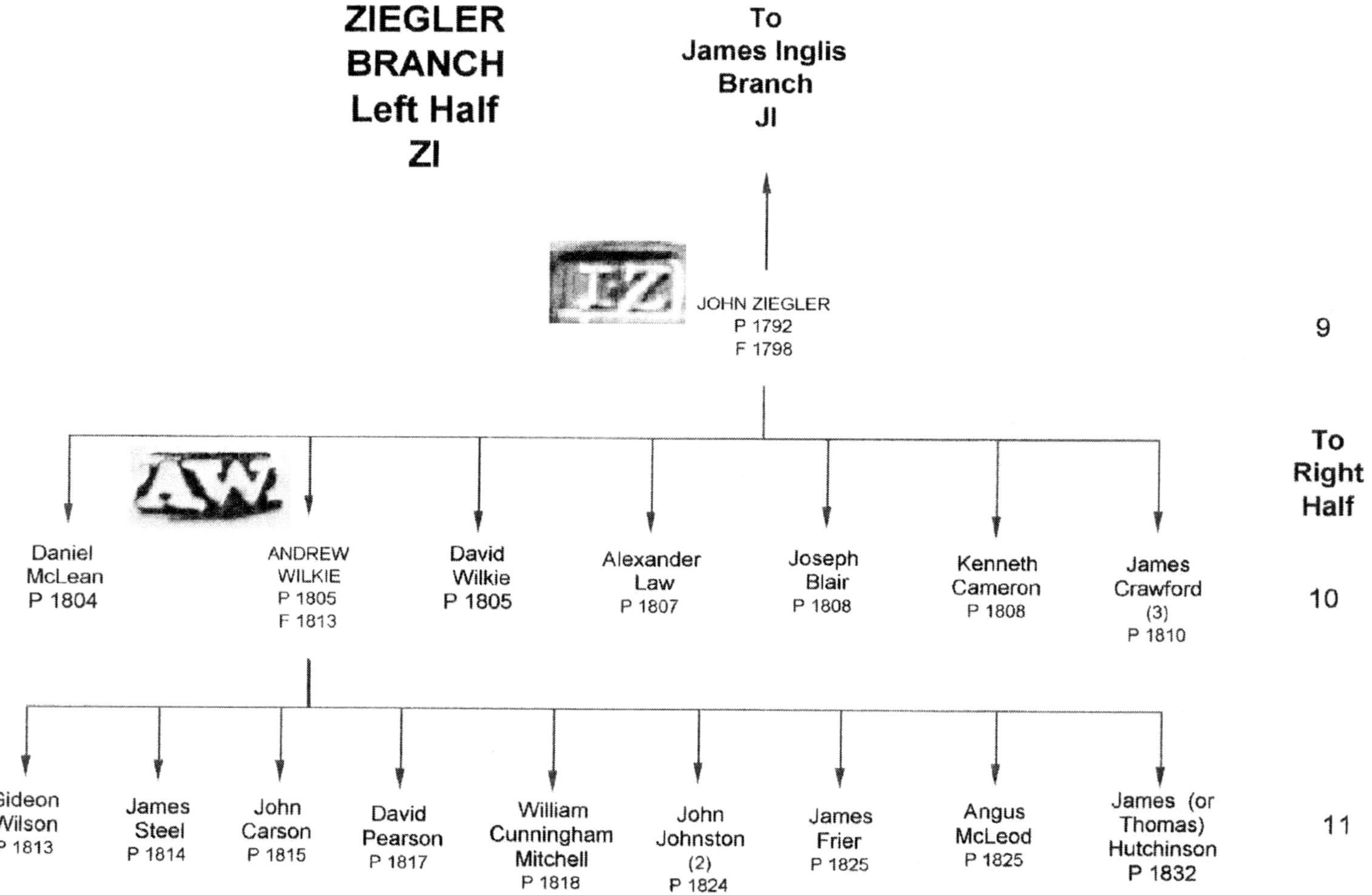
ZIEGLER
BRANCH
Left Half
ZI
To
James Inglis
Branch
JI
JOHN ZIEGLER
P 1792
F 1798
9
To
Right
Half
Daniel McLean P 1804
ANDREW WILKIE P 1805 F 1813
David Wilkie P 1805
Alexander Law P 1807
Joseph Blair P 1808
Kenneth Cameron P 1808
James Crawford (3) P 1810
10
Gideon Wilson P 1813
James Steel P 1814
John Carson P 1815
David Pearson P 1817
William Cunningham Mitchell P 1818
John Johnston (2) P 1824
James Frier P 1825
Angus McLeod P 1825
James (or Thomas) Hutchinson P 1832
11

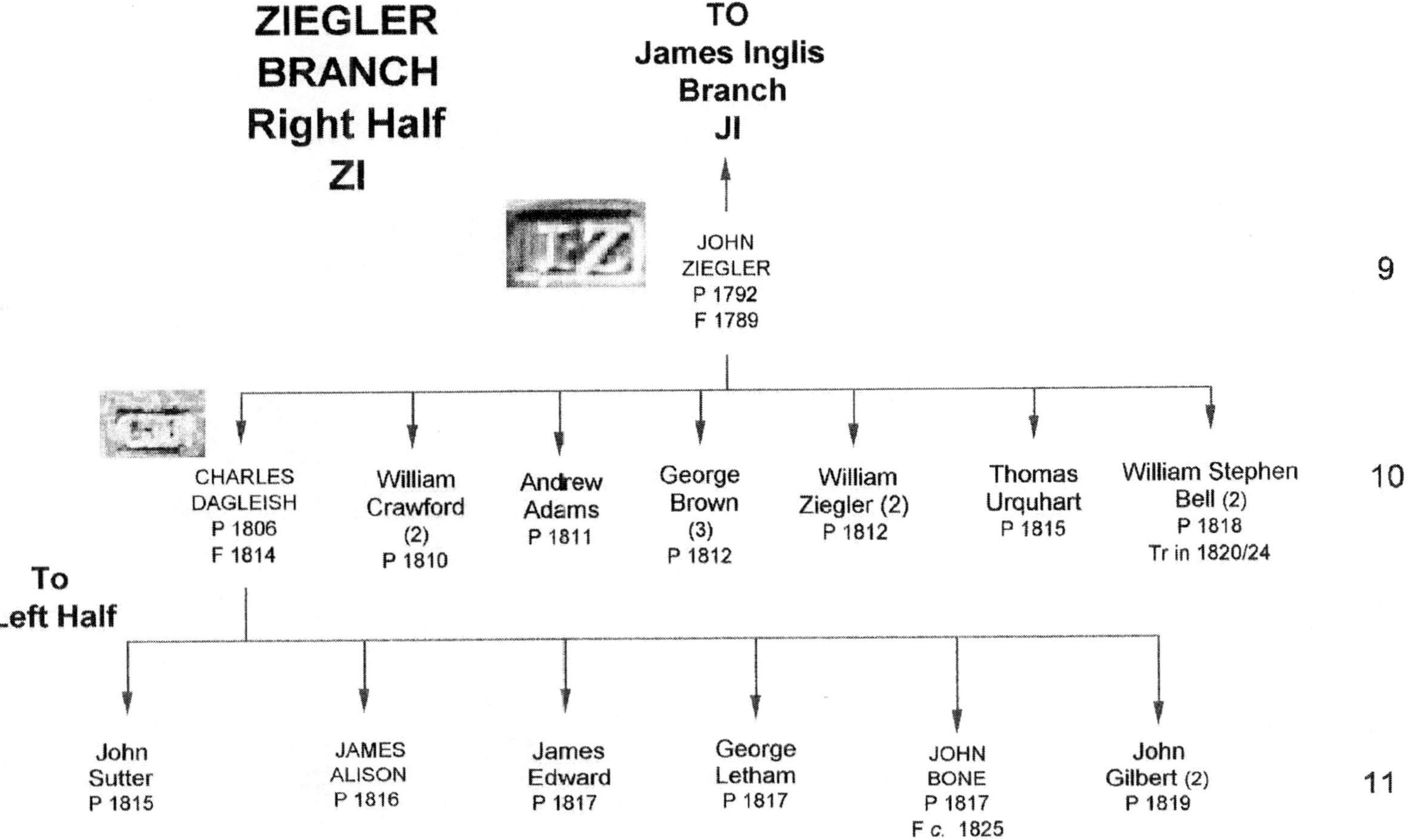
ZIEGLER
BRANCH
Right Half
ZI
TO
James Inglis
Branch
JI
JOHN
ZIEGLER
P 1792
F 1789
9
CHARLES
DAGLEISH
P 1806
F 1814
William
Crawford
(2)
P 1810
Andrew
Adams
P 1811
George
Brown
(3)
P 1812
William
Ziegler (2)
P 1812
Thomas
Urquhart
P 1815
William Stephen
Bell (2)
P 1818
Tr in 1820/24
10
To
Left Half
John
Sutter
P 1815
JAMES
ALISON
P 1816
James
Edward
P 1817
George
Letham
P 1817
JOHN
BONE
P 1817
F c. 1825
John
Gilbert (2)
P 1819
11

Assayed Output of Edinburgh Freemen Including Charts

Comparative Charts for Forty Freemen

The following four charts were constructed from data collected by Henry Steuart Fothringham taken from two of the Edinburgh Incorporation of Goldsmiths' Assay Master's Accounts volumes covering the years 1681-82 to 1701-02. The charts are divided alphabetically into groups of 10 goldsmiths per chart. The raw data was entered in the Incorporation volumes as the number of parcels presented at the assay office and the number of ounces assayed each year per freeman. In determining the annual averages of output some data were excluded. For example, if the freeman had less than three full years as a freeman and that included a partial year of less than six months, the partial year was not included in the calculation since this would unduly skew the per annum average. Additionally, widow's records were not included with the relevant freeman (e.g. Edward Cleghorne, William Law, George Yorstoun and Thomas Yorstoun) since this would have complicated interpretation of the freeman's actual output.

Utility and Restrictions of the Data

While the charts offer the opportunity to compare the output of approximately 10% of all the freemen in Edinburgh, this should be approached with some caution. Recognition of where the freeman's career fell relative to the 21 year period of data collection can be important. For example, a subset of the freemen included in these charts either began their career near the end of the period considered (e.g. Edward Penman) or ended a long distinguished career at the very beginning of the data collection years (e.g. Edward Cleghorne (1) and Alexander Reid (2)). In these cases, the annual average presented here may not reflect the output of these freemen either at the height of their careers or as averaged across the entire duration of their working period.

Interpreting the Data and Relevance to Collecting Today

Despite the restrictions mentioned, some patterns and trends are obvious. For example, George Main and Robert Inglis had parallel careers in terms of working period and in the training of important apprentices. Yet, their output of assayed silver was remarkably different. As is discussed in Dietert and Dietert *Silver Studies*, 2006, George Main was the postmaster of Scotland and appeared to have made his money in other trading related ventures. Between those obligations and possibly the predominant production of jewelry rather than hollowware in his shop, he sent only about 5% of the silver for assay when compared to Inglis. Nevertheless, George Main was an influential and apparently respected freeman and did serve as deacon of the Incorporation. In contrast with George Main and other lower-impact freemen like Adam Gordon, William Burton and William Wallace, other freemen were exceptional craftsmen who dominated the Edinburgh silver market over the period considered. These included James Cockburn, James Penman, Edward Cleghorne (1), Robert Bruce, Robert Inglis, Alexander Forbes, William Law (1), Colin McKenzie, Thomas Ker, and James Seaton. These men were among the elite craftsmen of the late 17th century. This hierarchy of contemporary output is fully consistent with the extant silver that has been catalogued for these freemen in the *Compendium of Scottish Silver*. Extant late 17th century silver is dominated by the very group of freemen with the highest output during the period from 1681-1702. As expected, little silver is seen from freemen like George Main, William Wallace and Adam Gordon.

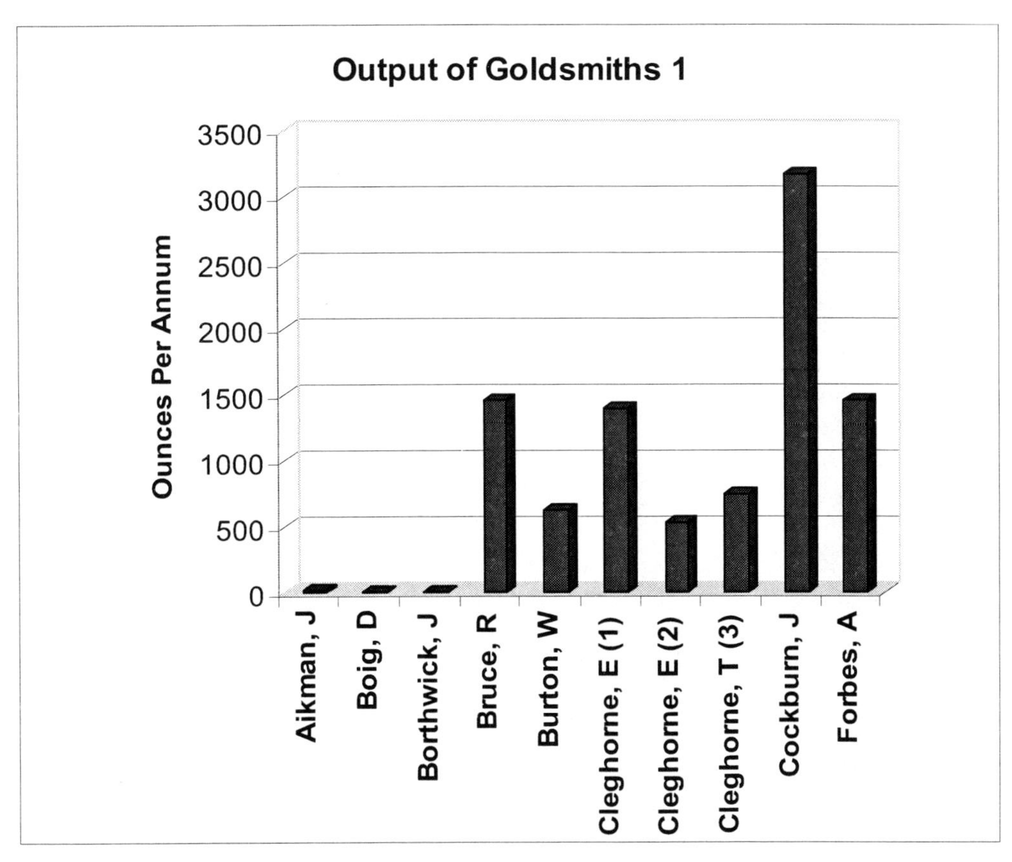
Output of Goldsmiths 1
Ounces Per Annum
3500
3000
2500
2000
1500
1000
500
0
Aikman, J
Boig, D
Borthwick, J
Bruce, R
Burton, W
Cleghorne, E (1)
Cleghorne, E (2)
Cleghorne, T (3)
Cockburn, J
Forbes, A

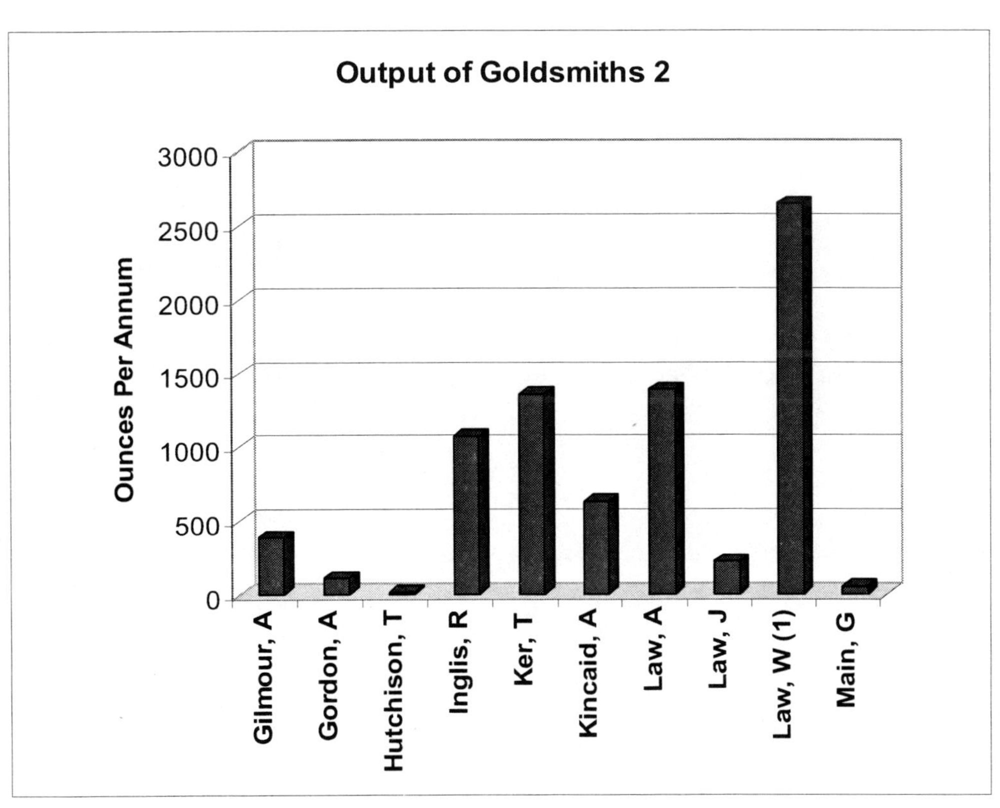
Output of Goldsmiths 2
Ounces Per Annum
3000
2500
2000
1500
1000
500
0
Gilmour, A
Gordon, A
Hutchison, T
Inglis, R
Ker, T
Kincaid, A
Law, A
Law, J
Law, W (1)
Main, G

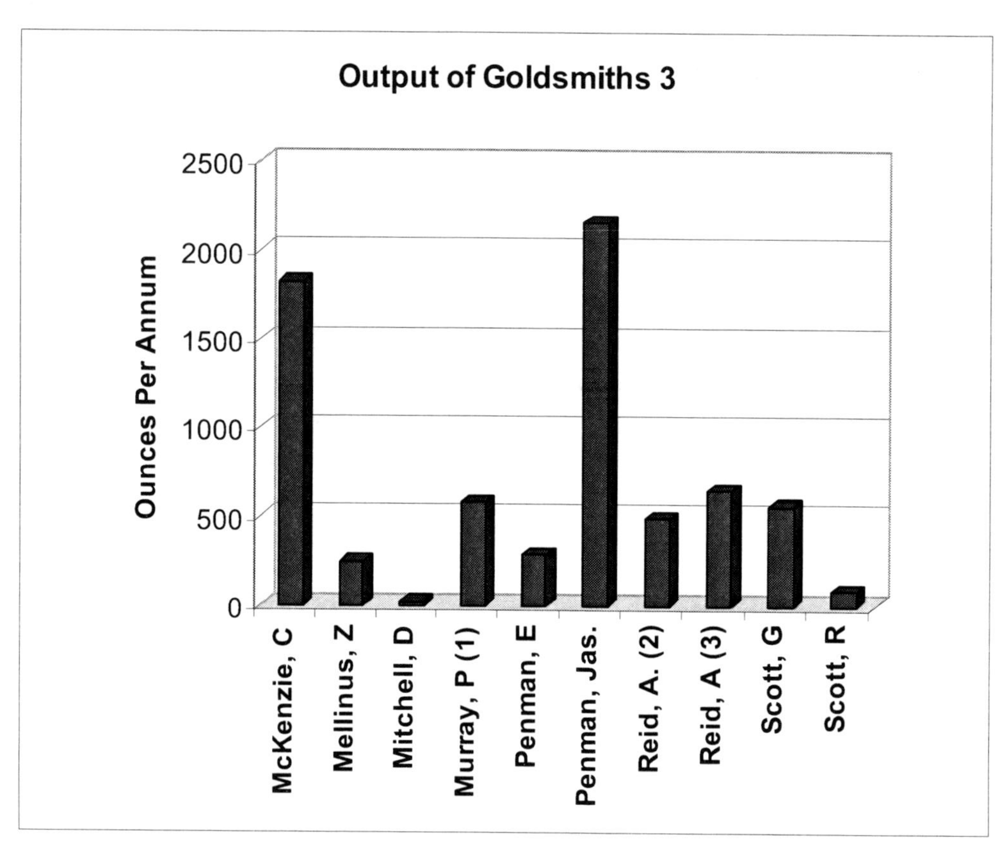
Output of Goldsmiths 3
Ounces Per Annum
2500
2000
1500
1000
500
0
McKenzie, C
Mellinus, Z
Mitchell, D
Murray, P (1)
Penman, E
Penman, Jas.
Reid, A. (2)
Reid, A (3)
Scott, G
Scott, R

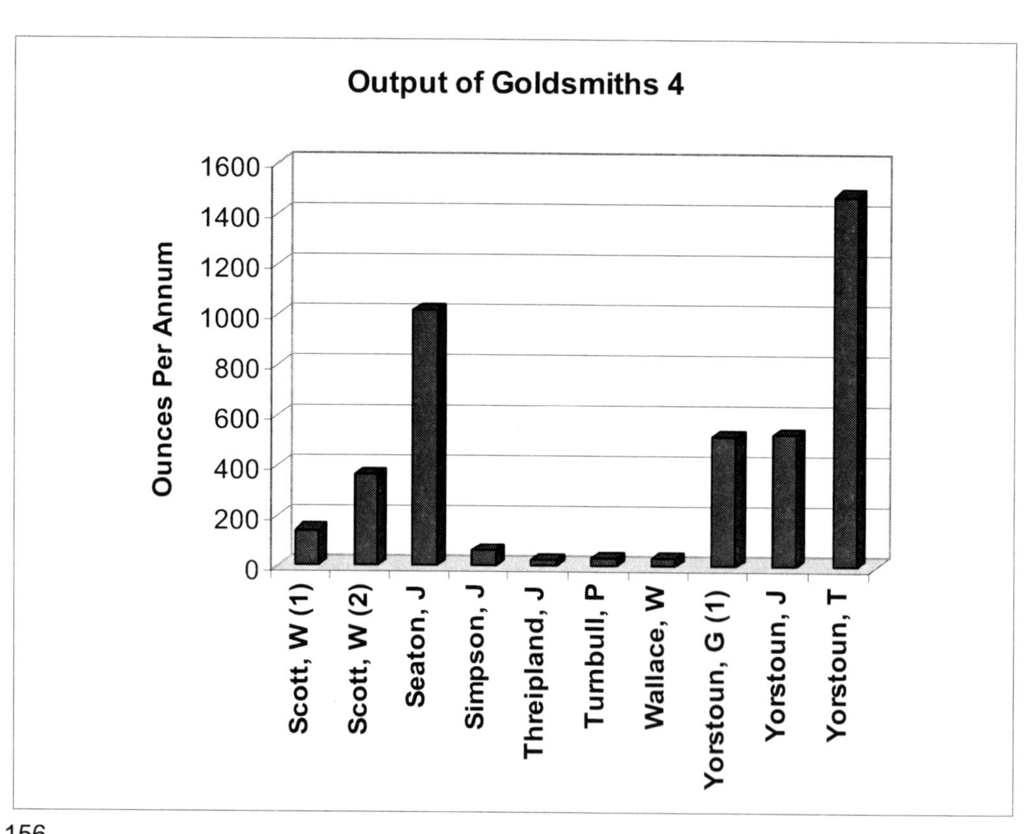
Output of Goldsmiths 4
Ounces Per Annum
1600
1400
1200
1000
800
600
400
200
0
Scott, W (1)
Scott, W (2)
Seaton, J
Simpson, J
Threipland, J
Turnbull, P
Wallace, W
Yorstoun, G (1)
Yorstoun, J
Yorstoun, T

Number of Freemen Goldsmiths Compared to the Population of Edinburgh*

The following table shows a comparison of the approximate number of Edinburgh freemen goldsmiths compared to the approximate Edinburgh population between the years 1525 and 1953. Both the ratio of numbers of freemen to 10,000 residents and the percentage of the 1525 ratio are shown for comparison. Note there was relative stability in the ratio from the 17th century to the mid-18th century. But after Culloden in 1746 and the subsequent land confiscation, there was a sharp decline in the numbers of freemen per 10,000 residents. Part of this was due to various economic factors in Scotland as well as heightened competition from other goldsmithing centers such as London and Glasgow. But an additional factor contributing to the decline was a change in town rules leading to an increased percentage of unfree men working as goldsmiths and jewelers in Edinburgh. This was most apparent from 1790 on.

	Approximate # Freemen	Approximate Edinburgh Population	# Freemen/ 10,000 Residents	Percentage of the 1525 Ratio
1525	16	*c.* 12,000**	13.3	100
1560	18	15,000	12.0	90
1600	23	20,000	11.5	86
1630	28	*c.* 30,000**	9.3	70
1694	29	47,000	6.2	47
1730	34	*c.* 53,000**	6.4	48
1755	35	57,000	6.1	46
1791	23	82,000	2.8	21
1821	23	112,000	2.3	17
1851	32	160,000	2.1	16
1881	15	228,000	0.7	5
1901	19	317,000	0.6	5
1931	12	440,000	0.3	2
1953	5	455,000	0.1	1

* Population numbers for 1755-1953 are derived from the Edinburgh City Council population statistics. The 1560 estimate is from W. Stanford Reid, 1973. The 1600 estimate from Prof. Keith Brown, "Crown and Clans - A Nation Left to Its Demons" 8 June 2003. The Scotsman. The 1694 estimate is from Helen M. Dingwall, 1994. Note some later population estimates may include Leith.

** Interpolated estimates: for the year 1525 of between 10K (1500) and 15K (1560), for the year 1630 of between 20K (1600) and 47K (1694) and for the year 1730 of between 47K (1694) and 57K (1755).

Demographics of Apprentices and Freemen: Their Father and/or Mother Did Matter

Guide to Family Data

Who Were the Apprentices and How Were They Selected?

Research into the families of individual apprentices and freemen will be reported in detail in the second volume of this book series. Understanding family associations as related to the goldsmiths is important not only for genealogical research but also as it pertained to the booking of apprentices. As will be shown in volume II of this series, apprentices were not booked randomly but rather were usually a son, cousin, nephew or more distant relative of the master, a neighbor from the village of the master's origin or connected to the master via family business ventures. Family relationships based on maternal lines were at least as important as the father's, if not more so, when compared to paternal relationships. Additionally, maternal line relationships cannot be identified by a cursory comparison of apprentice and freeman surnames.

Individual vs. Group Information on Families

Family information in volume II will be important for those interested in identifying and/or tracking ancestors or in understanding family structure among known ancestors. However, the composite results for the apprentices and freemen as groups were quite telling and are presented here.

Database for the Demographic Comparisons

Incorporation, town and parish records have been valuable resources for the purpose of examining family structures. Historical records such as the booking of apprentices, the granting of freedom by the Incorporation and the awarding of town burgess tickets as well as the recording of births, baptisms and marriages have provided a significant amount of information concerning the families of these individuals. For example, at least some family information has been catalogued for approximately 90% of all the goldsmiths' apprentices. Additionally, the father's profession or status was found for greater than 75% of the apprentices and freemen. The more than 900 fathers represented in the analysis of professions provides a rich data set for comparing the father's status as a general factor in determining the booking of apprentices and the probability of the son becoming a freeman of the City of Edinburgh Incorporation of Goldsmiths. Beyond that, there are approximately 154 different job titles represented among the 900-plus fathers of the apprentices.

Professions Represented

A glossary of the professions is provided on succeeding pages. Several "job" titles such as Baxter and baker could be linked or pooled together. Others reflected slightly different positions surrounding a related occupational goal (e.g. farmer vs. fermorer). Obviously in later years, newer professions such as "gas manager" or tobacco "auctioneer" emerged that were not specified in the 1500s. While the range of professions represented was huge [see the Table of Professions], only a few were really significant among the group of apprentices and freemen.

Key Professions and/or Societal Status

Comparisons of the profession and/or social status are shown in two charts. One includes the data for all apprentices and freemen combined. The second shows the results only for those apprentices who became freemen. A comparison of the two may be pertinent to issues concerning the required burgess ticket, financing of the shop and patron support for work. All of these were needed to establish a viable business as a freeman goldsmith.

Three professions/societal status groups are overwhelmingly predominant among fathers of the apprentices and freemen. The largest group was the goldsmiths themselves (19%). These are followed by a group comprising landed individuals and including the titled lords, landed gentry and significant property owners (16%). The third significant group of fathers was the merchants (13%). Higher education was a plus as a goldsmith so it is not surprising that the sons of lawyers (including the group of advocates called writers) as well as teachers/professors, and the clergy were somewhat represented particularly if considered together. Other Hammermen such as wrights also had greater than 1% of the proportion and tailors were also above 1%. But few other professions had a real impact.

Family Success

If the data for freemen alone are compared against the larger group of apprentices plus freemen, then the same three groups (goldsmiths, landed gentry and merchants) are still the most prevalent. No other group even comes close to these. However, the relative proportions among the top three father's professions are dramatically changed when only freemen are considered. The landed gentry and the merchants had almost the identical percentages as were found for the fathers of combined apprentices and freemen (13-15%). But the goldsmiths were almost 40% of the fathers of freemen. Some artificial skewing of the data is possible since it might be more likely that a freeman's son would have been identified as such in the Incorporation's records. However, that possible bias is unlikely to explain the doubling of the percentage among goldsmith's sons for those apprentices granted their freedom vs. the combined apprentice-freeman group. This suggests that having a goldsmith for a father was a positive factor in a son remaining in Edinburgh and at least starting his career as a freeman. As a group, a greater percentage of sons of landed gentry and merchants may well have 1) followed careers closer to their father's work, 2) become established as journeyman goldsmiths or 3) become goldsmiths outside of Edinburgh.

ALL FATHER'S PROFESSIONS

PROFESSION	COUNT
Advocate	5
Aide	1
Apothecary	1
Attorney	1
Auctioneer	2
Baillie	2
Bank messenger	1
Banker	1
Barber	15
Baxter, Baker	1
Becker	1
Book seller	2
Bookbinder	2
Booker	1
Bottle blower	1
Box keeper	6
Brewer	6
Builder	3
Burgess	38
Butcher	1
Butler	3
Cabinetmaker	5
Candlemaker	1
Carpenter	1
Carter	1
Carver	2
Causeway layer	1
Chairmaster	1
Clerk	4
Coachman	2
Contractor	1
Cook	1
Cooper	1
Coppersmith	1
Cork cutter	1
Dagmaker, dagmaster	1
Distiller	1
Doctor of Medicine	2
Doorkeeper for Exchequer	1
Doctor	1
Draper	1
Dressmaker	1

ALL FATHER'S PROFESSIONS (cont)

PROFESSION	COUNT
Dressmaker	1
Drummer	1
Engraver	1
Factor to General	1
Farmer	19
Farrier	1
Feltmaker	1
Fermourner	5
Feuar	1
Fishing rod maker	3
Flaxdresser	2
Flesher	1
Gardener	7
Gas manager	1
Gilder	2
Glassblower	1
Glazer	1
Glover	4
Goldsmith	182
Grocer	6
Guideman	1
Guild officer	1
Haberdasher	1
Hatter	1
Indweller	18
Innkeeper	2
Jeweler	6
Joiner	1
Keeper of gowns	2
Labourer	1
Laird	2
Landed gentry	152
Land surveyor	1
Lapidary	1
Linen printer	1
Litster, Dyer	8
Lorymer	1
Malt maker	1
Maltman	3
Manufacturer	3
Mariner	1
Mason	5
Master of the Revels	1
Master waker	1
Merchant	127

ALL FATHER'S PROFESSIONS (cont)

PROFESSION	COUNT
Military	9
Minister	21
Music-master	1
Nailer	1
Of that Ilk	2
Officer in Customs	1
Officer in Excise office	4
Overseer of salmon fishing	1
Painter	4
Pawnbroker	4
Pewterer, Peuterer	2
Port seller	1
Porter	2
Portioner	5
Printer	3
Professor of music	1
Quarrier	1
Riding officer	1
Saddler	4
Sawyer	3
Schoolmaster	2
Sculptor	1
Servant	5
Servitor	2
Sheriff	1
Shipmaster	3
Shoemaker, Cordiner	2
Sievewright	1
Silk Dyer	1
Silver engraver	1
Silver plater	2
Silversmith	6
Skinner	4
Skipper	3
Slater	1
Smith	7
Spirit dealer	5
Stabler	3
Staymaker	1
Tacksman	1
Tailor	23
Tanner	1
Tavern keeper	1
Teacher of English	1
Tenant	10
Ticket porter	1
Tobacconist	1
Toll keeper	1

ALL FATHER'S PROFESSIONS (cont)

PROFESSION	COUNT
Toolmaker	2
Town clerk	2
Treasurer	1
Turnkey, Jailer	1
Victual maker	1
Vintner	14
Watchcase maker	1
Watchmaker	2
Weatherglass manufacturer	2
Weaver	10
Wheelwright	1
Whiteiron smith	1
Wigmaker	2
Wine cooper	1
Wooden clockmaker	1
Wool merchant	1
Workman	1
Wright	20
Writer	18
Writer to the Signet	8
Total	**959**

MOST FREQUENT FATHER'S PROFESSIONS OVERALL

PROFESSIONS	PERCENTAGE
Barber	1.56
Burgess	3.96
Farmer	1.98
Goldsmith	18.96
Indweller	1.88
Landed gentry	15.83
Merchant	13.23
Tailor	2.40
Tenant	1.04
Vintner	1.46
Weaver	1.04
Wright	2.08
Writer	1.88

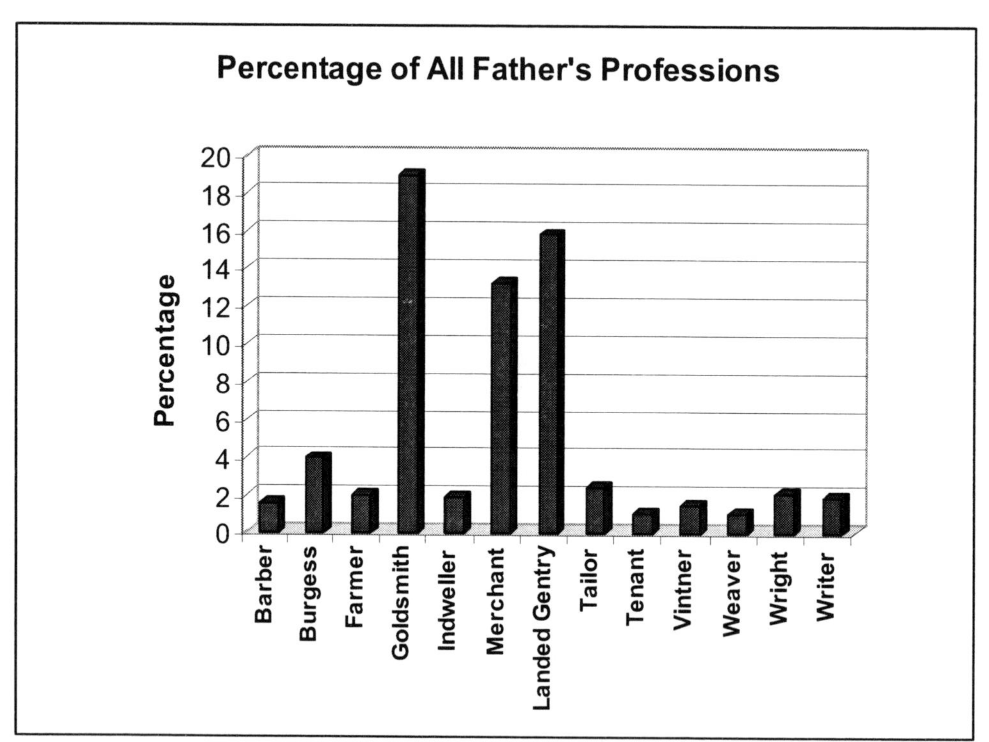

FREEMEN FATHER'S PROFESSIONS

PROFESSIONS	COUNT
Advocate	1
Baillie	2
Bank messenger	1
Barber	1
Baxter, Baker	6
Book seller	1
Brewer	3
Builder	1
Brass Founder	1
Cabinet maker	1
Candlemaker	1
Carter	1
Clerk	1
Cook	1
Cooper	1
Engraver	1
Factor to General	1
Farmer	4
Fermourner, Fermerer	2
Fishing rod maker	1
Gardener	2
Gas manager	1
Glover	1
Goldsmith	125
Indweller	2
Joiner	1
Landed gentry	46
Litster, Dyer, Dyster	2
Lorymer	1
Maltman	2
Mason	2
Merchant	43
Military	1
Minister	8
Music-master	1
Painter	2
Pewterer, Peuterer	1
Portioner	1
Professor of music	1
Saddler	1
Sawyer	1
Schoolmaster	1
Shipmaster	1
Shoemaker, Cordiner	1

FREEMEN FATHER'S PROFESSIONS (cont)

PROFESSIONS	COUNT
Skinner	1
Skipper	1
Smith	4
Spirit dealer	2
Tailor	11
Teacher of English	1
Tenant	2
Victual maker	1
Vintner	1
Weaver	2
Wigmaker	2
Wooden clockmaker	1
Wright	5
Writer	3
Total	**317**

MOST COMMON FATHER'S PROFESSIONS AMONG FREEMEN

PROFESSIONS	PERCENTAGE
Baxter, Baker	1.89
Goldsmith	39.43
Landed gentry	14.51
Merchant	13.56
Tailor	3.47
Wright	1.58

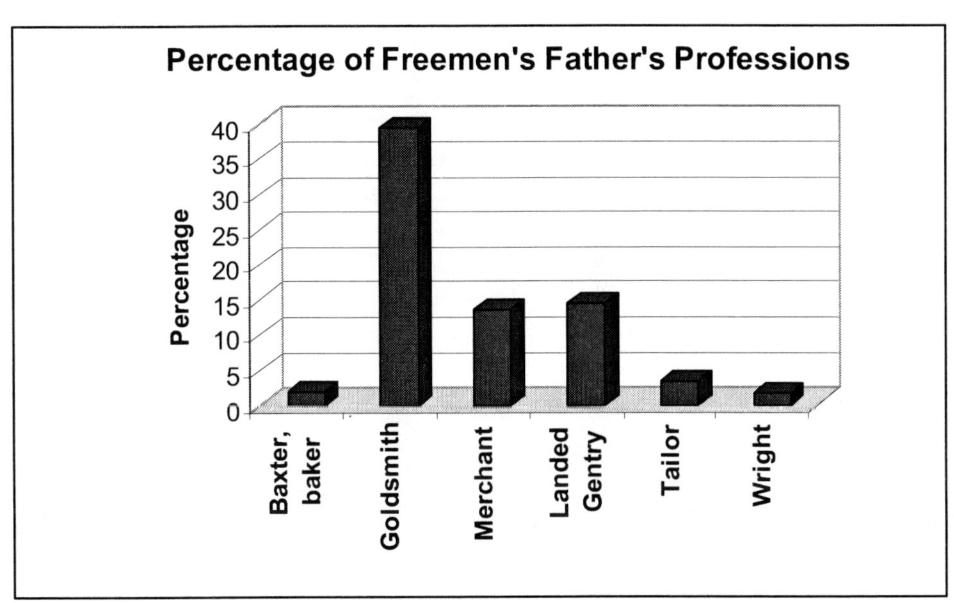

Edinburgh Apprentices Working Elsewhere

One of the interesting observations in examining the more than 1100 Edinburgh-trained apprentices to goldsmiths and freemen was that the number of freemen goldsmiths in the city itself was remarkably static even over centuries. Between 1525 and 1900 the number of freemen ranged from a low of about 15 to a high of approximately 35. This meant that even as the population increased dramatically, the support for these craftsmen as business owners was not growing at the same rate. As a result, many talented apprentices completing their indentures were left with the options of pursuing a long-term career as a journeyman in a freeman's shop or working as a goldsmith elsewhere. The expansion of British Empire around the globe brought excellent opportunity for the latter. The following table provides a list of Edinburgh apprentices, journeymen, and some freemen who were either known to have worked in the trade elsewhere or whose names and working periods match those of foreign goldsmiths and jewelers suspected of emigrating from Scotland. They are arranged chronologically by the beginning year of their indentures (Indent.) in Edinburgh. Note that the appearance of one of these goldsmiths in foreign lands does not necessarily reflect their immigration and establishment of a business. For example, the Edinburgh apprentice and Glasgow goldsmith, James Napier, apparently traveled to South Carolina briefly in conjunction with his brother's death and the probate of his will. But he never worked there as a goldsmith. Others may have had temporary business dealings in British colonies and not necessarily established permanent shops. Still others may have returned to Britain after brief stays or emigrated late in life in retirement. It is hoped that the information in the following table will help spur a more detailed examination of the impact of Edinburgh goldsmith training across the UK and within the Commonwealth and former British colonies.

Edinburgh Apprentices Potentially Working Elsewhere

Apprentice/Journeyman	Indent. Year	Destination	Est. Arrival
Bruce, Patrick	1552	Possibly Gateshead	*c.*1562
Heriot, Patrick	1586	Genoa, Italy	*c.*1620
Heriot, George (3)	1588	London	1603
Stalker, William (2)	1591	Perth then Glasgow	1605 then 1607
Chaip, Andrew	1600	Perth	*c.*1610
Wallace, David	1608	Dumfries	*c.*1625
Heriot, Alexander	1611	London	*c.*1640
Jackson, Alexander	1630	Possibly London	1643
Lindsay, John (2)	1631	Probably London	1663
Merstoun, Andrew	1649	Londonderry, Ireland	*c.*1681-1688
Strachen, Alexander	1675	Possibly London	1695
Cumming, Thomas (1)	1678	Glasgow	1682
Campbell, John (1)	1679	London	1691
Law, John (2)	1679	London, then Paris as banker	1691
Eckford, John [J]	1690s	London	*c.*1710
Ker, Robert	1694	Possibly London	1712
Guthrie, James	1700	Elgin	1712
Simpson, Alexander	1700	Glasgow	1723
Robertson, George	1703	Possibly Aberdeen	*c.*1710
Drummond, Andrew	1704	London	1712
Bruce, David	1705	London goldsmith-banker	1742
Ker, Alexander	1708	Williamsburg, Virginia	1717-1738
Gotlieff-Biltzing, Johan [J]	1709	Glasgow	*c.*1715
Scott, James	1709	Newcastle	1720
Inglis, James	1710	London	*c* .740-50
McKenzie, Roderick	1712	Possibly Ireland Briefly	*c.*1722
Inglis, ?	*c.*1712	Newcastle	*c.*1725
Main, John	1714	Cadiz, Spain	1734
Ramsay, John	1714	Possibly Glasgow then London	*c.*1718 then *c.*1726
Gilchrist, Archibald	1716	Probably London	1731
Abercromby, Robert	1717	London via Newcastle	1731
Fergusson, James	1717	Perth	1727
McDonald, Donald	1717	London	*c.*1725
McKenzie, Charles	1717	Possibly London	1736
Pollock, John	1719	London	1734
Anderson, James	1720	London	1765
Napier, James	1720	Glasgow	*c.*1730
Sutherland, John	1723	Possibly London	1753
Duncan, William	1724	Jamaica	1740s
Inglis, Alexander	1724	St. Kitts	*c.*1735
Allan, Charles	*c.*1724	Jamaica	1740s
Duncan, John	1725	Jamaica	1750s
Innes, Robert	1725	London	1743
Gordon, George	1727	Jamaica	1740s
Shiells, Gavin	1727	London	*c.*1730s-50s

Edinburgh Apprentices Potentially Working Elsewhere (cont.)

Apprentice/Journeyman	Indent. Year	Destination	Est. Arrival
Kincaid, John	1728	Possibly London	*c.*1743
Dickson, Charles (2)	1730	London	1752
Drysdale, Thomas	1731	Glasgow	1745
Hathorn, Henry	1731	Jamaica	1740s
Hay, Michael	1733	Jamaica	1740s
Campbell, Archibald	1734	Jamaica	1740s
Clark, John	1734	Possibly Newcastle then Lisbon	before 1760;by 1769
Stewart, William	1735	Possibly London	1762
Mitchelson, James (2)	1736	London	*c.*1745-51
Colquhoun, John	1737	Newcastle	*c.*1746
Glen, James	1737	Glasgow	*c.*1745
Rutherford, James	1737	Charleston, South Carolina	*c.*1751
Steven, John	1737	Dundee	*c.*1745
Coutts, David	1739	Dumfries	1753
Geddes/Giddes, Charles	1739	Possibly London	1760
Heriot, Joseph	1739	London	1750
Sommervail, James	1739	London	1762
Robertson, George (4)	1740	Possibly London	1755
Buchanan, Walter	1742	Jamaica	1750s
Clephan, Thomas	1743	Glasgow	*c.*1752
Colquhoun, Humphrey	1744	Jamaica	1760s
Dick, George	1744	Jamaica	1750s-60s
Moore, Robert	1744	Possibly London	1765
Murray, George	1746	Possibly London &/or Newcastle	1755
Bruce, Alexander	1747	Possibly Newcastle	1754
Robertson, John	1747	Newcastle	1772
Douglas, William	1748	Possibly London	1776
Murdoch, William	1748	Possibly Glasgow	1762
Stirling, John	1749	Possibly London	1773
Crichton, William	1750	Possibly London	1765
Dick, Charles	1750	London	1765
Jackson, Orlando	1750	London	1759
Jeffrey, William	1751	Glasgow	1757
Oliphant, James	1751	Charleston, South Carolina	1767
Paton, Alexander	1751	Jamaica	1760s
Roxburgh, John	1751	Jamaica	1760s
Sanders, Archibald	1751	Jamaica	1770s
Anderson, John	1753	London	1765
Craw, William	1753	Canongate and Dumfries	1760, 1769
Downie, David	1753	Augusta, Georgia	1795
Clark, Robert	1754	Halifax, Canada	*c.*1780
Taylor, James	1754	Glasgow	1762
White, John	1754	Possibly London	1772
Young, Adam	1754	Glasgow	1763
Denhame, William	1755	Jamaica	1760s
Wilson, Robert (1)	1758/1765	Glasgow	1778

Edinburgh Apprentices Potentially Working Elsewhere (cont.)

Apprentice/Journeyman	Indent. Year	Destination	Est. Arrival
Finlayson, Henry	1760	Savannah, Georgia	*c.*1774
Sommervail, Francis	1760	Newcastle	by 1771
Cumming, Thomas (2)	1761	Newcastle, Glasgow	before 1777
Wilson, Alexander	1761	Jamaica	1780s-90s
Beech, Patrick	1762	Newcastle	1778
Porter, Thomas	1762	Newcastle	1793
Tweedie, Walter	1762	London	1775
Dickson, Robert	1763	Perth	1779
Robertson, Alexander	1763	Possibly Dumfries	1787
Taws, William	1764	Dundee	*c.*1781
Taylor, John	1764	Glasgow then St. Eustatius	*c.*1773
Borthwick, Thomas	1766	Inverness	*c.*1772
Edward, Henry	1766	Newcastle	1772
Aitken, Alexander	1767	Glasgow	*c.*1775
Hood, Thomas	1768	Possibly Duns, Berwickshire	*c.*1775
Irvine, John	1768	London	1773
Clephan, Charles [J]	*c.*1768	Glasgow	*c.*1772
Hector, John	*1769*	Charleston, South Carolina	*c.*1774
Reid, Christian	1769	Newcastle	1778
Adie, John	1770	Calcutta, India	1781
Hewitt, William	1770	Glasgow	1812
Hunter, John Adams	1770	Dumfries	1776
Swan, Robert	1776	Left Scotland possibly for India	1794
Douglas, James	c.1778	Dundee	*c.*1805
Bayne, George	1780	Possibly Montrose	1807
Hamilton, Robert	1787	Calcutta, India	1808
Graham, John	*c.*1790	Glasgow	1800
Downie, James	1792	Glasgow	1811
Gray, David	1792	Dumfries	1814
Robertson, James	1793	Possibly London	1826
Stewart, James	c1795	Glasgow	1807
Ritchie, Nicol	1799	Possibly Newcastle	before 1831
Beech, Lindsay	1799ca	Glasgow	*c.*1804
Douglas, Archibald	1800	London	1821
Farquaharson, James Russell	1804	London	*c.*1820
Edmond, Alexander	1805	Glasgow	*c.*1820
McKell, John	1805	Glasgow	1825
Allen, James	1806	Glasgow	1819
Dalgleish, Charles	1806	Dundee	1823
Wilson, John (2)	1807	London	1837
Stewart, John	1809	Possibly Aberdeen then Dumfries	*c.*1820
Fenwick, George (2)	1812	Tobago	1821
Watt, James Haldane	1814	New Zealand	*c.*1835
Sutter, John	1815	Liverpool	*c.*1831
Urquhart, Leonard	1815	Perth	1836
McLean, George	1816	Dumfries	before 1861

Edinburgh Apprentices Potentially Working Elsewhere (cont.)

Apprentice/Journeyman	Indent. Year	Destination	Est. Arrival
Smith, Thomas	1816	Possibly Greenock	1866
Dick, Alexander	1818	Sydney, Australia	1824
Frier, James	1818	America	1832
McLeod, Angus	1825	Inverness	*c.*1841
McLean, John Craig	1849	Dumfries	1864
Park, James Snodgrass	1852	S. 4th St., Brooklyn, NY USA	1870
Weir, Alexander White	1866	Possibly Ayr	*c.*1900s
Crichton, Michael	1868	Cannes, France	*c.*1890-1900
Pollock, Archibald (2)	1869	Aberdeen	*c.*1920
McLean, John Montgomery	1880	Dumfries	*c.*1890

APPENDIX A

Glossary of Ancient Professions

Advocate - a solicitor in a Law Court [*Old Occupations in Scotland*]; a professional pleader in a court of justice [*Dictionary of Ancient Occupations and Trades*]

Aide - an assistant usually to a military officer or official,[modified from *Merriam Webster Dictionary*]

Apothecary - a historical name for a medical practitioner who formulates and dispenses *material medica* to physicians, surgeons and patients [modified from *Merriam-Webster Online*]

Attorney - an advocate; a lawyer in court [*ScotlandsPeople.gov.uk*]

Auctioneer - one who runs sales where the goods go to the highest bidder [*ScotlandsPeople.gov.uk*]

Baillie - a magistrate in a Scottish burgh [*Old Occupations in Scotland*]

Bank messenger - a person employed to convey official dispatches or to go on other official or special errands [*Economic History Review 4*, pp399-428 1934]

Banker - one owning or running a financial house [*ScotlandsPeople.gov.uk*]

Barber - one who shaves others; later cutting of hair and rough surgery [*ScotlandsPeople.gov.uk*]

Baxter, Baker - Baxter was originally the feminine form of Baker; someone who bakes breads, rolls, and other grain products for sale [*Old Occupations in Scotland*]

Becker - Probably intended to be “baker”

Book seller - one who sells books to the public [*ScotlandsPeople.gov.uk*]

Bookbinder - one who practices the art or trade of binding books [*Merriam-Webster Online Dictionary*]

Booker - the “bookie” accepting gambling bets [*Old Occupations in Scotland*]

Bottle blower - one who makes bottles of blown glass [derived from *ScotlandsPeople.gov.uk*]

Box keeper - treasurer of a trade association [*Old Occupations in Scotland*]

Brewer - one who prepares beer or ale [*Merriam-Webster Online*]

Builder - one that constructs dwellings and buildings [modified from *Merriam-Webster Online*]

Burgess - a man listed as a merchant or a craftsman in a town burgh [*Old Occupations in Scotland*]; a holder either of land or a house in a burgh, with special judicial privileges and a part to play in running the burgh [*Dictionary of Ancient Occupations and Trades*]

Butcher - one who kills animals for meat and sells it [*ScotlandsPeople.gov.uk*]

Butler - a domestic servant with widely diverse duties commensurate with the size of the Household [*Dictionary of Ancient Occupations and Trades*]

Cabinet maker - a maker of wooden furniture [*Old Occupations in Scotland*]

Candlemaker - one who makes candles [*ScotlandsPeople.gov.uk*]

Carpenter - one who works with wood and/or makes things from wood [*ScotlandsPeople.gov.uk*]

Carter - a man who worked with horse and cart on farms or in towns [*Old Occupations in Scotland*]

Carver - one who cuts patterns into wood [*ScotlandsPeople.gov.uk*]

Causeway layer - a man who built town roads (causeways) with stone setts [*Old Occupations in Scotland*]

Chairmaster - one of two persons who carried a sedan chair and passenger [*Old Occupations in Scotland*]

Clerk - a person employed to keep records or accounts [*Dictionary of Ancient Occupations and Trades*]

Coachman - one who drives a passenger vehicle [*ScotlandsPeople.gov.uk*]

Contractor - one that contracts to perform work such as erecting buildings [modified from *Merriam-Webster Online*]

Cook - one who prepares generally hot food [*ScotlandsPeople.gov.uk*]

Glossary of Ancient Professions (cont.)

Cooper - a maker of barrels and casks, often for distillers [*Old Occupations in Scotland*]
Coppersmith - one who works with copper [*ScotlandsPeople.gov.uk*]
Cork cutter - worked in cutting and preparing imported raw cork bark from Portugal [*Old Occupations in Scotland*]
Dagmaker, Dagmaster - a maker of dags or pistols [*Old Occupations in Scotland*]; a mitten maker usually for fishermen [*ScotlandsPeople.gov.uk*]
Distiller - a person or company whose business it is to extract alcoholic liquors by distillation [*Dictionary of Ancient Occupations and Trades*]
Doctor of Medicine - usually a medical practitioner [*ScotlandsPeople.gov.uk*]
Doorkeeper for Exchequer - possibly the guard at the door of the treasury
Doctor - usually a medical practitioner [*ScotlandsPeople.gov.uk*]
Draper - a dealer in fabrics and sewing materials [*Old Occupations in Scotland*]
Dressmaker - a person who makes women's clothes [*Oxford Dictionary*]
Drummer - a person who plays the drum and is employed by the town or army [*ScotlandsPeople.gov.uk*]
Engraver - one who cuts or carves on a hard surface such as a metal [*Oxford Dictionary*]
Factor to the General - estate agent for a landowner; collector of rents [*Old Occupations in Scotland*]
Farmer - one who tends and farms including livestock and crops [*ScotlandsPeople.gov.uk*]
Farrier - a blacksmith who shoes horses [*Old Occupations in Scotland*]
Feltmaker - one who makes cloth without a loom [*ScotlandsPeople.gov.uk*]
Fermourner - a farmer possibly with additional property [modified from, *ScotlandsPeople.gov.uk*]
Feuar - a landholder under the feudal system who paid a feu (fee) to the overlord [*Old Occupations in Scotland*]
Fishing rod maker – one who makes tapering rods for fishing [modified from *Oxford English Dictionary*]
Flaxdresser - one who prepares flax for working [*ScotlandsPeople.gov.uk*]
Flesher - a butcher [*Old Occupations in Scotland*]
Gardener - one employed to tend a garden [*ScotlandsPeople.gov.uk*]
Gas manager - presumably an overseer of Victorian-era street lighting
Gilder - a person who impressed gold leaf or gilt to overlay an item [*Old Occupations in Scotland*]
Glassblower - one who makes blown glass objects by hand [modified from, *ScotlandsPeople.gov.uk*]
Glazer - a window glassman [*Dictionary of Ancient Occupations and Trades*]
Glover - a maker of gloves [*Old Occupations in Scotland]*
Goldsmith - one who works with gold and silver [modified from, *ScotlandsPeople.gov.uk*]
Grocer - a dealer in food and household provisions [*Dictionary of Ancient Occupations and Trades*]
Guid(e)man - an owner of tenant of a farm [*ScotlandsPeople.gov.uk*]
Guild officer - one who is elected to a post of responsibility in a guild [*ScotlandsPeople.gov.uk*]
Haberdasher - a seller of small clothing wares and sewing materials [*Old Occupations in Scotland*]; a dealer in men's clothing [*Dictionary of Ancient Occupations and Trades*]
Hatter - a maker of hats [*Old Occupations in Scotland*]
Indweller - an inhabitant of a city, town or burgh [modified from *ScotlandsPeople.gov.uk*]
Innkeeper - one in charge of an inn [*ScotlandsPeople.gov.uk*]
Jeweler - a maker or repairer of jewelry also involving silver and watches [*Chambers Dictionary*]
Joiner - a person who makes furniture and light woodwork [*Dictionary of Ancient Occupations and Trades*]
Keeper of gowns - one in charge of maintaining or guarding gowns [modified from *ScotlandsPeople.gov.uk*]

Glossary of Ancient Professions (cont.)

Labourer - a person doing unskilled, manual labor for pay [*Dictionary of Ancient Occupations and Trades*]
Laird – rural estate landowner, usually in the Highlands [*Old Occupations in Scotland*]
Land surveyor - one who estimates or measures areas of land [*ScotlandsPeople.gov.uk*]
Lapidary - a worker who cuts, polishes, and engraves precious stones [*Merriam-Webster Online Dictionary*]
Linen printer - one who prints patterns on linen [*ScotlandsPeople.gov.uk*]
Litster, Dyer - a dyer of cloth [*Old Occupations in Scotland*]
Lorymer - a maker of horse gear and tack [*Dictionary of Ancient Occupations and Trades*]
Malt maker - someone who prepares malt for brewing [*Old Occupations in Scotland*]
Maltman - one who processed barley into malt for brewing [*ScotlandsPeople.gov.uk*]
Manufacturer - a maker [*ScotlandsPeople.gov.uk*]
Mariner - a person who works on a ship; a sailor [*ScotlandsPeople.gov.uk*]
Mason - a person who cuts and lays stone [*Old Occupations in Scotland*]
Master of the Revels - a supervisor of court entertainment [*Encyclopedia Britannica*]
Master waker - a master fuller of cloth [*ScotlandsPeople.gov.uk*]
Merchant - a retail trader, dealer, and storekeeper [*Dictionary of Ancient Occupations and Trades*]
Military - soldiers, members of the armed forcers [modified from *Merriam Webster*]
Minister - a member of the clergy [*Dictionary of Ancient Occupations and Trades*]
Music master - one who teaches music to others [*ScotlandsPeople.gov.uk*]
Nailer - a blacksmith who made nails by cutting and shaping metal [*Old Occupations in Scotland*]
Landed gentry "Of that ilk..." - one whose surname is the same as that of his estate [*Glossary from Clan McAlister*]
Landed gentry "Of...." – denoting possession of or ownership as with an estate owner [modified from *Webster Dictionary 1913*]
Officer in Customs - one who collects revenues on goods for the custom-house [*ScotlandsPeople.gov.uk*]
Officer in the Excise office - tax collector [*Old Occupations in Scotland*]
Overseer of salmon fishing - a person in charge of salmon fishing for an area [modified from, *ScotlandsPeople.gov.uk*]
Painter - an artist; a maker of portraits [*ScotlandsPeople.gov.uk*]
Pawnbroker - one who makes loans on the security personal property [*Merriam-Webster Online Dictionary*]
Pewterer, peuterer - a worker in pewter [*Old Occupations in Scotland*]
Port seller - one who sells mild beer [modified from, *ScotlandsPeople.gov.uk*]
Porter - a baggage carrier, or gate keeper [*Old Occupations in Scotland*]
Portioner - the owner of land, previously divided amongst co-heirs [*Old Occupations in Scotland*]; one who possesses part of a property which had been originally divided among co-heirs [*Dictionary of Ancient Occupations and Trades*]
Printer - one who prints books, pictures, posters, etc [*ScotlandsPeople.gov.uk*]
Professor of music - senior teacher of music in a college or university [modified from, *ScotlandsPeople.gov.uk*]
Quarrier - a person who works in a quarry[*ScotlandsPeople.gov.uk*]
Riding officer - a mounted customs officer who patrolled the coast [*ScotlandsPeople.gov.uk*]
Saddler - a person who makes and repairs horse saddles and leathers [*Old Occupations in Scotland*]
Sawyer - a worker in a sawmill or timber pit [*Old Occupations in Scotland*]
Schoolmaster - a teacher, often the head teacher, in a school [*ScotlandsPeople.gov.uk*]
Sculptor - one who makes figures in wood, stone, or metal [modified from *ScotlandsPeople.gov.uk*]

Glossary of Ancient Professions (cont.)

Servant - one privately employed to perform domestic services [*Dictionary of Ancient Occupations and Trades*]; also a journeyman working for a freeman
Servitor - a clerk or secretary [*Old Occupations in Scotland*]; also a personal servant
Sheriff - the chief officer of Crown in the country [*Old Occupations in Scotland*]
Shipmaster - the owner or captain of a ship [*Old Occupations in Scotland*]
Shoemaker, Cordiner - someone who makes shoes or works in cordwain [*Glossary from Clan McAlister*]
Sievewright - a person who made sieves (also spelled seive) [*ScotlandsPeople.gov.uk*]
Silk Dyer - one who prepares dyes and dyes silk [*ScotlandsPeople.gov.uk*]
Silver engraver - one who decorates silver through cutting or carving the surface [*Oxford Dictionary*]
Silver plater - one who coats metal with a thin coat of silver [modified from *Oxford Dictionary*]
Silversmith - one who works with silver [*ScotlandsPeople.gov.uk*]
Skinner - a flayer of animal hides for leather [*Old Occupations in Scotland*]
Skipper - the master or captain of a boat or small ship [*ScotlandsPeople.gov.uk*]
Slater - a person who prepares and fits roof slates and other slates [*ScotlandsPeople.gov.uk*]
Smith - a metal worker, usually a blacksmith [*Old Occupations in Scotland*]
Spirit dealer - a dealer in spirits, wines and ale [*Old Occupations in Scotland*]
Stabler - a person who stables horses for others [*ScotlandsPeople.gov.uk*]
Staymaker - a maker of corsets that used boning supports [*ScotlandsPeople.gov.uk*]
Tacksman - a farm tenant who sublet rents or tacks [*Old Occupations in Scotland*]
Tailor - one who makes, alters or repairs articles of clothing [*Dictionary of Ancient Occupations and Trades*]
Tanner - a person who cures hides to produce leather [*ScotlandsPeople.gov.uk*]
Tavern keeper - an innkeeper [modified from, *ScotlandsPeople.gov.uk*]
Teacher of English - an instructor of English usually in a school [modified from, *ScotlandsPeople.gov.uk*]
Tenant - one who rents land or property from a landlord [*Old Occupations in Scotland*]
Ticket porter - one who sees to the carrying of tickets [modified from, *ScotlandsPeople.gov.uk*]
Tobacconist - one who sells tobacco and related products to the public [*ScotlandsPeople.gov.uk*]
Toll keeper - one in charge of receipts gathered at a toll gate [modified from, *ScotlandsPeople.gov.uk*]
Toolmaker - one who makes tools, a machinist [*Merriam Webster Online Dictionary*]
Town clerk - a legal advisor to the town council [*ScotlandsPeople.gov.uk*]
Treasurer - one who looks after money for an organization [*ScotlandsPeople.gov.uk*]
Turnkey, Jailer - the person in charge of the keys of the prison; a jailer [*Merriam Webster Online Dictionary*]
Victual maker - a supplier of food and provisions [*Old Occupations in Scotland*]
Vintner - a wine merchant [*Old Occupations in Scotland*]
Watchcase maker - one who makes and repairs watches cases [modified from, *ScotlandsPeople.gov.uk*]
Watchmaker - a person who makes and repairs watches and clocks [*ScotlandsPeople.gov.uk*]
Weatherglass manufacturer - a person who made barometers and other instruments that told the state of the weather [*Merriam Webster Online Dictionary*]
Weaver - someone who made cloth from yarns of wool, cotton, silk, etc.; the operator of hand loom or textile mill power looms [*Old Occupations in Scotland*]
Wheelwright - a maker or repairer of wheels [*Old Occupations in Scotland*]
Whiteiron smith - a tin smith [*Encyclopedia of Genealogy*]
Wigmaker - one who makes wigs and hairpieces for men and women [*ScotlandsPeople.gov.uk*]

Glossary of Ancient Professions (cont.)

Wine cooper - a person who made wooden casks or barrels for wine [*Merriam Webster Online Dictionary*]
Wooden clockmaker - one who makes wooden timepieces [modified from, *ScotlandsPeople.gov.uk*]
Wool merchant - one who deals in wool [*ScotlandsPeople.gov.uk*]
Workman - a laborer [*ScotlandsPeople.gov.uk*]
Wright - a joiner or carpenter [*Old Occupations in Scotland*]
Writer - a solicitor [*Old Occupations in Scotland*]
Writer to the Signet - a solicitor for the Signet [*Old Occupations in Scotland*]

APPENDIX B

List of Maker's Marks in this Volume

Maker's Marks in Training Diagrams

Adam Craig	George Robertson (2)
Adam Lamb	Gilbert Kirkwood
Alexander Aitchison (1)	Henry Bethune
Alexander Aitchison (2)	Henry Bruce Kirkwood
Alexander Campbell	Hugh Gordon
Alexander Forbes	Hugh Lindsay
Alexander Gardner	Hugh Penman
Alexander Henderson	Jame McKay
Alexander Kincaid	James Cockburn
Alexander Reid (2)	James Dennistoun (1)
Alexander Scott	James Douglas
Alexander Simpson	James Gilliland
Alexander Spence	James Glen
Alexander Ziegler	James Hewitt
Andrew Wilkie	James Hill
Archibald Ure	James Ker
Benjamin Couts	James McKenzie (1)
Charles Dalgleish	James Mitchell
Charles Dickson (1) - Dundee	James Mitchelson
Charles Dickson (2)	James Penman
Charles Robb & Son	James Reid
Colin McKenzie	James Symontoun
Daniel Ker	James Tait (1)
David Boige	James Weems
David Gray - Dumfries	James Welsh
David Heriot	John Borthwick
David Mitchell	John Clark (1)
Dougal Ged	James Frasier
Ebenezer Oliphant	John Howden
Edward Cleghorne	John Lindsay
Edward Lothian	James Mosman (3)
Edward Penman	John Pollock - London
George Carstairs	John Robertson - Newcastle
George Christie George Cleghorne	John Rollo
George Crawford (1)	John Scott (1)
George Fenwick (1)	John Seaton
George McHattie	John Taylor
George Paton	John Warlaw
George Robertson (1)	John Yorstoun

John Yorstoun	Samuel Weir
John Ziegler	Thomas Borthwick - Inverness
Kenneth McKenzie	Thomas Cleghorne (1)
Lawrence Oliphant	Thomas Cleghorne (3)
Lindsay Beech	Thomas Duffus
Nicol Trotter	Thomas Ker
Patrick Borthwick Patrick Graham (Graeme)	Walker Crichton
Patrick Murray (1)	William & Patrick Cunningham (1)
Patrick Murray (3)	William & Patrick Cunningham (2)
Patrick Robertson	William Auld
Patrick Sutherland	William Aytoun
Peter Mathie	William Burton
Peter Spaulding	William Dempster
Robert Abercromby - London	William Edmonstoun
Robert Bruce	William Ged William Law (2)
Robert Gordon	William Marshall (2)
Robert Hamilton - Calcutta	William Robertson
Robert Inglis	William Taylor
Robert Low	Zacharius Mellinus

Maker's Marks in the Appendix

Adam Elder or Alexander Edmonstoun (3) Charles Duncan or Charles Dickson (1)	John Seaton-second mark used
Edward Cleghorne's widow - Marion Mitchell	Matthew Craw
Edward Penman--earliest used	McKay, Cunningham & Co
Edward Lothian & Patrick Robertson (L & R) George and Michael Crichton	Richard Haxton
Hamilton & Inches	Robert Low-variant mark
James Ker and Wm. Dempster (K & D)	Wm Davie or Wm Dempster block letters
James Mitchelson - variant	Wm. Davie or Wm. Dempster script letters
James Mitchelson - late (or James McKenzie 1)	William Jamieson or John Main (WI or IM in an oval)
John McDonald	William Ker (or Daniel Ker) "KER"

APPENDIX C

ADDITIONAL EDINBURGH MARKS

Adam Elder or Alexander Edmonstoun (3) - 

Charles Duncan or Charles Dickson (1) - 

Edward Cleghorne's widow, Marion Mitchell - 

Edward Penman – earliest mark 

Edward Lothian and Patrick Robertson – partnership mark 

George and Michael Crichton - 

Hamilton and Inches – 

James Hamilton and Robert Inches (unfreeman)

James Ker and William Dempster, his son-in-law - 

James Mitchelson – variant mark 

James Mitchelson – last mark or James McKenzie first mark 

John McDonald – unfreeman 

John Seaton – second mark 

Ker – William or Daniel 

Matthew Craw – unfreeman 

Richard Haxton – unfreeman 

William Davie or William Dempster - 

William Davie or William Dempster - 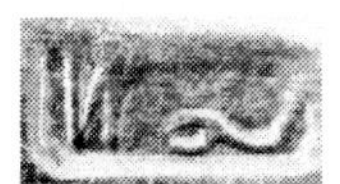

William Jamieson – or John Main (inverted)  

WORKS CONSULTED

Books

Black, George G. The Surnames of Scotland: Their Origin, Meaning and History. The New York Public Library. New York: 1946.

Burke, Sir. Bernard. Burke's Genealogical and Heraldic History of the Landed Gentry. Edited by Peter Townsend, 18th Edition. 1965-92 three volumes. Burke's Peerage, London.

Burke, Sir Bernard. Burke's Genealogical and Heraldic History of the Peerage, Baronetage and Knightage. Burke's Peerage Limited, London. 7th, 37th, 73rd, 89th, 95, 99th-104th Editions. (via Cornell University Library System).

Burton, E. Milby. South Carolina Silversmiths 1690-1860. The Charles E. Tuttle Company, Inc. Rutland, VT: 1968.

Cutton, George Barton. The Silversmiths of Virginia 1694-1850. The Dietz Press, Inc. Richmond, VA: 1952.

Darling, Herbert F (compiler). New York State Silversmiths. The Darling Foundation of New York State Early American Silversmiths and Silver. Eggertsville, NY: 1964.

Dietert, Rodney R. and Dietert, Janice M. Compendium of Scottish Silver v.1 & 2. Internet-First University Press. Ithaca, NY: 2006.

Fothringham, Henry Steuart (Ed.) Edinburgh Goldsmiths' Minutes 1525-1700. Scottish Record Society. New Series. v.29. Edinburgh: 2006.

Gilhooley, James. A Directory of Edinburgh in 1752. Edinburgh University Press. Edinburgh: 1988.

Gill, Margaret A.V. A Directory of Newcastle Goldsmiths. Newcastle: 1980.

Grimwade, Arthur G. London Goldsmiths 1697-1837 Their Lives and Marks. 3rd Edition. Faber & Faber. London: 1990

Harrington, Jessie. Silversmiths of Delaware 1700-1850 & Old Church Silver in Delaware. National Society of Colonial Dames of America in the State of Delaware. The Hadden Craftmen, Inc. Camden, NJ: 1939.

Hiatt, Noble W. and Lucy F. The Silversmiths of Kentucky 1785-1850. The Standard Printing Company. Louisville, KY: 1954.

Kimber, Edward The Peerage of Scotland: a genealogical and historical account of all the peers of that ancient kingdom; ... Together with a like account of all the attainted peers; and a complete alphabetical list of those nobles of Scotland whose titles are extinct. ... Printed for J. Almon; T. Cadell; R. Baldwin, S.

Crowder, Robinson and Roberts, S. Bladon, and Johnson and Davenport. London: 1767.

Macfarlane, Walter. Genealogical Collections Concerning Families in Scotland (in 2 vols.) Scottish History Society v.33-34. Edinburgh: 1900.

Maitland, William. The History of Edinburgh, from its Foundation to the Present Time. Containing a faithful Relation of the Publick Transactions of the Citizens... With the Several Accounts of the Parishes of the Canongate, St. Cuthberts, and other districts within the Suburbs of Edinburgh.... Printed by Hamilton, Balfour & Neill, for the Author, MDCCLIII. Edinburgh: 1753.

Scott, Hew. Fasti Ecclesiae Scoticanae: the Succession of Ministers in the Church of Scotland from the Reformation. Oliver and Boyd. Edinburgh: 1915-1981.

Smith, John. Monumental Inscriptions in St. Cuthbeth's Churchyard, Edinburgh. Scottish Record Society. Two volumes. Sir James Balfour Paul (Ed.), Printed for the Society by the J. Skinner Co. Edinburgh: 1915-1919.

Watt, Donald Emslie Robertson. Fasti Ecclesiae Scoticanae medii aevi ad annum. 1638. Scottish Record Society. Printed for the Society by Smith and Ritchie Ltd. Edinburgh: 1969.

Wilkinson, Wynyard R. T. Indian Colonial Silver. European Silversmiths in India (1790-1860) and Their Marks. Argent Press. London: 1973.
................................The Makers of Indian Colonial Silver, a Register of European Goldsmiths, Silversmiths, Jewellers, Watchmakers and Clockmakers in India and Their Marks 1760-1860. London: 1987.

Periodicals

Henry Steuart Fothringham: "The Records of the Incorporation of Goldsmiths of the City of Edinburgh". In Silver Society Journal, no.5 (Spring 1994), pp.187-194.

Bullock, Helen. Palmer House Historical Report. Colonial Williamsburg Foundation Library Research Report Series - 1133. Colonial Williamsburg Foundation Library. Williamsburg, VA 1990 (via Colonial Williamsburg Digital History Archive) 2006-2007

Electronic Resources

Aberdeen Directories 1824-25, 1827-30. Electronic version via http://www.ancestry.com 2006-2007

Aberdeen, Scotland Register of Testaments, 1715-1800. Electronic version via http://www.ancestry.com 2006-2007

Angus Directories 1829, 1830. Electronic version via http://www.ancestry.com 2006-2007.

Argyll, Scotland Parish and Probate Records. Electronic version via http://www.ancestry.com 2006-2007

Ayr Directory 1830. Electronic version via http://www.ancestry.com 2006-2007

Banff-shire, Scotland Parish and Probate Records. Electronic version via http://www.ancestry.com 2006-2007

Canongate Burials 1820-1851
Electronic version at http://www.scotsfind.org 2006

Censuses for England and Wales 1841-1901. Electronic versions via http://www.ancestry.com 2006-2007

Census Records of the United States 1790-1930. Electronic digital version via http://www.ancestry.com 2005-2007

Dictionary of Ancient Occupations and Trades.
http://www.freepages.geneaology.rootsweb.com/~da4vis/Sources/Occupations.html 2006-2007.

Dumfries-shire, Scotland Parish and Probate Records, Electronic version via http://www.ancestry.com 2006-2007

Dumbartonshire, Scotland Parish and Probate Records. Electronic version via http://www.ancestry.com 2006-2007

Dundee Directories 1782, 1809, 1818, 1822k, 1824, 1829. Electronic versions via http://www.ancestry.com 2006-2007

Edinburgh Advertiser, various years 1771-1829. Electronic indexed digital versions via http://www.ancestry.com 2006-2007

Edinburgh Courant, 1884. Electronic digital version via http://www.ancestry.com 2006-2007

Edinburgh Directories for 1774, 1776, 1778, 1780, 1782, 1794, 1797, 1800, 1801, 1804, 1805-1830. Electronic versions via http://www.ancestry.com 2006-2007 1805-1831.

Edinburgh Weekly Journal, 1801-1808. Electronic digital version via http://www.ancestry.com 2006-2007

England and Wales Birth, Marriage and Death Indexes 1837-1983. Electronic version via http://www.ancestry.com 2006-2007

Glasgow Directories for 1801, 1803-07, 1809-1830. Electronic versions via http://www.ancestry.com 2006-2007

Glossary of Obsolete or Uncommon Scots Words Occurring in the Dictionary of Names. Clan McAlister of America. http://www.clanmcalister.org/glossary.html 2006-2007.

Greenock Directories 1815, 1820, 1828. Electronic version via http://www.ancestry.com 2006-2007

Grant, Francis J. (Ed.) Parish of Holyroodhouse or Canongate Marriage Register 1564-1800. Scottish Record Society
Electronic version at http://www.scotsfind.org 2006

Grant, Francis J. The Commissariot Record of Edinburgh. Register of Testaments Part I. Volumes 1-35. 1514-1600. British Record Society-Scottish Section.
Electronic version via http://www.scotsfind.org 2005-2006

International Genealogical Index (IDI). Electronic site via http://www.familysearch.org 2005-2007

Kinross-shire, Scotland parish and Probate Records. Electronic versions via http://www.ancestry.com 2006-2007

Lanarkshire Parish and Probate Records. Electronic version via http://www.ancestry.com 2006-2007

London Directory 1790. Electronic version via http://www.ancestry.com 2006-2007

Middlesex England parish and Probate Records. Electronic version via http://www.ancestry.com 2006-2007

Midlothian, Scotland Parish and Probate Records. Electronic version via http://www.ancestry.com 2006-2007

Moray, Scotland Parish and Probate Records. Electronic version via http://www.ancestry.com 2006-2007

Nairnshire, Scotland Parish and Probate Records. Electronic versions via http://www.ancestry.com 2006-2007

Occupations for Scottish Genealogical Research. Electronic resource via the Scottish Government site representing the National Archives of Scotland at http://www.scotlandspeople.gov.uk 2006-2007

Old Occupations in Scotland http://www.scotsroots.com/occupations.htm 2006-2007.

Paisley Directories 1810, 1812, 1820, 1823, 1827, 1828. Electronic version via http://www.ancestry.com 2006-2007

Parish Registers of birth/baptisms and bann and marriages 1553-1854 electronic versions via the Scottish Government site representing the National Archives of Scotland http://www.scotlandspeople.gov.uk 2004-2007

Paton, Henry (Ed.) Register of Interments in the Greyfriars Burying Ground 1658-1700. 1902, Scottish Record Society
Electronic version via http://www.scotsfind.org 2005-2006

Register of Wills and Testaments 1513-1901. Electronic version and digitalized images of wills available via the Scottish Government site representing the National Archives of Scotland http://www.scotlandspeople.gov.uk 2006-2007

Renfrewshire Directories 1829-1830. Electronic version via http://www.ancestry.com 2006-2007

Renfrewshire, Scotland Parish and Probate Records. Electronic version via http://www.ancestry.com 2006-2007

Robertson, D. South Leith Records 1588-1700. 1911
Electronic version via http://www.scotsfind.org 2006

Scottish censuses of 1841 and 1851 via the electronic site www.ancestry.com 2006-2007 http://www.scotlandspeople.gov.uk

Scottish censuses 1841-1901. Electronic versions via the Scottish government site representing the National Archives of Scotland
http://www.scotlandspeople.gov.uk 2006

Selkirkshire, Scotland Parish and Probate Records. Electronic version via http://www.ancestry.com 2006-2007

Statutory registers of births 1855-1906, marriages 1855-1931 and deaths 1855-1956. Electronic version via the Scottish Government site representing the National Archives of Scotland http://www.scotlandspeople.gov.uk 2004-2007

Stirlingshire, Scotland Parish and Probate Records. Electronic version via http://www.ancestry.com 2006-2007

Sutherland, Scotland Parish and Probate Records. Electronic version via http://www.ancestry.com 2006-2007

The Register of Apprentices for the City of Edinburgh
1583-1666 Edited by Francis J. Grant, 1906 Scottish Record Society
1666-1700 Edited by Charles B. Boog Watson, 1929 Scottish Record Society
1701-1755 Edited by Charles B. Boog Watson, Scottish Record Society
1755-1800 Edinburgh Edinburgh by Dr. Marguerite Wood

All above electronic versions on http://www.scotsfind.org 2004-2006 and www.ancestry.com 2006-2007

The Register of Edinburgh Burgesses 1406-1841 Edited by Charles B Boog Watson, 1929, 1930 Scottish Record Society
Electronic version at http://www.scotsfind.org 2005-2006 and www.ancestry.com 2006

The Register of Edinburgh Marriages
1595-1700 Edited by Henry Paton 1905 Scottish Record Society
1700-1751 Edited by Henry Paton 1908 Scottish Record Society
1751-1800 Francis J. Grant Scottish Record Society
All electronic versions via scotsfind.org 2004-2006 as well as via http://www.ancestry.com

Original Records (Non-Published Sources)

Laws of the Incorporation (and miscellaneous accompanying newspaper articles, documents and hand notations). Deacon's Library of the Incorporation of Goldsmiths of the City of Edinburgh.

Research Materials of Mr. Robert B. Barker, London.

Research Notes of Mr. Stewart Maxwell.

Minute Books of the Incorporation of Goldsmiths of the City of Edinburgh

Vol. 1	31/01/1525/6-16/09/1738	National Archives of Scotland (NAS) GD1/482/1
Vol. 2	05/04/1727 - 14/02/1744	NAS GD1/482/2
Vol. 3	17/02/1743 - 23/05/1749	NAS GD1/482/3
Vol. 4	16/09/1738 - 29/04/1758	NAS GD1/482/4
Vol. 5	21/12/1757 - 16/08/1768	NAS GD1/482/5
Vol. 6	13/09/1768 - 09/09/1790	NAS GD1/482/6
Vol. 7	08/09/1789 - 11/02/1794	NAS GD1/482/7
Vol. 8	16/01/1794 - 24/07/1805	NAS GD1/482/8
Vol. 9	14/09/1805 - 25/10/1820	NAS GD1/482/9
Vol. 10	11/12/1820 - 01/11/1826	NAS GD1/482/10
Vol. 11	20/11/1826 - 17/05/1836	NAS GD1/482/11
Vol. 12	17/06/1836 - 10/12/1850-51	NAS GD1/482/12
Vol. 13	10/02/1851 - 16/02/1864	
Vol. 14	23/05/1864 - 14/08/1883	
Vol. 15	23/08/1883 - 28/05/1901	
Vol. 16	25/07/1901 - 14/08/1928	
Vol. 17	?	
Vol. 18	08/12/1953 - 31/12/1976	

Assay Master's Accounts of the Incorporation of Goldsmiths of the City of Edinburgh

Assay Master's Accounts, vol.1: 21/10/1681 - 30/09/1690 NAS GD1/482/15
Assay Master's Accounts, vol.2: 01/10/1690 - 22/09/1702 NAS GD1/482/16

Assay-Office Day Books of the Incorporation of Goldsmiths of the City of Edinburgh

Vol.1 *Missing (Apr.1891 - Sep.1904)*
Vol.2 03/10/1904 - 30/08/1912
Vol.3 02/09/1912 - 31/05/1922
Vol.4 17/06/1922 - 13/05/1932
Vol.5 16/05/1932 - 25/05/1950
Vol.6 25/05/1950 - 30/12/1960
Vol.7
Vol.8 1971-1977

Assay-Office Duty Books of the Incorporation of Goldsmiths of the City of Edinburgh

Vol. 1: 02/12/1799 - 04/10/1805
Vol. 2 *Missing (Oct.1805 - Oct.1811)*
Vol. 3 02/10/1811 - 13/03/1818
Vol. 4 16/03/1818 - 24/09/1827
Vol. 5 26/09/1827 - 16/07/1841
Vol. 6 19/07/1841 - 25/09/1857
Vol. 7 28/09/1857 - 22/06/1866
Vol. 8 25/06/1866 - 10/11/1875
Vol. 9 12/11/1875 - 24/06/1885
Vol.10 26/06/1885 - 25/05/1887
Vol.11 27/04/1883 - 16/12/1887
Vol.12 01/04/1887 - 03/04/1891

Apprentice Registers of the Incorporation of Goldsmiths of the City of Edinburgh

Apprentice Register, 24/03/1694 - 12/07/1786 NAS GD1/482/13
Register of Goldsmiths' Apprentices, 1793-1860 NAS GD1/482/27
Book of Discharged Indentures, 1825 - 1833
Bundle of 19 original Indenture Papers of Apprentices (numbered), 1786-1815 } NAS GD1/482/26
Bundle of 23 original Indenture Papers of Apprentices (un-numbered), 1816-1871} NAS GD1/482/26
Record of Admission of Freemen, 1770-1800 NAS GD1/482/14

Book of Registrations of the Incorporation of Goldsmiths of the City of Edinburgh

Book of Registrations, Vol. 1: 02/03/1847 - 02/04/1902
Book of Registrations, Vol. 2: 1903 - 1935
Book of Registrations, Vol. 3: 1935 - ?

Boxmaster's Accounts of the Incorporation of Goldsmiths of the City of Edinburgh
Boxmaster's Accounts, vol. 1, 1716-17 to 1822-23 National Archives of Scotland (NAS) GD1/482/24
Boxmaster's Accounts, vol. 2, 1823-24 to 1872-73
Boxmaster's Accounts, vol. 3, 1873-74 to 1931-32

1800-1860 Register of Apprentices of the City of Edinburgh. City of Edinburgh. Archives pertaining to goldsmiths as extracted by Henry Steuart Fothringham, O.B.E.

Manuscript of the 1800-1860 Register of Apprentices of the City of Edinburgh by the late Dr. Marguerite Wood, City of Edinburgh Archives